Photo of Rabbi Regina Jonas, probably taken after 1939

This photograph of Regina Jonas was one of only two she placed with her documents.
Jonas's rubber stamp on the back of the image includes the additional name Sara,
which the Nazis forced all Jewish women to use beginning on January 1, 1939:
"Rabbiner [rabbi] Regina Sara Jonas."
Reproduction: Margit Billeb

FRÄULEIN RABBINER JONAS

JONAS

The Story of the First Woman Rabbi

Elisa Klapheck

o

Translated from the German by
Toby Axelrod

An Arthur Kurzweil Book

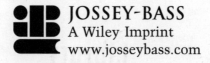

JOSSEY-BASS
A Wiley Imprint
www.josseybass.com

Published by Jossey-Bass
A Wiley Imprint
989 Market Street, San Francisco, CA 94103-1741   www.josseybass.com

This book is translated from the original German book *Fräulein Rabbiner Jonas* under the
Judische Memoiren series published by Hentrich & Hentrich.

Photograph on page 15 by Silke Helmerdig.

Reproduction on page 57 is a gift of Jonas's former pupil Ilse Ehrlich-Kochanczyk to the
author.

Reproduction on page 81, Památník Terezín © Zuzana Dvoráková.

Reproductions on pages 82–85 are used by permission of Yad Vashem Archives.

All other photographs and reproductions are courtesy Stiftung Neue Synagoge Berlin-Cen-
trum Judaicum (CJA).

Jossey-Bass books and products are available through most bookstores. To contact Jossey-
Bass directly call our Customer Care Department within the U.S. at 800-956-7739, outside the U.S. at 317-572-3986, or fax 317-572-4002.

Jossey-Bass also publishes its books in a variety of electronic formats. Some content that
appears in print may not be available in electronic books.

Library of Congress Cataloging-in-Publication Data
Jonas, Regina, 1902–1944. [Fräulein Rabbiner Jonas. English]
Fräulein Rabbiner Jonas: the story of the first woman rabbi
/ Elisa Klapheck; translated from the German by Toby Axelrod.
p. cm. "An Arthur Kurzweil book."
Includes bibliographical references and index.
ISBN 0-7879-6987-7
1. Rabbis—Office. 2. Women rabbis. 3. Jonas, Regina,
1902–1944. 4. Women rabbis—Germany—Biography. 5.
Jews—Germany—Berlin—Biography. 6. Judaism—Germany—
Berlin—History—20th century. I. Klapheck, Elisa. II. Title.
BM652.J6613 2004
296'.092—dc22
2004014533

Printed in the United States of America
FIRST EDITION
HB Printing   10 9 8 7 6 5 4 3 2 1

CONTENTS

LIST OF PHOTOS AND TRANSLATIONS

FOREWORD

IT WAS IN THE EARLY 1960s, during my bar mitzvah lessons with Rabbi Martin Riesenburger in a room of the administration building of the Weissensee Jewish Cemetery in Berlin, that I asked my teacher about one Rabbinerin Jonas,[1] who supposedly had lived in our city. Somehow, the name must have come up in a conversation at home.

I clearly remember Riesenburger's answer: "You wouldn't understand. I will tell you later, when you are older." That is the kind of answer that every child loves, and I am still annoyed with myself that I did not persist with my questions. Riesenburger might well have been able to share many details from his close knowledge of the Berlin Jewish Community of the 1930s and 1940s.

Martin Riesenburger died on April 14, 1965. In his memoirs, *Das Licht verlöschte nicht* [The Light Did Not Fade] (recently rereleased),[2] the name of Jonas is not mentioned.

Nearly thirty years passed before I became aware that a collection of Regina Jonas's papers had survived, and that it existed within the holdings of the Gesamtarchiv der deutschen Juden [Central Archive of German Jewry], which in 1958 was moved to the German Central Archive in Potsdam (later called the State Archive of the German Democratic Republic) and in the spring of 1996 was delivered by the Federal Archive of Germany to the Centrum Judaicum.[3] Of course, the Jonas estate was not originally part of the Gesamtarchiv, but her documents were in that vicinity because, in all likelihood, a few days before her deportation to Theresienstadt on November 6, 1942, Jonas either had given her most important papers to the remaining Jewish communal administration for safekeeping, at Oranienburger Strasse in Berlin Mitte, or had given them to a trusted contact who then brought the material there.

Shortly before her deportation, Jonas had agonized over what to do with the papers, and she discussed it in her correspondence with her friend Rabbi Dr. Joseph Norden of Hamburg,[4] as Elisa Klapheck tells us in her biography of Jonas. "I have not yet heard that one cannot take papers along," Norden wrote in a letter, of which only a fragment remains. "Just in case, I advise you to . . . them somewhere." One automatically wants to fill in the missing word to read "deposit them somewhere."

Of the correspondence between Rabbi Jonas and Rabbi Norden, only his letters remain, some of them torn fragments; Regina Jonas's letters to Joseph Norden apparently have not survived. The epistolary pair were, as Elisa Klapheck describes in depth, very close friends; Norden's letters provide ample and eloquent evidence. Jonas's papers also contain a photograph, which—as I was able to determine—was taken in 1939 of Rabbi Joseph Norden and Rabbi Joseph Zwi Carlebach.[5]

Regina Jonas likely entertained the hope that she eventually would be able to reclaim her documents. But this was not to be: from Theresienstadt, Rabbi Jonas was deported to Auschwitz on October 12, 1944, and murdered there.

☙ ☙ ☙

We will not cover all the details of Regina Jonas's biography here. There are several new undertakings, and in particular the work of Elisa Klapheck in this volume, that serve this purpose.[6]

The life and work of Regina Jonas remain in the memory of several people who came into contact with her. As is often the case, eyewitnesses contradict each other. Günther Ruschin describes her as a "nice and humorous woman with large, dark eyes";[7] my mother, Marie Simon (née Jalowicz), recalled the "odd manner" of Jonas the "martyr," and then continued, "Everyone in the Old Synagogue knew she was a rabbi, and frequently members of the board referred to her as *Fräulein* Rabbiner Jonas.[8] The word *Fräulein* [a diminutive] was expressed in an unpleasant, I would almost say a bit snide manner, but one must keep sight of the historical context: today it is common to refer to women—even unmarried women—as 'Frau' [Mrs.]. The argument was that all men are addressed as 'Herr'—unmarried men are not called 'Herrchen' or 'Herrlein' [diminutive forms]. So why 'Fräulein'? In those days, it was fully common to address or refer to single women, even if they had earned a doctoral degree, as 'Fräulein Doktor.' As everyone knows, the tone makes the music. It was all about the way this word *Fräulein* was expressed—not always but sometimes in a somewhat mocking way."

As a very young woman, Marie Jalowicz had the impression "that Regina Jonas was fairly unsure of herself." Her situation was certainly very difficult for, from the Orthodox standpoint, though Jonas was ordained, as a woman she could perform no cultic functions. "That is like a contradiction in terms, but this contradiction could be mediated in that she made her contribution as a teacher of religion."[9]

Clearly it is difficult to assign Rabbi Jonas to her proper place in Berlin Jewish history: some reject her vehemently, while others raise her to the heavens and turn her into a cult figure. As is often the case, the truth lies somewhere between the two. Jonas was, as her contemporary James Yaakov Rosenthal once said in reference to the Reform movement, a "fascinating phenomenon on the colorful palette of Berlin Jewry."[10]

The fortunate coincidence through which Jonas's documents were preserved has allowed the first serious examination of the life of the first woman ordained as a rabbi. She studied from 1924 to 1930 at Berlin's Hochschule für die Wissenschaft des Judentums [Academy for the Science of Judaism]. It is interesting to note that, as far as we know, Regina Jonas pursued no other university education, in contrast to the common practice of rabbinical students in Germany, as required by Jewish educational authorities.

The centerpiece of Jonas's documents is the required halachic dissertation that she delivered in the summer of 1930 to Eduard Baneth of the Academy for the Science of Judaism, and which received a grade of "good." Maren Krüger wrote that Baneth "probably intended to grant her an ordination after an oral exam, but his death in 1930 thwarted this plan."[11] But there is no proof for Krüger's assertion! Only later did Jonas receive her ordination—on December 27, 1935. The question of whether an ordination would have taken place if the situation for Jews in Germany had not worsened after 1933 cannot be answered, but must be asked.

The manuscript of Jonas's halachic exam, "Can Women Serve as Rabbis?", which Elisa Klapheck correctly calls a "treatise," seems in some sense to be an unfinished work. It appears clear to me that this is not the paper she handed in for her degree; it is also not a copy of that paper. It is likely that the many corrections on the manuscript were made by other people and then partly included in a final version. But it is also not out of the question that the many handwritten comments, corrections, and additions that undoubtedly are in Jonas's own hand were added much later and for other purposes.

One must agree with Elisa Klapheck when she says in her Preliminary Notes, "Perhaps the work is only a draft that she presented to her acquaintances for their critical review, so she could rework it once again."

Though this might not have been the final version, nevertheless the editor and publisher have decided to publish Jonas's text with comments, edited according to the highest standard. Elisa Klapheck verified the relevant quotes and explanations and placed them in a greater context, as far as it was possible for her to do so. As publishers of the first edition, we felt it would be acceptable if some citations were difficult to verify due to inexact titles and editions.

Regina Jonas, who was not a feminist by today's standards, certainly is one of those characters in Berlin Jewish history who are of great interest to Jews around the world today. A manuscript and a collection of papers such as this, housed in the Stiftung Neue Synagoge Berlin—Centrum Judaicum, must not remain hidden and unexamined. It is one of our most important tasks to bring such material to the light of day. For doing just that, Elisa Klapheck—a competent member of the Jewish Community to which Regina Jonas also belonged and in which she was a blessing—deserves our gratitude.

Hermann Simon, Director
Stiftung Neue Synagoge Berlin—Centrum Judaicum

NOTES

1. Editor's note: *rabbinerin* is the female form of the title "rabbi" in German. There is no direct translation into English.

2. Martin Riesenburger, *Das Licht verlöschte nicht: Erinnerungen an ein Berliner Rabbinerleben* [The Light Did Not Fade: In Remembrance of the Life of a Berlin Rabbi], ed. Andreas Nachama and Hermann Simon, Jüdische Memoiren, Band 5 (Teetz: Hentrich & Hentrich, 2003).

3. On the Gesamtarchiv, see Barbara Welker, "Das Gesamtarchiv der deutschen Juden" [The Central Archive of German Jewry] in *Tuet auf die Pforten,* the book accompanying the exhibit by the Stiftung Neue Synagoge Berlin—Centrum Judaicum (Berlin: Hermann Simon and Jochen Boberg, 1995), 227 ff.

4. Born June 17, 1870, in Hamburg; deported to Theresienstadt on July 15, 1942; died there on February 7, 1943.

5. My thanks go to Dr. Ina Lorenz of the Institute for the History of German Jews, in Hamburg, for her collegial help in confirming the identities of those in the photo.

6. To mention two, Katharina von Kellenbach, "Jonas, Regina," in *Jüdische Frauen im 19. und 20. Jahrhundert, Lexikon zu Leben und Werk* [Jewish Women in the Nineteenth and Twentieth Centuries: An Encyclopedia of

Lives and Work], ed. Jutta Dick and Marina Sassenberg (Reinbeck bei Hamburg: Rowohlt, 1993); and Maren Krüger, "Regina Jonas. Die erste Rabbinerin in Deutschland 1935–1942" [Regina Jonas: The First Female Rabbi in Germany 1935–1942], in *Tuet auf die Pforten,* 146 ff.

7. Hermann Simon's conversation with Günther Ruschin, May 20, 1999.

8. Editor's note: *rabbiner* is the male form of the title "rabbi" in German.

9. Hermann Simon's interview with Marie Simon (née Jalowicz; b. April 4, 1922, d. September 16, 1998), on July 30, 1998; see details in "The Story of Regina Jonas" in this book.

10. See James Yaakov Rosenthal, "Jüdische Reformgemeinde zu Berlin" [Berlin's Jewish Reform Community], in *Die Berliner Privatsynagogen und ihre Rabbiner 1671–1971* [Berlin's Private Synagogues and Their Rabbis 1671–1971], ed. Max M. Sinasohn (Jerusalem, 1971), 39.

11. Maren Krüger, "Regina Jonas," 146.

In memory of my mother,
Lilo Klapheck, née Lang,
who collected Rabbinic literature
and left it to me

ACKNOWLEDGMENTS

NATIONAL SOCIALISM led to the murder of millions, but it could not destroy their spirit. More than half a century after Regina Jonas's death in Auschwitz, she taught and guided me—with her work "Can Women Serve as Rabbis?"—through the ages of rabbinical writings. This fascinating and intensive learning experience, when I worked on the German edition of this book in 1998, would not have been possible without Dr. Hermann Simon, director of the Stiftung Neue Synagoge Berlin—Centrum Judaicum, who not only provided access to Regina Jonas's archival material but also stood by me during my research and even involved his own family in the work. I was particularly grateful for the interview he conducted with his mother, Prof. Dr. Marie Simon (née Jalowicz), who shortly before her death recounted her impressions of Regina Jonas in the Alte Synagoge [Old Synagogue] on Heidereutergasse. I am also indebted to his father, Prof. Dr. Heinrich Simon, for his tremendous help in proofreading my translations from the Hebrew sources.

In addition, Prof. Dr. Rabbi Nathan Peter Levinson and Prof. Dr. Pnina Navè-Levinson were to a great degree responsible for bringing the German edition to life, through their professional guidance. Sadly, Pnina, a childhood friend of Marie Simon, also has passed away in the meantime. Shortly before her death, she, too, answered questions about Regina Jonas, from whom she took private Hebrew lessons in the 1930s.

I will never forget the many inspiring hours spent with Israel-Meir Miller, the Ba'al Koreh [Torah reader] of the orthodox Joachimstaler Strasse Synagogue in Berlin, who studied Talmud, Rambam, Tur, and *Shulchan Aruch* with me for an entire summer. I will always cherish the memory of those supremely Jewish moments of exhilaration when, after hours of intense concentration, suddenly we would crack the nut of a particular Tosafot. I also wish to thank the head of the Library of the Jewish Community of Berlin, Arkady Fried, who helped find the relevant rabbinical texts, using his CD-ROM collection.

One of my best experiences relates to my contact with Dr. Katharina von Kellenbach, who researched Regina Jonas long before I did. She shared her notes and research—up to the deportation lists, which she found only after intensive efforts—with the comment that "we women can only move ahead if we work together." Also greatly inspiring were my many conversations with Lara Dämmig and Dr. Rachel Monika Herweg, who with me initiated Bet Debora Berlin, the historical first conference of European female rabbis, cantors, scholars, and other spiritually interested Jewish women and men, which took place in May 1999. At the conference, I also received important tips from two former students of the Academy for the Science of Judaism, Shoshana Ronen (née Susi Elbogen) and Ilse Perlman (née Selier). Much unexpected inspiration came from friends, including Reingard Jäkl, who deciphered some of Regina Jonas's more difficult handwriting.

My great thanks go to Alan Rinzler and Arthur Kurzweil, who immediately recognized the importance of making this book available to an English-speaking public. A particular learning experience was the cooperation between Toby Axelrod and me. Toby not only translated this book into English but also engaged me in reconsidering how to present a German theme to an American audience, making me more aware of my subjective German perspective and of the occasional need to take a different approach. Her influence made its way into the final text.

Furthermore, I am indebted to Andrea Flint for her sensitive thoroughness in editing and proofreading and to Rebecca Allen for her careful and expert review of the sources cited by Regina Jonas in her treatise.

When I started six and a half years ago to place queries in German-language newspapers read by survivors of the Shoah, I didn't expect such a great response. My thanks go to the following eyewitnesses who, from 1998 onward, shared in letters and conversations their recollections of Regina Jonas, whether recounting firsthand experiences or those of family and friends. An asterisk indicates the person corresponded by letter with Dr. Katharina von Kellenbach.

- Shalom Albeck (Jerusalem, Israel)—son of Prof. Dr. Chanoch Albeck, former lecturer at the Academy for the Science of Judaism

- Rabbi Ted (Theodor) Alexander (San Francisco, United States)— son of Hugo Alexander, former president of the board of the Rykestrasse Synagogue

- Gad Beck (Berlin, Germany)—former slave laborer under the Nazis, together with Regina Jonas

- Eva Berg (née Fischer) (Bustan Hagalil, Israel)—pupil of Regina Jonas

- Jack Brotzen (Oceanside, United States)—son of Karl Brotzen, former member of the board of the Neue Synagoge of Berlin
- Herta Budwig (née Ciefer) (Berlin, Germany)—pupil of Regina Jonas
- Bernhard H. Burton (original name Burstein) (Manhasset Hills, United States)—former patient of the Jewish Hospital in Berlin
- Ruth Callmann (San Francisco, United States)—pupil of Regina Jonas
- Margaret H. Collin (Tucson, United States)—sang in the choir of the "Neue Synagoge"*
- Else Davidsohn (née Coper) (Hamburg, Germany)—schoolmate of Regina Jonas
- Ilse Ehrlich-Kochanczyk (Griesheim, Germany)—pupil of Regina Jonas
- Karla Emanuel-Rosenstock (Wembley Park, Great Britain)—daughter of a friend of Regina Jonas
- John Fink (originally Hans Finke) (Chicago, United States)—pupil of Regina Jonas
- Rita Friedman (née Nagler) (Berkeley, United States)—pupil of Regina Jonas
- Ursula de Hecht (née Behrendt) (Buenos Aires, Argentina)—pupil of Regina Jonas
- Hanna Hochfeld (San Francisco, United States)—daughter of Rabbi Dr. Joseph Norden
- Siegbert Kaffe (Santiago de Chile, Chile)—pupil of Regina Jonas
- Miriam Knöpfle (née Magafiner) (Albuquerque, United States)—pupil of Regina Jonas*
- Gisela Lavie (née Müller) (Haifa, Israel)—pupil of Regina Jonas
- Dr. I. O. Lehman (Cincinnati, United States)—classmate of Regina Jonas at the Academy for the Science of Judaism*
- Gerda Levinsohn-Marcus (née Schustermann) (Jerusalem, Israel)—pupil of Regina Jonas who encountered her later in the Theresienstadt concentration camp
- Prof. Dr. Rabbi Nathan Peter Levinson (originally Lewinsky) (Jerusalem, Israel; and Berlin, Germany)—encountered Regina Jonas when he was a rabbinical student

- Prof. Dr. Pnina Navè Levinson (née Paula Fass) (Jerusalem, Israel; and Berlin, Germany)—pupil of Regina Jonas

- Lieselott Lilian Levy (Philadelphia, United States)—pupil of Regina Jonas*

- Hanna and Dieter Renning (Turlock, United States)—Rabbi Dr. Joseph Norden's granddaughter and her husband

- Günther Ruschin (Berlin, Germany)—encountered Regina Jonas in the Levetzowstrasse Synagogue

- Ernst Joshua Samosh (North York, Canada)—brother of a friend of Regina Jonas

- Meta Schiowitz (née Wolny) (Berlin, Germany)—pupil of Regina Jonas

- Margot Schramm (née Camnetzer) (Pembroke Pines, United States)—pupil of Regina Jonas

- Ruth Sherman (née Epstein) (Burbank, United States)—neighbor of Regina Jonas in Krausnickstrasse

- Herta Shriner (née Lewin) (New York, United States)—pupil of Regina Jonas

- Prof. Dr. Marie Simon (née Jalowicz) (Berlin, Germany)—encountered Regina Jonas in the Alte Synagoge

- Susanne Spatz (née Flörsheim) (Newton Center, United States)—pupil of Regina Jonas

- Gisela Stone (née Langer) (Century Village, United States)—pupil of Abraham Jonas*

- Hans Walter (Mansfield, United States)—pupil of Regina Jonas

- Gerda Zielke (née Roth) (Berlin, Germany)—pupil of Regina Jonas

- Betty Zinvirt (Berlin, Germany)—granddaughter of Margot Kurzweg, a pupil of Regina Jonas

With their recollections, these witnesses have contributed to preserving the memory of Regina Jonas.

E.K.

*Fräulein Regina Jonas, our first female preacher
since Deborah, who not only is a gifted speaker
but also can preach well, often and with humor—
and who has pleased absolutely everyone.*

—Dedication in a book that the medical doctor
Arje Jehuda presented to Regina Jonas in 1931
in the summer resort of Bad Reichenhall

*I have always wondered why our rabbis do not speak
in a lively manner—your talk at the end of the holiday
gave me my answer. A speech can only affect people
when one works together with them,
feeling and suffering. Jews will understand such
sermons, and when your listeners say to each other
upon exiting the temple, "Wasn't she right," and
"She was indeed right," then it is not only recognition
but also gratefulness.*

—From a letter from congregant Alfred Salinger
to Regina Jonas on May 25, 1942

Photo of Rabbi Regina Jonas, presumably taken at the beginning of 1936

This photo of Regina Jonas appears to have been taken shortly after her ordination in December 1935. On the reverse is written "18. Febr. 36, Iranishe Str. 3. Jüd. Altersheim, Rosenberg" [February 18, 1936, Jewish Senior Home, Rosenberg, at Iranische Str. 3] together with a Hebrew citation from Exodus (3:14): "I shall be who I shall be." Reproduction: Margit Billeb

PART ONE

MY JOURNEY
TOWARD REGINA JONAS

I WILL NEVER FORGET my ambivalent feelings at the closing scene of the film *Yentl*. For most of the film, I was transported back to the eastern European shtetl where Yentl is portrayed famously as a young girl struggling to have the education and opportunities that were only permitted in those days to boys. But suddenly, in the final moments, I watched Barbra Streisand seated in the hold of a ship, together with other Jewish immigrants, heading for America. The actress begins to sing the song that by now is so well known: "Papa, can you hear me?" She rises and goes to the ship's deck, where she stands by the railing and brings the song to its ecstatic conclusion. The camera slowly draws back until the expanse of ocean fills the screen. The boat traverses the horizon. The end.

Was that the right thing to do? To leave? To retreat? To start life again somewhere else? Did Yentl have no chance in Europe? Did a young woman who had just conquered the world of the Talmud on her own turf, and who had triumphantly stood her ground with men, inevitably have to leave the scene?

The filming of Isaac Bashevis Singer's story took place almost four decades after the Shoah, the murder of European Jewry by the Nazis. As a Jew who had grown up in Germany, I had conflicting feelings as I sat in the Hamburg movie theater that day, but my knowledge of recent history would not permit me to find words to express my ambivalence. Naturally, as a Jewish member of the audience, I *had to be* grateful.

Thank God Yentl got out of Europe on time! Thank God she and her descendants were spared from the tragedies looming on the European horizon: pogroms, anti-Semitism, persecution, culminating finally in the Nazi death camps.

But something in me resisted this message. I knew the answer contained in the film's conclusion could not be the right one for a woman like me, a Jewish feminist in Germany in 1983.

The Shoah, which almost completely extinguished Jewish life in Europe, resonated wordlessly in the film's final scenes, adding to the sense of relief at Yentl's emigration. But the story contained a second, subtler message. Long before "gender" had become a term used in feminist discourse, Yentl had traversed gender's traditional, accepted boundaries. As a girl dressed in a man's clothing—as a "yeshiva *bocher*"—she immersed herself in a male world of learning, thus reclaiming a spiritual inheritance that had been passed down exclusively among men for centuries. And this all happened in "old Europe," supposedly a forbidden zone for such pursuits. Following the logic of the film's conclusion, Yentl the troublemaker, Yentl the rebellious woman, ultimately must leave Europe, thereby also leaving the old ways undisturbed.

But was this the only and unavoidable response to the challenge? Was Europe so hardened by convention that Judaism, too, would be unable to open new doors in Europe? And what was the situation now, for me?

In fact, back in the 1980s, when I saw the film, it was unimaginable for a Jewish woman in Germany to conquer the world of the Talmud—because fathers were no longer handing down Jewish tradition to their sons, let alone to their daughters. It never even occurred to most of us younger women that a female Jewish scholar could become a rabbi, because hardly any men would take on such a task either. Not only had the Shoah almost completely destroyed European Jewry in the physical sense; spiritually, too, Jewry was devastated to its core.

The few survivors who rebuilt their lives after 1945 on the ruined foundations of German Jewry came not only from Germany but from all across central and eastern Europe. Most ended up staying by chance, not by choice, in the land of the murderers, and most were too deeply wounded in their souls to develop an active, positive Judaism ready to take on contemporary challenges. In addition, these survivors carried with them memories and traditions from their destroyed homes. These memories gave them stability, but did not provide a vision for the future. Postwar Jewry arose against the backdrop of these many, varied memories.

We children of survivors grew up with the attitude that at best we were an "epilogue." Our "Jewish upbringing" often fostered an inferiority complex, according to which we no longer really existed. Relatives from Israel or America helped confirm this complex, so that we developed neither self-confidence in our Jewishness nor an appreciation of the fact that what once had existed could still be meaningful for us. The answer, for those who wanted a *real* Jewish life, was—just like Yentl—to set out for America, or better yet, Israel. The very idea of promoting equality for women in the Jewish tradition in postwar Germany seemed laughable, particularly because tradition as such lay shattered, and few could picture creating Jewish life from these broken shards.

Thank God, Yentl left Europe just in time, so that the seedlings she and other Jewish women planted at least could thrive in the United States!

But this was not the entire answer.

Wouldn't Yentl encounter similar reservations among men in America as in Europe? Were not female rabbis in the United States—at least until the 1970s—just as little accepted as in Europe? In Yentl's day, was not the struggle for equality between the sexes in Judaism only starting on both sides of the ocean?

Between Yentl's generation and mine lay the abyss of the Shoah. But between the film *Yentl* and the publishing of this book today, an event occurred that changed our outlook: the fall of the Berlin Wall in November 1989. Before, few thought European Jewry would ever thrive again, to pick up where it left off in 1933. But unlike Yentl, who had to leave at the end of the story, European Jews in my generation have reasons to stay.

Some of those reasons were revealed like long-hidden treasures when, after the end of the communist dictatorship in the East, the archives of the former East Germany were opened. In 1989 the remaining Gesamtarchiv der deutschen Juden (Central Archive of German Jewry) was located in Potsdam. Seven years later, in 1996, this archive was given to the Stiftung Neue Synagoge Berlin—Centrum Judaicum. The archive contained sensational material. And the most remarkable rediscovery was—in my view—the first female rabbi in the world: Regina Jonas.

☙☙☙

In 1989 the name Regina Jonas was barely known anymore. She was born on August 3, 1902, in Berlin and murdered in Auschwitz, most likely on October 15, 1944. Jonas had given her documents presumably to the Berlin Jewish Community for safekeeping in 1942 shortly before her deportation to the Theresienstadt concentration camp. Most probably, these fourteen files were transferred from the Berlin Jewish Community to the archive, where they lay for five decades without awaking anyone's interest.

In particular, there were two outstanding documents. First, there was Jonas's eighty-eight-page halachic treatise, "Can Women Serve as Rabbis?" Jonas had written this in 1930 as her final paper for the Berlin Hochschule für die Wissenschaft des Judentums [Academy for the Science of Judaism]. There, Jonas made the historical first attempt to argue, on the basis of Halacha, or Jewish religious law, for the emancipation of women up to and including admission to the rabbinate. The second groundbreaking document in this collection was a certificate of ordination, written in Hebrew. According to this document, Regina Jonas became the first female rabbi in the world on December 27, 1935. A leading liberal rabbi of that day, Max Dienemann, had signed the document.

In addition, Jonas's files contained letters from most of the renowned contemporary German rabbis. Some letters were from Jonas's teachers, including her professors at the Academy for the Science of Judaism, including Leo Baeck, Eduard Baneth, and Harry Torczyner (Tur Sinai); others were from colleagues with whom Jonas had worked closely: rabbis Max Weyl, Isidor Bleichrode, Felix Singermann, and Joseph Norden; and many letters were from people who had supported Jonas's courage and persistence during years of struggle for recognition as a rabbi.

As sensational as the discovery was, it also evoked a sense of deep disappointment. Why had no survivor of the Nazi regime spoken about Regina Jonas? Why was her story suppressed for decades? When Hebrew Union College in Cincinnati ordained Sally Priesand in 1972, the press celebrated her as "the first woman rabbi of the world." Why did hardly any of those who knew better not correct this information? Why should it have taken more than a half-century before Regina Jonas could be restored to her proper place in Jewish history?

Wasn't Regina Jonas someone of whom surviving German Jews could be proud? Why did Leo Baeck, who survived Theresienstadt and spoke out for liberal Judaism, never mention his former student who suffered with him at the concentration camp? Jonas had worked closely in Theresienstadt with the Viennese psychoanalyst Viktor Frankl, whose postwar publication and autobiography *Ein Psychologe erlebt das Konzentrationslager* [A Psychologist Experiences the Concentration Camp], published in English as *Man's Search for Meaning,* revolved around his experiences in the concentration camp, from which Frankl developed his own approach to therapy. Why is there not a single reference to Regina Jonas in this book? Frankl certainly had not forgotten her. In an interview in 1991 with the German-American theologian Katharina von Kellenbach after the rediscovery of Jonas's works, not only did Frankl remember very well the female rabbi in Theresienstadt, but one of her sermons had moved him so much that he could even repeat it in detail.

Why was Regina Jonas kept from us? And who else have we younger women been denied? In the early 1990s, several Jewish women—including myself—organized within the Berlin Jewish Community to press for equality for women in the synagogues and services. Why did none of Regina Jonas's former students, of whom quite a few still lived in Berlin, inform us that we were following in her tradition, that we in fact were only picking up a debate that had begun decades ago?

‍§ § §

I have two answers to these questions. The first is shame. The survivor generation had cut itself off emotionally from German Jewry and suppressed its memory. Its members were ashamed to have believed in a country that had abused their trust so terribly, inflicting the most horrible trauma on Jewry. To remember Regina Jonas would be to recall a time when hope for the future had been transformed into murderous self-betrayal. For many, this was too painful.

The second answer is also shame. Even today, a woman who steps out of line and succeeds in a male domain quickly becomes an embarrassment—particularly if she calls attention to controversial subjects. During my research, I sensed that some eyewitnesses—both men and women—had felt threatened by Jonas's public breaking of taboos. Instead of taking her seriously, they portrayed her as a negative exception, one of those unconventional, high-achieving women with unpleasant attributes, such as "hysterical," "odd-looking," "eccentric," and so on.

Perhaps only a new generation of Jews who choose to live in Germany—a generation that no longer struggles with the inferiority complex of "still" living in Germany, but rather that deliberately connects with its spiritual heritage on the very ground where it was generated—can appreciate the message of Regina Jonas's life.

As time passes and the pain begins to fade, the messages left to us by victims of the Shoah become more complex. Some of these messages—such as "staying"—can be reevaluated and seen in a new light only in my generation. Regina Jonas did not leave—unlike Yentl. She stayed at the cost of her own life. Jonas always refused to flee. She, like many other rabbis in Nazi Germany, could have left; perhaps she could even have made a career in the United States. But she did not leave. She saw her life's work as staying with those of her people who were in need, and she took the same path of suffering that cost the lives of more than fifty-five thousand Berlin Jews who were murdered in German concentration and extermination camps.

For many Jews, it certainly took courage to leave Nazi Germany. But Jonas's decision to stay displayed a courage of its own, which is meaningful for me and the generation of younger German Jews. Her commitment to Jewish life in Germany contains seeds that can regenerate in us, contradicting decades of insistence that there can be no more Jewish life in the land of the Nazi perpetrators.

To stay as an act of resistance.

To stay as a way of holding on to a greater past, a past that must not be sacrificed due to current circumstances—the epitome of the Jewish leit-motif.

To stay as an antiheroic act, an act that contradicts the dramatic, almost kitschy film and fantasy scenes of persecution, decline, flight, and death, and instead focuses on the daily ups and downs of life.

To stay as a radical constructive approach.

My generation would stay, hold on, rebuild, perhaps even take new directions. And Regina Jonas bequeathed to my peers and me exactly the right bridge.

❧ ❧ ❧

In 1998, while I was helping prepare the first Bet Debora conference in Berlin for female rabbis, cantors, scholars, and spiritually interested Jews, Dr. Hermann Simon, director of the Stiftung Neue Synagoge Berlin—Centrum Judaicum, asked me to examine the unpublished work of Regina Jonas that had been revealed by our new access to the East German archives. He wanted me to write a biography about her, and then to edit and write a commentary on her halachic treatise, "Can Women Serve as Rabbis?"

As great as the silence of remaining eyewitnesses, colleagues, students, and friends of Regina Jonas had been, so was their excitement now over the fact that a book about Jonas would be published. It was crazy. Suddenly, dozens of voices were raised—for or against Regina Jonas. These aging opponents or supporters of the first female rabbi in the world argued so vehemently that I began to feel that, even after more than half a century, the provocation of a woman entering the rabbinate was as stirring as if it had occurred yesterday.

Initially, negative attitudes predominated—including, to my astonishment, those of a significant number of women. One of Jonas's contemporaries, who also had studied at the Academy for the Science of Judaism and later became a professor for Jewish studies, described Jonas as a "hysterical person" whose only goal was to "show herself off against the men." A former pupil of Jonas who also became a professor of Jewish studies considered Jonas's treatise, "Can Woman Serve as Rabbis?", to be "nothing special" and her arguments to be "cold coffee" compared with today's publications by American Jewish feminists. Some of Jonas's male colleagues, too, stressed that "no one took her seriously" and added that her certificate of ordination was not genuine. At a podium discussion to which I was invited and where I mentioned the name Regina Jonas in passing, the son of a cantor who was Jonas's contemporary interrupted me and warned me not to use the term *Rabbinerin* [female rabbi] casually. Jonas was "no *Rabbinerin*," she was "only a preacher!" He emphasized that Leo Baeck "did *not*" sign Regina Jonas's original Hebrew certificate of ordination but "only the translation" into German. And he added that Max Dienemann "accomplished single-handedly" an ordination that remained extremely questionable among German Jews. Furthermore, he said, the Jewish Community only allowed Regina Jonas to preach in the synagogues because during the Nazi period many rabbis had fled abroad or were imprisoned, creating a great need for rabbis. The same man expressed his opinion in a letter to a German Jewish newspaper, in response to which Jonas's supporters raised their voices. "This is total nonsense!" Rabbi Ted (Theodor) Alexander of San Francisco railed in a letter to the newspaper. "The man has no idea!" On the contrary: many rabbis stood behind Jonas and not only respected her as their equal but saw Dienemann's step as "long overdue." As a youth, Rabbi Alexander, today of Congregation B'nay Emunah, went to the same synagogue on Shabbat with Regina Jonas. In an enthusiastic letter to me, he expressed his joy over Jonas's triumph in becoming a rabbi, noting that his daughter also has become a rabbi. Rabbi Nathan Peter Levinson, who also knew Regina Jonas well as a young man, likewise expressed to me his belated appreciation for Jonas. Her ordination cleared the way for new developments in Judaism and ended up encouraging many women—including his wife, Pnina—to follow a similar path. Pnina Navè Levinson herself was a pupil of Regina Jonas in Berlin and was the first to put out Jewish feminist publications in postwar Germany.

The "Jonas case" brought the denominational coordinates of Germany's pre-1939 rabbinical system back into play. Orthodox and liberal Judaism—both of which had moderate and radical forces—suddenly faced off against each other again in the context of the 1920s and 1930s. Not one rabbi from this period was without an opinion about the ordination of women. Once again, the great authorities of those days took their positions vis-à-vis the scandal. And the debate took place in German—my language. I was able to perceive and appreciate all the optimistic innocence with which one could, even in the early 1930s, feel in touch with the most important developments in Judaism.

I felt almost wistful when I saw how much "further along" the Jews in Germany had been, just how much had been possible then, just which struggles were remaining but had at least been discussed, themes for which there was little recognition today in Germany, barely any understanding. Had these possibilities become obsolete through the destruction of the Shoah? Or could it be that if we wish to have a vibrant Judaism here today, we must connect with the very themes taken up by Regina Jonas and others—in other words, to reattach ourselves to this heritage?

I started to feel a foundation under my feet, a base on which not just I but all Jews in Germany today could have been standing had there been no Shoah. It seemed only natural that Judaism would be able to develop under new terms. Because if they could see new horizons back then, why should I not have the same possibilities today? Rescuing Jonas from oblivion opened new doors.

Word soon got out about my research. In 1998 I had placed ads in German-Jewish newspapers worldwide, and people reacted with letters, e-mail, and phone calls. The responses continue to this day. In all, there have been more than forty contacts.

The response was unexpected, because virtually nobody had spoken about Regina Jonas for decades. And as an editor of *jüdisches berlin* magazine, I knew that very few people ever respond to authors' queries. But very quickly, people reacted. It was as if they all had been waiting to say something about Regina Jonas, whether good or bad. The story moved them in a way that the ordination of Sally Priesand had not, because Regina Jonas was ordained in Germany—specifically, in Berlin. It was a way for all these older people to reconnect with their own past.

Here too, I experienced as much approval of Jonas as aggression against her. One woman who was a forced laborer in 1941 together with Regina Jonas utterly refused to speak with me. One should let the "blanket of forgetfulness" cover Regina Jonas, because "everything she did as a woman was forbidden!" Such silences made me realize how much open rejection Regina Jonas had to endure from other Jews even during the Shoah, and I also saw how little compassion they showed for her sixty years after her murder. Still, numerous former religious-school pupils reported how much Jonas's lessons had meant to them, particularly in those dark days in Nazi Germany. For many girls, this unusual religion teacher became a lifelong role model.

A former pupil of Jonas who taught at Berlin's Jewish kindergarten after the war referred to Jonas's "modern pedagogic style," which was already noteworthy then and drew many girls back to Judaism. For example, Jonas wrote a play that her pupils performed with great enthusiasm every year for Chanukah. The kindergarten teacher told me that for decades she had tried to find a copy of the play because it had been more effective than many contemporary teaching methods at instilling a joy in Judaism among children.

I also learned much about the relativity of oral history. Often, the descriptions revealed more about the witnesses themselves than about Regina Jonas. It was astonishing how much weight many former pupils gave to Jonas's appearance. And here I made an interesting observation. Those students who had been preadolescent had an overwhelmingly positive recollection of their "unforgettably beautiful" and "impressive" teacher, who managed to "make learning unbelievably interesting." For the older girls, in whom sexuality and competition over boys played a role, negative memories predominated of a teacher who clearly was threatening, who did not set an example as a wife or mother but instead agitated for professional equality with men. Even today I detected some disrespectful giggling and nasty comments in the descriptions of those then-adolescent young women. Regina Jonas supposedly did not take care of herself, her wardrobe left much to be desired, and even her hair supposedly stood on end.

It hardly mattered whether the memories were positive or negative: I was amazed at the deep impression Regina Jonas had left in these women and at how vividly they could describe their former teacher sixty years later. Several former pupils could even recite their lines from the Chanukah play.

Just as the eyewitnesses described the controversy surrounding Regina Jonas as if it had taken place only yesterday, so did Regina Jonas become ever more present to me as a person—even physically. When I visited the places where she lived and worked, it sometimes felt as if she were accompanying me—as if she actively pushed me toward the most important questions. I asked myself how she would have related to my Jewish feminist positions: a women's Rosh Chodesh group (new month celebration), experiments with Hebrew liturgy, feminine terms for God, new rituals for new lifestyles. How would she have responded if she could have been a guest of honor at our first Bet Debora conference in May 1999? She would certainly have been deeply moved to find a younger generation in Germany carrying Jewish tradition into the future. Her dream would have been fulfilled. It was always her goal as a rabbi to enable women to have an active role in Judaism, because this promised the revival of tradition.

Regina Jonas probably would have been somewhat amazed by our new ideas, considering she was herself quite conventional, if not conservative. She was never out to change the Jewish religion. Rather, she wanted to reactivate Judaism against the backdrop of the "immoral" ways of the "Roaring Twenties," to reinstill moral values in the Jewish youth of Berlin. Thus, she even argued that a female rabbi should remain single in order to exemplify the ideal of *zniut*—dignified restraint and chastity. This view of course later conflicted with her love relationship with Rabbi Joseph Norden of Hamburg, who was a widower and much older than she. Nevertheless, "higher morality" remained her lifelong ideal. And in this respect she trusted women more than men. Correspondingly, she argued for the female rabbinate as a "cultural necessity." Here again she was amazingly modern and open to new possibilities. In her halachic treatise, "Can Women Serve as Rabbis?", Jonas managed more or less to reconcile the emancipation of women with principles of Jewish religious law.

But she would certainly not have missed the chance to step up to the *bima* with us younger women during the Shabbat service at Bet Debora. Yes, she would have joined in, and she would have discovered to her satisfaction that most of the debates that take place today in the United States and in Israel about the female rabbinate were already handled in her treatise.

Today, orthodox Jewish women are seeking halachic arguments with which they can advance the cause of women entering the rabbinate. Jonas's halachic treatise provides them with valuable suggestions. Today, rabbis discuss the pros and cons of a male or female title: in Hebrew, *Rabbanit, Rav,* or *Rabah;* and in German, *Rabbiner* or *Rabbinerin.* This theme, which emerged in Jonas's 1930 writings, was taken up recently by Rabbi Moshe Zemer of Israel. In other respects, too, Regina Jonas's life and work has been well received, with interesting results. The Hadassah International Research Institute of Jewish Women at Brandeis University published Gudrun Maierhof's article about Regina Jonas's activities as a rabbi in the Nazi period. Currently, a doctoral candidate is comparing Jonas with other religious female thinkers during the Shoah, including Edith Stein.

However, with the discovery of Jonas's writings, not only must Jewish history be rewritten with regard to the female rabbinate, but a new chapter of Jewish life in Germany must be written too, for me and many others whose families remained after the Shoah: the chapter connecting us with our predecessors. True, the discussion about women in the rabbinate today is far more advanced in the United States. But the U.S. experience cannot be translated directly to the European context. We who have stayed have to write that new chapter by ourselves, based on our own experiences.

Unlike in the United States, where female candidates now make up the majority in liberal rabbinical seminaries, Europe still must fight for the acceptance of women in the rabbinate. In Germany, at any rate, this book already has contributed greatly to this purpose. Thanks to the name

Regina Jonas, the subject of *Rabbinerin* is no longer quite so provocative, because a woman already was accepted to the rabbinate many decades ago. The next wave of German-speaking female rabbis, starting with Daniela Thau in the 1980s and Bea Wyler in the mid-1990s, and continuing with Eveline Goodman-Thau and Gesa Ederberg, now could refer back to Regina Jonas and were no longer seen as "taboo breakers" in the full sense of the word.

It seems that both the Jewish and non-Jewish public were waiting for this book to arrive: almost all the major newspapers dedicated space to the themes of Regina Jonas and women in the German and European rabbinate today. The October 1999 German first edition was snatched up within a few weeks, making a second printing necessary in the spring of 2000. Then, in the fall of 2003, Berlin publisher Hentrich & Hentrich came out with the third edition of Jonas's biography. To this day I am invited to deliver talks about Regina Jonas on an almost monthly basis. Audiences range from liberal Jews to committed Christians to feminist politicians. In launching the second Bet Debora conference in 2001, I unveiled a memorial plaque at Rabbinerin Jonas's former home, on Krausnickstrasse 6. Germany's first female cantor, Avitall Gerstetter, sang at the ceremony. This, too, drew the attention of German media, and the plaque is an attraction for many tourists today.

The present English-language edition of the book contains numerous extensions of the first version in German. I have extended and amended it with a view toward the reader who may not be familiar with the German context of the 1920s and 1930s. Where necessary I have added detailed explanations. In addition, more witnesses emerged in response to the first publication. Their recollections are included in this U.S. edition. I wish to mention in particular the children and grandchildren of Rabbi Dr. Joseph Norden, Regina Jonas's lover. Not long after the publication of the second edition, I received a call from Dr. Ulrike Schrader, the director of the Alte Synagoge in Wuppertal-Elberfeld, the synagogue where Norden served for years as a rabbi before serving in Hamburg. She seemed astonished that Norden had been together with Jonas, and she reported that Norden has grandchildren, and that one of his five children was still alive. She then invited me to deliver a talk on Regina Jonas in Wuppertal, and invited Norden's granddaughter in California, Hanna Renning, and her husband, Dieter. Hanna brought along letters from her grandfather from 1940 to 1942 in which Norden told his children about his relationship with Regina Jonas. Some of these letters were written while Jonas was spending her vacation with Norden in his home in Hamburg. They even contained handwritten comments from Jonas herself. Independent of their content, the letters were sensational for me, because virtually all the letters in Jonas's collection of documents, including of course Norden's, were written *to* Regina Jonas. There are almost none that she wrote to others. On the basis of these letters and the new information they provided, I have completely reworked the passages on the love relationship between Jonas and Norden.

჻ ჻ ჻

Regina Jonas has influenced and changed my life as few others have. Not only have I grown spiritually through the subject of the book, seeing certain things today differently from a decade ago, before I became involved in this project, but my confrontation with Regina Jonas, which, admittedly, led temporarily to an overidentification with the first female rabbi in Jewish history, also brought me to a decision of great significance in my own life. While working on this book, I often thought I heard her voice with its pleasant "sonorous" ring, which so many of her former pupils still remembered well. This voice seemed to prod me: "And what about you? Could you not also serve as a rabbi?" In fact, almost sixty years after she was murdered in Auschwitz, Regina Jonas became my teacher and trailblazer. In a symbolic fulfillment of her role, my own rabbinical ordination under the Aleph Rabbinic Program coincided with the publication of this U.S. edition.

In this context, the publication of this book is also an expression of a greater development—the renewal of a German, a European Jewry that no longer stands only on the ruins of the Shoah, that is no longer imprisoned by the trauma of the destruction, but that builds bridges to a great past. That development is spurred by the initiatives of Jews across Europe today. Bet Debora is only one of them. In all of Europe's largest cities, new Jewish communities or groups have formed in which women and men connect—on an equal basis—with their Jewish heritage. It is still too early to say how European Jewry will look in the decades ahead. But there is no doubt that, with this renewal, some great names of the past are returning—as if they had only been waiting to reach out to the generation that would stay.

The author unveiling a plaque to Regina Jonas

The author unveiling a plaque to Regina Jonas at Jonas's former residence in Berlin, Krausnickstrasse 6, at the beginning of the second Bet Debora conference, June 2001.

THE STORY OF REGINA JONAS

God has placed abilities and callings in our hearts,
without regard to gender. Thus each of us has the duty,
whether man or woman, to realize those gifts God has given.

Regina Jonas, June 23, 1938

JUDAISM TEACHES THAT God did not decide who would lead his people of Israel into the next era by rank, power, riches, or birthright. After all, Jacob was only the second born, David was the youngest and least outstanding of his clan, and Rabbi Akiva was a simple shepherd. Yet Jacob became one of the three patriarchs, David became king of Israel, and Rabbi Akiva became a founder of rabbinic Judaism.

These transformations express the epitome of Jewish ethics: the image of God is revealed in every person, regardless of social status. But Jewish tradition also has a conservative orientation. Every generation looks back, honors the teachings of its divinely inspired predecessors, and holds up these teachings as irrevocable, eternally valid statutes. Still, God's ways are not the same as those of people. And so the people of Israel are ever surprised when someone in whom the Jewish core message becomes reality follows a different path from that apparently prescribed by tradition.

Unlike most Jewish activists who struggled for the emancipation of women in Germany before and after World War I, Regina Jonas did not come from a distinguished family. She also had no rabbinical forefathers in her family tree to legitimize her daring decision to become the first female rabbi. Nor did she have a family fortune in the background to ease her down a career path strewn with obstacles.

❧ ❧ ❧

One can only speculate about Jonas's childhood, based on scanty evidence. Her birth certificate, an entry in the card catalog of Berlin's Jewish cemetery in Weissensee reporting the death and burial of her father, Berlin address books indicating where Regina's family lived, and a few statements related to the Nazi census of 1938–1939 reveal isolated details about Jonas's early years. In a 1939 interview, well after she had become a rabbi, Jonas said she came from a "strictly religious home." Her friend and lover, Rabbi Dr. Joseph Norden of Hamburg, with whom she corresponded intensively from 1939 until his deportation in June 1942, remarked in one of his letters about her "difficult youth." Her mother told a journalist who wrote an article after Jonas passed the rabbinical exam on December 26, 1935, that even as a "little girl" Regina was already behaving like a minister, influencing her classmates. But these few details provide only a blurry image.

So it seems Jonas emerged literally from nothing, in the 1920s, into the world of rabbinical Jewish scholarship.

Born in Berlin on August 3, 1902, Jonas grew up in an area where no cultivated or well-to-do Jewish Berliner would normally visit. At any rate, those who grew up before World War I in the Scheunenviertel [lit., the district of barns; an area of horse barns that later became a living area] had to learn early on how to fend for themselves. In this shabby, grungy quarter "behind Alexanderplatz," poverty was the rule. The apartments often had never even been provided with a sink, whole families lived in one room, and several parties had to share a toilet located in the hallway or in the backyard. The population density of the Scheunenviertel was five times higher than the average for Berlin. The various apartment buildings often opened out into several courtyards, the innermost of which were the most dark and narrow.

In Berlin city records from the time around World War I, the name "Wolf Jonas" is not found in every year. If all entries regarding Wolf Jonas actually refer to Regina's father, her family must have moved constantly within these first years. One reason could have been the "dry living" principle. Poor families were permitted to live up to two years in newly built houses, until the walls had "dried out" and the apartments could be rented at a higher rate. Living in these damp rooms had disastrous health consequences, and it was no accident that Regina's father died of tuberculosis.

At the time of Regina's birth, her family lived in Lothringer Strasse 59 (today Torstrasse); afterward they registered the address of Linienstrasse 24, followed by Grenadierstrasse 4; they lived temporarily in Strassburger

Strasse 43a in the adjacent Prenzlauer Berg district, then in Grenadier-strasse 25, and finally in Alte Schönhauser Strasse 21. Even today these street names evoke the flickering shadows of Berlin's fascinating, lively but dangerous poor quarter. From a moral standpoint, a childhood in the Scheunenviertel provided contradictory impressions. Amidst the misery, Berlin's underworld and women of ill repute had settled. Gang activity, prostitution, crime, and police raids were an everyday occurrence.

Today there is a special genre of nostalgia literature about the *Miljöh*—milieu—of the Scheunenviertel, particularly focusing on dives like the narrow bar on Mulackstrasse called the "Mulack-Ritze"—or "Mulack-Slit"—in which famous artists, including the Berlin caricaturist Heinrich Zille as well as the Expressionist Georg Grosz, found inspiration both before and after World War I.

At the same time, the Scheunenviertel was a place of Jewish piety. Even before the massive Jewish immigration from Russia and Poland made its impact, many Jews lived here. In the houses were hidden numerous small private synagogues and prayer rooms, where Jewish men prayed and studied. From the turn of the century, the Scheunenviertel increasingly took on an eastern-European Jewish atmosphere. The streets were filled with Yiddish-speaking people who had fled pogroms in the czarist region.

By the time of the Kristallnacht pogrom on November 9–10, 1938, this culture had been destroyed. Only today does one begin to realize that there were people of great learning among these refugees, people who ran their own *Stibls,* or small synagogues, where they taught their students and disciples.

Regina's parents were originally not from Berlin, but they had not come as refugees from Russia or Poland. Wolf Jonas, a "businessman" by trade, was born in 1843 in Bütow in the state of Pommern; his wife, Sara Jonas, thirty-three years his junior, was born in 1876 in Böchingen in the state of Bavaria. Regina also had a brother, Abraham, who was two years older than she. Exactly what Wolf Jonas did to feed his family is not clear from the available documents. The term "businessman" could just as easily mean *Bauchladenhändler* [street vendors who carried their wares on a tray attached around their waist] as it could mean department store owner, though the latter would not have been likely in the case of Wolf Jonas. Given their housing conditions, the family must have been impoverished. But it is very likely that Regina's father regularly visited one of the many small private synagogues in the Scheunenviertel and raised his children with a profound sense of religiosity.

Jewish men had lived a double existence for centuries, according to the maxim *"Torah im derech erez"*—Torah study in connection with a worldly profession. Ideally, a man should learn a worldly trade in order to feed his family. The remaining time, however, should be dedicated to the study of Torah and Talmud. Every child from a "strictly religious home" knew these two different worlds. Whatever the impact of the social relationship of poverty and insecurity, within a hostile, anti-Jewish environment, the moment one delved into the world of Hebrew letters, from which teachings and statutes of eternal validity were molded, a sphere of exhilarating, spiritual riches became available to any Jew, regardless of social status.

In the 1939 interview, Regina Jonas did not elaborate on what it meant for her to have grown up in a "strictly religious home." The description does not at all suggest submission to a tough regime of discipline, but rather implies an introduction to the holy writings and Jewish teachings at a very early age. In a strictly observant Jewish family, a child was forced to develop an awareness of a sharp dividing line according to which every aspect of daily life either is sanctified by benedictions and ritual regulations or is considered unfit, impossible to purify. No matter how religious her father was, Regina Jonas grew up with this spiritual principle of differentiation on which the entire Halacha—Jewish religious law—is based and around which most rabbinic confrontations have revolved since talmudic days. Wolf Jonas certainly recited the morning prayer daily, and the family held to the strict Jewish dietary laws, *kashrut* [kosher], dividing milk from meat products and eating meat only from animals that had been slaughtered according to Jewish law, when they could afford meat at all. No matter which synagogue the family attended on Shabbat, whether a small private synagogue in the Scheunenviertel or Berlin's large Orthodox synagogue in Heidereutergasse, Jonas's mother lit Shabbat candles every Friday evening and her father blessed the wine and challah before the meal.

However, for many German Jews, being "strictly religious" in the Orthodox way didn't at all contradict being modern at the same time. It is more than likely that Regina's father was open to the new ideas about religious education for girls and even was himself her first teacher. Regina was not the only one in the family to pursue a religious career; her older brother, Abraham, also became a religious instructor. On Regina's birth certificate, her religion is listed as "mosaic," a term that had replaced the word "Jewish" in official forms and that reflected the self-image of most Berlin Jews, Prussian citizens whose Jewish background was only a matter of religion, not a matter of peoplehood. Certainly Regina's parents, too, hoped for a future for their child that would combine a traditional Jewish identity with that of a citizen with equal rights in a modern Prussia.

Evidently living in the current of their time, they gave their daughter a Latin name (*Regina* means "queen") rather than a Jewish one, which—if names are an omen—speaks for itself. It seems that Regina did not have an additional Jewish name in memory of a grandmother or aunt, as is common in Ashkenazi Jewish tradition. Later, in some letters written to her in Hebrew, she was addressed as "Rifka"—Rebekka, which sounded similar to her given name. But her Talmud professor, Eduard Baneth, as well as some of her rabbinical colleagues, referred to her in their Hebrew letters as "Malka," which means "queen" and suggests that she had no other name besides Regina. And in the original Hebrew text of her rabbinic diploma, she is referred to as "Reyne" [pure woman], a Yiddish name that sounds like "queen" in French *[reine]*.

&&&

On November 3, 1913, Wolf Jonas died of chronic tuberculosis of the lung. He received a poor man's "third-class" burial in Berlin's Weissensee Cemetery, for which Sara Jonas paid in installments to the Jewish Community. The path to the field in which Regina's father was buried passes between many stately, artistically embellished grave sites of Berlin's wealthy Jewish families. How did the then twelve-year-old Regina react to such contrasts? No eyewitnesses who knew Regina Jonas in Berlin saw any evidence that she was ashamed of her parents' poverty or that she felt disadvantaged. Wolf Jonas received only a small grave marker of unpolished, light sandstone, which today stands like a tree stump in the earth surrounded by all the other proud gravestones in that row (J-IV, row 14), with only the name of the deceased incised upon it. There was no rabbi at the funeral and no one was sent by the Jewish Community to chant El Male Rachamim, the prayer of mourning.

Perhaps it was her father's death that wakened young Regina's longing for the "religion of her fathers," and perhaps this combined with her mother's dream of a regal future for her daughter, blending together fruitfully in her choice to become a rabbi. But perhaps Regina Jonas was driven by something else entirely. In any case, her relationships to several much older father figures, who at the same time were her rabbinic mentors—and one of whom even became her lover—is a recurring theme in her life.

In the Jüdische Mädchen-Mittelschule [Jewish Girls' School] in the front building of the Orthodox synagogue on Kaiserstrasse, which Regina Jonas attended during World War I, other students were impressed by her boundless enthusiasm for everything that had to do with Judaism. Else Coper, a former classmate, remembered how Jonas vied for attention in the subjects of Hebrew, religion, and Jewish history, and how the other girls in the class enjoyed it when Jonas was able to show off her knowledge to the teachers. In these areas she had straight A's. She had less interest in the other subjects. Her attention appeared to be oriented almost solely to Jewish religion. As her mother noted, she already leaned toward the rabbinic calling even at this young age, and told the other girls of her plan to study and become a rabbi. She must have been so convincing that her classmates found nothing unusual about this career goal, and it did not even occur to them that a woman's way toward this goal could be barred.

The emancipation of Jewry and the emancipation of women often are seen as one result of the same spiritual-ideological premise. Modern citizenship was linked to the idea of equal rights as the natural right of every human being. It is no accident that in France, the driving force of emancipation in continental Europe, Olympe de Gouge formulated in 1791, shortly after the French Revolution, the "Déclaration des droits de la femme et de la citoyenne" [Declaration of the Rights of the Woman and Female Citizen], and that the Jews of the French province of Alsace, who were inclined to modern citizenship and considered themselves to be French patriots, petitioned for equal rights shortly after the revolution.

It would take, however, much more than proclamations, petitions, and even legal steps to make equality a reality. Even after World War I, when German women had gained suffrage, not all university faculties were completely open to them. It was not until 1921, for example, that women who studied law were permitted to do their *Referendariat* [practical year in court] and final exam, the prerequisite in Germany for running a law office as a lawyer. Despite the eventual access for women to all academic disciplines during the course of the Weimar Republic, the female role as wife and mother conflicted with the idea of equal rights. Female teachers, for example, had to be single by law. Once they married, they had to quit their job. This is one reason why all female teachers were "Fräulein"— "Miss"—indicating their independent status. The inequality of the sexes was also mirrored by the statutes of the Jewish communities in Germany. Although women already had received general suffrage in 1919, it was not until 1926 that Jewish women in Berlin were permitted to vote for the elections of the *Repräsentantenversammlung* [community parliament].[1]

Equal rights for Jews were achieved at the same slow pace. During the time of the German emperor (1871–1918), Jews were placed in the same legal category as the Christian majority. However, apart from some very rare exceptions, they had no chance to pursue a career in the state bureaucracy, let alone in the military and other institutions that were considered to be highly representative for Germany. For Jewish men, it was still almost impossible to become a university professor. Apart from the infamous *Judenerhebung* [census for Jews] during World War I, which aimed to investigate whether a large proportion of Jews had tried to evade their military service, the discrimination against Jews can be demonstrated by the financial situation of the clergy. While the Reich paid for Christian pastors and ministers to visit soldiers in the field, Jewish communities had to pay for their own *Feldrabbiner*. However, most Jews identified with the German Empire and believed they had a hopeful future ahead of them. In order to finally establish themselves in society, Jews of all social levels focused on education—a pillar of their tradition. Even children from poor families pursued a high school diploma and aimed for a university education.

For women it was also a time of social upheaval. The "surplus of women," due to the greater number of girls born, had increased after World War I due to the loss of soldiers. Even women from middle-class homes could no longer simply count on marriage and an economically secure life as wife and mother. Many widows of fallen soldiers were forced to go to work. Meanwhile, a first generation of female students already had entered the universities. Almost all of these young women could claim to be the first in their fields. Long before World War I, the first middle-class women's movement had begun. They fought for women's right to vote, for political equality, and for the right to choose a career. And Jewish women were among the most active in this movement.

In 1904 Bertha Pappenheim founded the Jewish Women's League.[2] Pappenheim is famous today as Sigmund Freud's "Anna O." Recent publications, including Marianne Brentzel's book *Anna O., Bertha Pappenheim, Biographie,*[3] demonstrate that Pappenheim, while undergoing psychoanalysis as a young woman, discovered the healing effect of self-analysis through talking, as opposed to other popular methods of the day, such as hypnosis. According to Brentzel, it was Pappenheim who invented the "talking cure," which Freud then adopted. Another result of her psychoanalytic treatment was her emancipation as a Jewish woman. In her day, Jewish feminist women favored the social fields as a way to make an impact on society. Pappenheim founded such important institutions as a home for Jewish unwed mothers in Isenburg, where they could get a professional education, and the *Zentralwohlfartsstelle* [Central Welfare Board of the Jewish Community], which remains the main social welfare office for Jews in Germany today. She combated the so-called white slavery of eastern European Jewish women who were forced to be prostitutes in Germany, and attacked the double moral standards of Jewish men, who apparently were among their clients. Pappenheim is in many aspects comparable to the American Henrietta Szold, with the exception that she was not a Zionist but remained deeply committed to Jewish life in the Diaspora even during the Nazi period.[4]

Pappenheim, too, was deeply religious, even Orthodox, but modern and feminist. She wrote thousands of prayers and religious thoughts, which express her struggles as a woman and a Jewish feminist of her day.[5] In 1919 she pressed Frankfurt's Orthodox Rabbi Nehemia Nobel to declare that Judaism allow women both active voting rights and the right to run for office—a document that was cited from then on in every debate about equal rights for Jewish women.

But it would never have occurred to Pappenheim that women also have equal rights in areas of ritual and can serve the same functions as do men in the synagogue, much less that they could preach from the pulpit as rabbis. As did most feminists of her time, she rejected the concept of an "equality" of the sexes, but rather demanded gender "equivalence." Women should try to pursue careers related to their "female nature," particularly in social realms—welfare work, youth work, and emergency services for the most needy members of society. That women were particularly capable in such realms was an argument that also found expression in Regina Jonas's thinking and her later rabbinical self-image.

During Jonas's school years, no one in Germany saw the "women's question" as neutral—not even the pupils in the Jewish Girls' School in Kaiserstrasse. They experienced the resignation of the emperor in 1918, the proclamation of the Weimar Republic, and the first democratic elections, which also admitted women. And they also were poised before the decision of whether to pursue a career after their schooling. For Jonas there was no question that she would seek a high school diploma. But it seems that she did not immediately enter an institute of higher education after finishing secondary school.

It appears she left the Jewish Girls' School at Kaiserstrasse in about 1918. It was only in 1920 that she entered the Public Oberlyzeum [*gymnasium*, or academic preparatory school] in Berlin-Weissensee. Perhaps in the interim she had attended a "home economics" school, something that many girls did in those days after finishing high school. It was not unusual for young women to complete their high school degree relatively late.

☙ ☙ ☙

Although after the death of her husband Sara Jonas was dependent on social welfare, she ultimately was able to create a relatively stable environment for her children. Even during the war, she moved with Abraham and Regina to Prenzlauer Berg, the area northeast of Alexanderplatz. In comparison to the former conditions in the Scheunenviertel, this was a solid neighborhood. The area outside Prenzlauer Tor had just been built in the final decades of the nineteenth century to make room for the city's extremely fast-growing population. This tenement district was home to, for the most part, a comfortable working class and lower-middle class; there was no extreme poverty, but there were ordinary civil servants, shop-keepers, and artisans—among them many Jews. Some better streets of Prenzlauer Berg were even lined with showy facades; some buildings had Belle Etage apartments and bay windows.

Sara Jonas's financial means permitted only a small place in the "sec-ond inner courtyard" of an apartment building. But it was the beginning of a more secure period, following years of instability, many moves from one poor dwelling to the next, the death of Wolf Jonas, and the impres-sions of the world war that had overshadowed Regina Jonas's school years. The family remained here for the next sixteen years.

On Shabbat, Sara Jonas went with her children to Rykestrasse Syna-gogue, one of the most beautiful houses of worship in Berlin, which was within walking distance and had been built for the Jewish population in Prenzlauer Berg around the turn of the century. The synagogue, which survived the Kristallnacht pogrom in 1938 and was reclaimed after the war by the Jewish Community in Communist East Germany, was then known as a "synthesis between tradition and present."

Despite original attempts, the congregation did not succeed in intro-ducing what liberal Jews called the *Neuer Ritus* [new rite]—including organ music and a mixed choir—because most members preferred the *Alter Ritus* [old rite]. Nevertheless, rabbis with a moderate bent regularly served here, including Rabbi Dr. Max Weyl (after 1917).

Though deeply rooted in traditional rabbinical writings, Weyl impressed the spirit of the synagogue with a series of innovations directly related to the status of women. Among other things, he committed him-self to the religious education of girls, introducing bat mitzvah celebra-tions for them—analogous to the bar mitzvah for boys—and later leading the girls' section of the Jewish Religious School in the front building of the Rykestrasse Synagogue complex.

He also encouraged Regina Jonas. Else Coper of the Jewish Girls' School in Kaiserstrasse even remembered that Regina Jonas had spoken of "working together" with Rabbi Weyl. Apparently, she became his assis-tant. Jonas always spoke of Weyl with great respect. He must have repre-sented her rabbinic ideal, at the same time fulfilling a kind of spiritual father function. When Weyl delivered a sermon on Shabbat in the

Rykestrasse Synagogue, one could be sure that Jonas would be there, sitting and listening together with her mother in the women's balcony.

Those who visited the synagogue in those days describe Weyl as an older, unmarried man, small, modest, and with a fine, integrated personality. He was not a charismatic speaker, but he was a good clergyman, in whom one could confide. Weyl had studied in Berlin's Orthodox Rabbinical Seminary, but took his exams at the Liberal Rabbinic Association. Thus, he represented a spiritual conjunction—referred to as "liberox" by Berlin Jews, at once traditional and progressive—which also fit Jonas's religious outlook. Weyl gave her private instruction and studied Talmud and other halachic works with her.

In those days, illnesses provided an excuse to write letters wishing a good recovery, and as Jonas was often ill, Weyl wrote her many letters and greeting cards, in which he answered her questions, such as "who was Captain Dreyfus?" But not only did he help Jonas bridge gaps in her knowledge, he also wrote about various rabbinic interpretations of biblical passages. Taken with her religious seriousness, but also somewhat taken aback by his bright student who so eagerly grasped rabbinical writings—a student whom he once described to a colleague as an "enormously ambitious lady"—he teased Jonas in one letter, in which he wished for her "liberalization," because "the term *liberal* comes from the word *free*"—but in this case she should only be "quickly freed" from her still "tormenting pains."

❧ ❧ ❧

In 1923, after three years at the Oberlyzeum Weissensee, Regina Jonas completed her graduation exams. Her grades were rather mediocre, dominated by Cs, whereas her instructors gave her a "very good" in both "behavior" and "attention." In addition, Jonas received "very good" marks for her achievements in "pedagogy." She continued her studies at the Oberlyzeum in the seminar on pedagogy for another year, passed the exams with "good" grades, and in March 1924 received a "teaching certificate for *Lyzeen*," high schools for university-bound students. This not only offered her future economic security but also was the first step into the rabbinate. Rabbis always have been first and foremost "teachers" of their religion (*rabbi* means "my teacher").

Certainly, the Berlin rabbis whom Regina Jonas knew in the *Kaiserzeit* [era of the emperor] and in the Weimar Republic practiced a spiritual function whose contours were not yet very old. In the course of centuries, the function of a rabbi had changed in numerous respects.

No rabbis are mentioned in the Hebrew Bible itself. In ancient Israel, priests embodied religious authority—the Cohanim and the Levi'im from the tribe of Levi. With the destruction of the Second Temple (70 CE), the expulsion of the Jews from Palestine, and the end of the cult of sacrifice, the priesthood lost its meaning. Priests were replaced with rabbis, an intellectual class of teachers that established major Talmud academies in Palestine and Babylonia. Even before the Middle Ages, the rabbi had incorporated the role of judgelike decision maker.

Europe's Jewish communities enjoyed autonomy concerning civil law; Halacha—Jewish religious law—ruled. The rabbis wrote responsa (see the Glossary) on legal matters and made decisions in conflict situations. As religious leaders, they also saw to it that community members upheld Jewish ritual laws, and they were empowered to excommunicate apostates. The modern concept of the nation, which gained acceptance in Europe from the time of the French Revolution and which granted Jews equal civil rights, did not tolerate autonomy for minorities and led to the rabbis' loss of power. Following their emancipation, many Jews wanted a new definition for the rabbinical role, convinced as they were by the words of the Enlightenment, especially regarding individual freedom.

The wish for redefinition of the rabbi's role was in no small way furthered by leading rabbis as well as by Germany's greatest Jewish emancipator, Moses Mendelssohn, himself. Just how thoroughly one practiced Jewish religion and ritual laws would depend henceforth on individual free will. To be sure, the rabbis should continue to serve as spiritual leaders in their communities and should teach Judaism and its laws. But instead of holding judicial power, the rabbi's role as preacher and minister would dominate, together with tasks in areas such as social work and youth work. In this way the rabbinate began to match the spiritual roles of the Christian churches. And it was this kind of modern rabbi whom Jonas encountered in the 1920s in Berlin.

Immediately following her graduation from the Oberlyzeum in 1924, Jonas entered the Academy for the Science of Judaism, Germany's liberal rabbinical seminary, and financed her studies from that point on by teaching Hebrew and religion. Her brother, Abraham, already worked as a teacher in the Jewish Boys' School in Grosse Hamburger Strasse. After 1925 Sara Jonas's entry in the Berlin city records changed. Apparently, Jonas's mother had experienced some difficulties in financing her daughter's further education. Her entry now bore the added, but vague description, "businesswoman." Sara Jonas's work is just as difficult to ascertain from the remaining documents as was the work of her late husband before her.

Along with Max Weyl, one of Regina Jonas's most important supporters was Rabbi Dr. Isidor Bleichrode of the Kottbusser Ufer Synagogue (today the Fraenkelufer Synagogue). Bleichrode, despite his conservative positions, still was prepared to make compromises with liberal Jews and— "asking no questions," as a former congregant recalled—dedicated himself particularly to the religious training of youth, holding youth services in a wing of the building dedicated to that purpose. As rector of the religious school in Annenstrasse, he hired both Abraham and Regina Jonas as teachers. It was not only Abraham who saw teaching as his calling. An invitation from the association known as ESRA (*Ehemalige Schüler der Religionsschule Annenstrasse* [Former Students of the Annenstrasse Religious School]) to a "Lecture by Miss Regina Jonas on 'Youth and Prayer,'" on January 9, 1924, shows that Jonas's educational views were bound with a deep sense of Jewish mission.

Following the presentation, Jonas noted the reaction of the audience on the invitation card: "Dr. Bleichrode (school rector) is impressed by the applause—they all wanted to be my student—'rhetorically perfect'—'[you] touched the heartstrings'—'an enthusiastic teacher.'" While the text of this lecture no longer exists, Jonas's legacy contains a later one on a similar theme. She delivered this talk about the meaning of Jewish symbols for the "receptive soul" of youth, titled "Echo of the Holidays," in 1938, by which time she was already a rabbi.

Even though fourteen years separate the two lectures, Jonas's formulations reveal that her desire to awaken Jewish souls had not diminished. In the lecture manuscript, she says, "Wrapped in Jewish symbols, the greatest ideas enter the hearts of Jewish people through their eyes and ears. People whose hearts have strayed from the path of life often find their way back to Judaism by following the thread of Jewish symbols. True, for many people the shofar, the death shroud, the sukkah, the *lulav,* and Simchat Torah often are covered with dust, like the strings of a once-splendid instrument of the soul stilled by the ashes of time. Those of us Jews, who still know how to strike the tone will bring back those notes, silenced long ago, to ring again at last in the depth of the lone Jewish heart."

It is not easy to grasp the personality of one who has dedicated her entire being to a godly calling. As a boy, Theodor (Ted) Alexander, today rabbi of Congregation B'nai Emunah in San Francisco, often came into contact with Jonas, who would visit his family on Shabbat afternoons. Alexander's father, Hugo Alexander, was president of the board of the Rykestrasse Synagogue in the 1920s. Jonas "was a very Orthodox woman," Ted Alexander recalled, who—in keeping with the absolute ban on working or physical exertion on Shabbat—"never carried a handbag on the Shabbat and tied her handkerchief around her wrist." Although Jonas was good-looking—with dark, soulful eyes, black hair gathered together at her neck, and a stately figure—Alexander never got the impression from her that she could be interested in men.

Despite her absolute acceptance of the demands God had placed on the Jewish people, and her perpetual emphasis on values such as selfless devotion to pure belief in God, humility, and chastity, Jonas was, said many of her former pupils of religion, both "amusing" and "down-to-earth," someone who loved to laugh and who despite the seriousness of teaching did not need to be strict. Meta Wolny emphasized that Jonas, unlike other teachers, never hit her students. Some pupils, such as Margot Camnetzer, recall Jonas as an "unforgettably beautiful person" with an "intelligent expression" and a "deep, pleasant voice." She knew how "to make teaching unbelievably interesting" and was "completely dedicated" to her work.

Others, such as Rita Nagler, found her a bit odd, if not even "eccentric":

> Where did she get this item of clothing, and what will she reveal next time she takes off her coat? In my head, I carry an image of a woman who sat on the desk, in a dark green velvety dress with short puffy sleeves, with extensions that tapered down to fit snugly around the arm. This extension of the sleeve she unbuttoned and detached in preparation for the class. One might think that the class tortured her mercilessly, as happened with so many of these unlucky people who did not understand children and who helplessly delivered their lessons as religion teachers who had to earn their bread through suffering. She must therefore have impressed us as a strong personality or she must have been so unusual as to have held our attention. We certainly did not understand or fully appreciate her.

Jonas's appearance fascinated many, even if some pupils mocked her, found her appearance sloppy, her gait inelegant, her wardrobe unfashionable. Gisela Müller suggested that Jonas lacked the Prussian discipline common among teachers. Sometimes she showed up late to her afternoon class—Jewish pupils in public schools in those days also received extracurricular religious education—and then she appeared to be "completely exhausted." She supposedly even ate her lunch, usually a sandwich, during the class. Her pupil Hans Finke remembered that she regularly "brought along a red apple and put it on the desk, which really made us jealous when times were bad." Marie Jalowicz, who often saw Jonas with her mother during services in the Orthodox Heidereutergasse Synagogue, likened her to a "mystic of the Middle Ages." When she crossed the street, "she was focused inward and her thoughts were not on her surroundings but wrapped up in other matters."

≈ ≈ ≈

Regina Jonas was also a challenge to her Academy professors. Even if she really only wanted to be a rabbi, she always had to have discussions about whether she—"as a woman"—*could* be a rabbi. In this, she won the sympathies of open-minded spirits such as Rabbi Dr. Leo Baeck and Talmud professor Rabbi Dr. Eduard Baneth, to whom Jonas regularly sent a Jewish New Year greeting card. Baeck himself had already helped promote the higher education of numerous young women. When it came to women who wanted to study at the Academy for the Science of Judaism, he presented an unusually open attitude. For example, he convinced Ellen Littman's parents to allow her to study, something they had at first resisted.[6] Littman was the first woman to complete a degree at this Academy. For a while she also had studied at the Jewish Theological Seminary in Breslau.

If Regina Jonas had had her way, she probably would have preferred the Orthodox rabbinical seminary. But that was unthinkable for a woman. In Germany, aside from the Jewish Theological Seminary in Breslau, the only program that admitted women was Berlin's Academy for the Science of Judaism, founded in 1872 in the liberal tradition. In 1906 the first female auditing student was enrolled there. Later up to sixteen women studied at the Academy at one time, and in 1921 the first three women became fully matriculated there. The Academy's *Forty-Second Yearbook,* marking fifty years since the opening of the Academy, noted that "the Academy allowed female auditors long before study for women was generally accepted at German universities. Recently, even the number of women pursuing degrees has grown. The majority of them sit in as auditors." The year with the highest number of women was probably 1932. Among a total of 155 students there were twenty-seven female students (1932 yearbook). At the Jewish Theological Seminary in Breslau, there were some thirteen women studying up to 1938.[7]

The theme of Jewish women's emancipation had already been raised in the Jewish Reform movement thanks to Abraham Geiger, one of the founders of the Academy, at the 1846 Rabbinical Convention in Breslau.[8] Geiger proposed changes related to the practice of religious laws and underscored the "full equality of women," which he compared to the civic emancipation of the Jews. In the further development of liberal Judaism,

entire sections of Halacha were declared ripe for reform regarding the
legal status of women, and major changes were made in the synagogue
service, including a modified liturgy, rejection of the blessing in the morning service in which men thank God for not creating them as women, the
development of bat mitzvah celebrations for girls, and introduction of
mixed choirs in the synagogue. In radical synagogues such as the Berlin
Reform Temple in Johannisstrasse or the Prinzregentenstrasse Synagogue,
there was even mixed seating.

Similar developments took place in England and the United States. By
the final decade of the nineteenth century, women entered American synagogues as lay preachers.[9] Among them was Ray Frank, acclaimed in the
press as the "first female rabbi in the world," although she was not
ordained. In 1903 Henrietta Szold became the first woman to study at the
Jewish Theological Seminary in New York. She signed a declaration
according to which she would not seek ordination after the end of her
studies. In 1922 Martha Neumark strove to be the first woman ordained
as a rabbi at the Hebrew Union College in Cincinnati, but this recognition was denied by the Board of Governors despite the support of the fac-
ulty. In 1928, by which time Regina Jonas had completed four and a half
years at the Academy for the Science of Judaism, the World Union for Progressive Judaism, long directed by Leo Baeck, held an International Conference in Berlin. On this occasion, a woman for the first time delivered a
sermon from a German synagogue pulpit—Lily Montagu, founder of the
liberal Jewish movement in England. She spoke in the Reform Temple in
Johannisstrasse.[10]

Despite all these developments, it barely occurred to anyone in the
1920s that women one day could also be rabbis. It was too unusual to
picture a woman in this position; it collided with the traditional image of
the rabbi as a father figure. Most women who studied at the Academy
wanted to be religion teachers or simply to deepen their knowledge of
Judaism. Even Susi Elbogen—daughter of Ismar Elbogen, the professor of
Jewish history—who in 1932 was one of about only twenty-seven women
out of 155 students matriculated at the Academy, had to admit more than
half a century later, "none of us would have taken a female rabbi seriously."[11] The same has been said by various rabbis today, such as Emil
Fackenheim, who studied at the Academy at that time—"no one would
have taken female rabbis seriously in those days."

Still and all, Jonas identified in body and soul with the rabbinical role—
as preacher or minister, as a legal scholar required to make decisions based
on religious law, and as a teacher of religion. Especially impressive were
her oratorical skills and her ability to transmit her own enthusiasm to her

listeners, at least for the duration of her speech. In her practice sermons at the Academy, Jonas did not need any notes, and later, too, she always spoke extemporaneously; even when delivering long lectures she managed to keep the attention of her audience. Max Weyl, who often interrupted his own lectures with the words, "It is written . . ." and then drew a piece of paper from the pocket of his trousers under his robe, held Jonas to a higher standard of discipline in this regard and pushed her to "work on an outline of her sermon or at least to sketch it out."

⁂

Jonas's declared intention to take the rabbinical exam at the end of her studies—apparently her dream since her school days—irritated everyone, but it did not lead only to stern disapproval. However, rabbis like Max Weyl, in the Rykestrasse Synagogue, and other influential personalities who were well inclined toward Jonas and other committed women, unexpectedly discovered how great the obstacles still were. For example, in 1931, Hugo Alexander pushed to have the first election of a woman—the schoolteacher Martha Ehrlich—as *Gabba'it,* a member of the synagogue board. But the rabbinate would not allow her to carry out ritual functions. She was not permitted to have a say in which men would be called to the Torah during the synagogue service. Nevertheless, she did have a seat of honor in the women's gallery, took part in all board meetings, and participated in their votes.

Hugo Alexander also had contact with Jonas's Academy teachers Chanoch Albeck and Ismar Elbogen. His son, Ted Alexander, remembers that his father often asked the probing question of whether these men would have the courage to hand Jonas the *Hatarat Hora'a,* or rabbinical diploma, after her studies. Both always answered with "We'll see. . . ."

Even the Talmud professor responsible for ordaining rabbinical candidates, Eduard Baneth, was not necessarily opposed to the ordination of women. It was he who in 1930 allowed Jonas to write her final halachic project on the question with which she had challenged both her classmates and instructors for six years: "Can Women Serve as Rabbis?" Given that Baneth gave Jonas a grade of "good" for this work, one must conclude that he could not have considered the possibility of ordination for women as being out of the question, because Jonas's work contained arguments derived from rabbinical writings that spoke for the ordination of women as rabbis.

The eighty-eight-page work had the character of a treatise and represented a historical first attempt to legitimize the rabbinical role for women from a halachic point of view. What was unusual about it was that Jonas did not fall back on liberal Jewish arguments. Any interpretation that the equality of women could only be realized through the rejection of parts of Halacha was out of the question for her. For Regina Jonas, the equality of women had to be grounded in Jewish religious law itself. She felt strongly that the female rabbinate should not ring in a new era, but rather should strengthen and continue an existing tradition. Because she connected Halacha with the emancipation of women, Jonas was able to achieve a considerable intertwining of the conservative, preservationist approach and modern demands. Her argumentation set itself apart both from the Orthodox rabbis and from the Reform movement, which assumed itself to be the only advocate of women's equality in Judaism.

Jonas presented her theme along the lines of a centuries-old rabbinical discussion. Her treatise took her deep into the world of the Talmud. In search of clues to a question never before dealt with in Judaism, she sifted through all the great halachic works in addition to the Talmud, the *Mishneh Torah* (Maimonides), the Tur (Jacob ben Asher), and the *Shulchan Aruch* (Joseph Karo). All of these multivolume collections of laws and commentary belong in the library of every rabbinical seminary and form the basis for the study of Halacha. But Jonas also cited books and responsa that were not necessarily familiar to an Academy student. Her later friend, Rabbi Dr. Joseph Norden, asked after reading the treatise whether Eduard Baneth had "given her tips," noting that "there are certain obscure quotes from works that one rarely has available."

As had countless generations of rabbis before her, Jonas also set to work with sharp logic in a complicated interplay of arguments and counterarguments. For the most part she confronted statements according to which women initially were barred from such rabbinical tasks as teaching or making decisions based on religious law. However, for Jonas's argumentation, it was not the ban itself that was decisive, but rather the reason for the ban.

If for example the rabbinical writings rejected women in the function of teacher, it was not based on their supposed incompetence, but rather on the fear that allowing women to teach would lead to awkward situations between men and women. Jonas suggested that the reasons for such explanations had changed over the centuries and that the bans based on these explanations therefore did not have an eternal validity. In doing so, Jonas also applied centuries-old halachic principles as, for example, "who is commanded to learn [study] is also commanded to teach." Usually such principles were used as an argument against women as teachers, for, according to the view of the rabbis, women were not "commanded to learn." But Jonas reversed the rabbi's argumentation by proving that women by Halacha always had to learn, at least, the halachic fields "that relate to them" and teach them to their daughters. However, as the "fields that relate to women" have today widened to "all fields," Jonas argued, women should be permitted to teach in general.

Jonas differentiated between inalterable statutes springing from God and "opinions" of individual rabbis. In response to misogynistic statements in the Talmud, she said that men also have not always contributed to the spiritual well-being of the Jewish people, and that particularly in her day in this regard there was much left to be desired.

With the first sentence of "Can Women Serve as Rabbis?", Jonas plunged with self-confidence into the use of the German term *Rabbinerin* [female rabbi] and suggested that this "new title for this calling" had not only to do with a woman dressed in the function of a man, but rather was about a career that could have a female identity. A key term repeated in her work was *zniut*—the Jewish ideal of humility, modesty, and also chaste behavior. Jonas saw in this both the special educational role of women and the link to her independent career. "There are even some things that women can say to youth, which cannot be said by the man in the pulpit. Her experiences, her psychological observations are profoundly different from those of a man, therefore she has a different style."

But Jonas felt that a woman as rabbi should remain single. She didn't question the role of the wife who dedicates her life to advancing her husband's career and to educating their children. But a woman should be able to choose freely between family and career; in particular, female virtues such as "tact, sympathy" should not be kept within the private sphere of the family. Rather, they should be put to use for responsible societal tasks in the service of improving humanity.

Jonas also emphasized the "necessity" of female rabbis. "One may assume that if a woman takes on such a position she will manage it with seriousness and love. Nowhere would it be denied that the woman has sensitivity, honesty of aspiration, willingness to sacrifice, love for humanity, and a sense of tact—the basic requirements for the job of rabbi."

"Can Women Serve as Rabbis?" is marked by an almost unencumbered sense of security with which Jonas represented her own convictions, without shying away from a confrontation with opposing views in the rabbinical discussion. On the first page, she wrote that she "personally love[s] this profession and would love to practice it if it were ever possible." On the last page, she concluded: "Aside from prejudice and unfamiliarity, there is almost nothing halachically opposed to the woman taking on the rabbinical role."

જ઼ જ઼ જ઼

As of July 1930, Regina Jonas had passed the general obligatory exams in religious history and education, the philosophy of religion, Jewish history and literature, the science of the Talmud, and Hebrew language and Bible study. She already had handed in her halachic work, "Can Women Serve as Rabbis?", and a biblical final paper with the title "Rashi's Lexicology." Her admirers waited anxiously to learn whether she would be admitted to the rabbinical exam. But on August 7, Eduard Baneth, who was in charge of rabbinical ordinations, died unexpectedly. His successor, Chanoch Albeck, represented a conservative viewpoint. Leo Baeck held back, because the task of ordination fell to the Talmud professor. He most likely wished to avoid controversy in the general rabbinical council, where as president he also represented Germany's Orthodox rabbis.[12] Shalom Albeck, who heard his father discussing the confrontation over Regina Jonas's ordination, said the Academy committee was dominated by fear of a scandal and the view that Jewry in Germany, despite being liberal, was not yet ready for a female rabbi. Thus, on December 12, 1930, Jonas received only a certificate of passing the "Academic Religion Teacher Exam" with a grade of "overall good."

It seems Leo Baeck did support Jonas with a policy of taking small steps. In the spring of 1931 he confirmed that Jonas, after participating in his homiletics practice course, achieved a grade of "very successful" in a series of practice sermons, showing herself to be "a thoughtful and gifted preacher." It is interesting to note the ambivalence with which the *Israelitisches Familienblatt* [Israelite Family Bulletin] reacted to this certificate. "Overnight, we have received the first Jewish woman preacher in Germany. As a little surprise, so to say," it began in a congratulatory tone. "Miss Jonas" already has "performed the function of preacher on the Shabbat" in three smaller German communities. But then the author criticized the fact that in Baeck's certificate it does not say "that this is only a teaching diploma and not a preaching diploma. . . . It could easily happen that other female teachers of religion who were trained at academies and seminaries would step up to the pulpit and claim that their educational establishments also qualified them for such work."[13]

That same year, Jonas delivered a talk for the Jüdischer Frauenbund [Jewish Women's League] about her halachic treatise on whether women could become rabbis. But this time the *Israelitisches Familienblatt* opposed her from the liberal view: "One may not use such arguments. One can say: New times demand new institutions, therefore also female rabbis. One can also say: Since we and countless valued rabbinical forces do not stick to tradition, why should we then allow ourselves to be stopped [by tradition] from ordaining women as rabbis, when we want to and believe we must do so? What one cannot say is this: A woman as rabbi—that is fully in the spirit of the Talmud and the Torah."[14] But that was exactly what Jonas always intended to prove.

In the meantime, Jonas taught at the upper level of Berlin's schools for girls and transmitted Jewish knowledge to her pupils—despite intimations of growing National Socialism—with unaffected pedagogic passion. Many still remember the annual Chanukah festival in which the theater piece *The Pearls of Judaism* was performed. Weeks before the holiday, Jonas would begin rehearsals with her pupils.

She had written *The Pearls of Judaism* herself—a collage of scenes depicting Jewish holidays, with much dancing. In the final scene, six girls remain on stage and toss veils at each other, which in the end fall into the shape of a Star of David. The performance usually took place in the auditorium of the Jewish Girls' School on Kaiserstrasse. Often, Leo Baeck and his wife, Natalie, were in the audience.

A report about the Chanukah festival in 1931 quoted Jonas's address to the parents. "The goal of the festival" is to "illustrate through pictures a pure, practical Judaism" for the pupils. She also referred to "the education of girls, as seen from the Jewish vantage point." Chanukah should be "a learning experience particularly for female youths, with their new rights and duties." Role models should be historical religious personalities "such as Hanna with her seven sons, Esther, Jephta's daughter, and Deborah."[15]

In 1933 Jonas was confronted with the new anti-Semitic regulations of National Socialism, as were all educators who taught Jewish subjects. The study of Hebrew, Jewish history, and religion took on a new importance, as they became part of a preparation for emigration to Palestine or were seen as a way to boost the self-image of disoriented children who came from nonreligious homes, giving them a basis for spiritual self-assertion. In addition, Jewish schools came under increasing pressure due to a doubling or even tripling of the student body because of the exclusion of Jewish children from public schools.

Many of Jonas's pupils had secular parents who forbade their children—even after 1933—to study Hebrew and Jewish religion. Susanne Flörsheim, who in those days attended the Auguste Viktoria Lyzeum, said

she would never forget how Jonas had "converted me." Jonas "spoke privately" to her about Hitler and made it "clear that the times are such that
one can no longer hold back." Then Jonas offered her a role in the
Chanukah performance. For Susanne Flörsheim this was the first contact
with Judaism. As far as she remembers, she played the role of a candle in
the nine-branched candelabra.

ॐ ॐ ॐ

Jonas did not give up her goal to become a rabbi. She continued to attend
the lectures and above all the Talmud seminars at the Academy, and in
addition she met for weekly study sessions with Rabbi Max Weyl. In the
apartment of Hugo Alexander she consulted within a circle of some
admirers about the possibility of a "private ordination" given by liberal
rabbis such as Max Dienemann, Georg Salzberger, or Caesar Seligmann.
A committee of three rabbis would deliver this in the traditional manner,
but such an ordination had a lower status within liberal Judaism than an
academic rabbinical diploma. Obviously such considerations were rejected
at first, perhaps also because the Berlin Jewish Community would not recognize a "private ordination."

It seems Jonas never considered emigration from Germany in the face
of the rise of anti-Semitism and the Nazis. Her entire focus and work were
oriented toward Jews in Germany. She saw her task as strengthening the
Jewish spiritual backbone against discrimination, by bringing Jews back
to the teachings of their religion. In addition, she felt responsible for her
aging mother, whom, as witnesses recall, Jonas would never have bur-
dened with starting a new life somewhere else. Many letters to Regina
Jonas contained "greetings to your mother," and some bore clues as to
how much Sara Jonas had sacrificed for her daughter in recent years. Since
1932 the two had lived in a wing of the building at Krausnickstrasse 6, a
side street off Oranienburger Strasse in Berlin-Mitte. Regina Jonas's
brother, Abraham, had rented his own apartment in Immanuelkirchstrasse
in Prenzlauer Berg.

The area around Oranienburger Strasse, with its magnificent New Synagogue, the largest Jewish house of worship in Germany, and its many
Jewish institutions—the community center, large and small synagogues,
rabbis' apartments, the Academy for the Science of Judaism, the Orthodox Rabbinical Seminary, and Jewish newspapers and publishers—had
turned this area into the Jerusalem of German Jews. The dream to live
here among fellow Jews and after stubborn struggles finally to become a

rabbi came true for Jonas at a time when Jewish life had already been delivered up for destruction by the Nazis.

In 1935, the year in which the Nuremberg racial laws were enacted, the liberal Rabbi Dr. Max Dienemann—known for his progressive position—declared himself ready to administer to Jonas the rabbinical exam—the additional final oral test, which she was not permitted to pass at the Academy in Berlin. He did this on behalf of the Liberaler Rabbiner-Verband [Liberal Rabbinic Association], of which he was manager. Jonas's supporters, such as Max Weyl, who decades earlier had passed the rabbinical exam of the Liberal Rabbinic Association, and Leo Baeck, may have used their influence behind the scenes. Jonas visited Dienemann on December 26 in his home in Offenbach, near Frankfurt on Main.

The exam theme had been given to her in a postcard sent in August: ciphers 87–106 and 151–154, codex Orach Chayim (regulations for prayer and the synagogue) written by Joseph Karo, author of the *Shulchan Aruch*. Dienemann reassured the rabbinical candidate: "We are not talking about 'memorized' knowledge. It depends on your showing how you decide a question, and how you trace the *passuk* [decision according to religious law] set down in the codex to its roots through the literature. Naturally we will also consider your work [the previous halachic treatise]. You don't have anything to worry about. Such a colloquium is essentially a conversation."

The exam, which would last "a few hours," was given to Jonas by Dienemann alone. There were clearly difficulties in advance for both to find a good date for the exam. Jonas had to teach in Berlin until the winter vacation, and she wanted to take advantage of a "cheaper vacation ticket." Because of Dienemann's full appointment calendar, only Christmas itself remained free, though he would have preferred a later appointment "in the quarter" or in the Easter vacation. It appears that Jonas pushed for an earlier date and so they agreed on December 26, 1935.

On the following day, Dienemann issued the *Hatarat Hora'a*—the rabbinical diploma—to Jonas. It states:

> And she never stopped studying, and Mr. Professor Baneth of blessed memory agreed, that from the standpoint of religious law one can answer that a woman can serve as a rabbi. He [Baneth] began to administer the oral exam, but before he could complete it, he was called away to eternity. And then she was sent to me by the Liberal Rabbinic Association, and I tested her and found that she can learn and understand how to deal with the pros and cons in a subject of religious law, and that she can refer to the sources when delivering a

religious decision. Because I have recognized that her heart is with
G-d and Israel, and that she delivers her soul for the goal that she has
set for herself, and that she is G-d fearing, and that she has passed the
exam I have given her in religious legal topics, I testify to her that she
is capable to answer questions of religious law (the Halacha) and *that
she is suitable to serve as a rabbi.* May G-d support her and stand by
her and be with her on all her paths.

※ ※ ※

From the circle of her liberally oriented colleagues and followers, Jonas
received numerous encouraging letters. The board of the Neue Synagoge
sent her a congratulatory note saying, "Jewry needs more than ever diligent, energetic people of conviction who work and fight for their ideals.
We are convinced that you offer the greatest hope in this regard." And
Leo Baeck, who from then on addressed Jonas in his letters as *"Liebes
Fräulein Kollegin"* [Dear Miss Colleague], congratulated her: "May you
achieve satisfaction and the fulfillment of your hopes through the position you have reached, or rather that you practically have conquered!"
Dienemann had reported to him about the exam. "To my joy, I heard that
you were tested seriously and that you did well." With his signature and
the stamp of the Academy for the Science of Judaism, Baeck certified
copies of Jonas's rabbinical diploma in 1941 and 1942.

Her former professor of Bible study, Harry Torczyner, who had signed
her Academy diploma and meanwhile had fled Germany, wrote from
Jerusalem, "So you have reached your goal at last. I myself do not have
(thank G-d) such delicate halachic problems to solve and do not need
myself to answer the question with which you confronted us for all those
years: Can a woman be a rabbi? Now, you are one. And I congratulate
you warmly on the fulfillment of your wishes. Hopefully this success and
its results will bring the satisfaction that you have earned through this
long struggle."

Many of Jonas's colleagues and acquaintances expressed their satisfaction. "Your exam with the Gaon [honorary title] of Offenbach is and
remains an earth-shaking event," stated one well-wisher. Numerous
women wrote with delight, "that finally the right person, one who is really
deserving, will stand at the pulpit," or "that it was possible for you as a
weak female to successfully come out on top against men, and above all
in a field otherwise relegated only for men." But men, too, expressed their
recognition. The Dresden Rabbi Albert Wolf invited her to visit him during the school vacation: "I would very much like to receive instruction

from you about the rabbinical rights of women." Rabbi Hermann Vogel-stein wrote, "You are as far as I know the first female rabbi, and I am not at all afraid of the competition. Once again, Dienemann has won a quiet victory for our views in Judaism."

Among the countless variations of address, however, there was also a slight undertone of insecurity about Jonas's title and its gender in German. One letter contained four possible modes of address: *"Liebes Fräulein Rabbiner! Liebe Frau Rabbiner! Liebes Fräulein Regina! Liebe Regina!"* [Dear Miss Rabbi! Dear Mrs. Rabbi! Dear Miss Regina! Dear Regina!]. Felix Singermann, Berlin's leading Orthodox rabbi, addressed her in his card, written in Hebrew, as *"Rabbanit"* [female rabbi]. The Orthodox former rector of the religious school in Annenstrasse, Isidor Bleichrode, who by then had moved to Jerusalem, called Jonas *"Rav,"* Hebrew for rabbi. Her longtime mentor, Max Weyl, addressed his effusive letter *"An die Rabbinerin Fräulein R. Jonas"* [to the Rabbi Miss R. Jonas]. Some joked in their letters: "Dear Miss Jonas, I congratulate Mrs. Rebbetzin [the rabbi's wife]. . . . Oh, excuse me! Mrs. Rabbi—because you alone have earned this awe-inspiring title deserving of respect."

Others honestly took great pains to find a fitting, respectful address for a woman—such as *"Liebe Frau Collega"* [Dear Mrs. Collega], *"Sehr geehrte Frau Rabbiner!"* [Honored Mrs. Rabbi!], *"Fräulein Rabbinerin"* [Miss Rabbi], or *"Fräulein Rabbi"* [Miss Rabbi]. Eyewitnesses contradict one another on how Regina Jonas herself wished to be addressed. Her former pupil Rita Nagler remembered that Jonas "repeatedly insisted that she be addressed as *'Fräulein Rabbinerin Jonas'* [Miss Rabbi Jonas] and never as *'Frau Rabbiner Jonas'* [Mrs. Rabbi], which might refer to the title of a husband.

Bernhard Burstein, a patient in the Jewish hospital in July 1940, reported that a "young woman visited" him "daily, and she introduced herself as *'Frau Rabbiner Jonas'* [Mrs. Rabbi Jonas] [not using the femi-nine form of the word, *Rabbinerin*]." Jonas clearly wavered between these possibilities—*"Rabbiner,"* in the masculine form, or *"Rabbinerin"* in the feminine form. She signed a letter to a journalist with *"Ihre Rabbiner Regina Jonas"* [Your Rabbi Regina Jonas].[16] Even her rubber stamp said *"Rabbiner Regina Jonas"* [Rabbi Regina Jonas]; and from 1939 on, when Jewish women were forced to take on the name "Sara," her stamp said *"Rabbiner Regina Sara Jonas,"* using the masculine form. In the archive of the memorial at the former ghetto and concentration camp of There-sienstadt was another document that she signed as *"Rabbinerin Regina Jonas,"* using the feminine form.[17] The most common form of address, however, was *"Fräulein Rabbiner Jonas"* [Miss Rabbi Jonas].

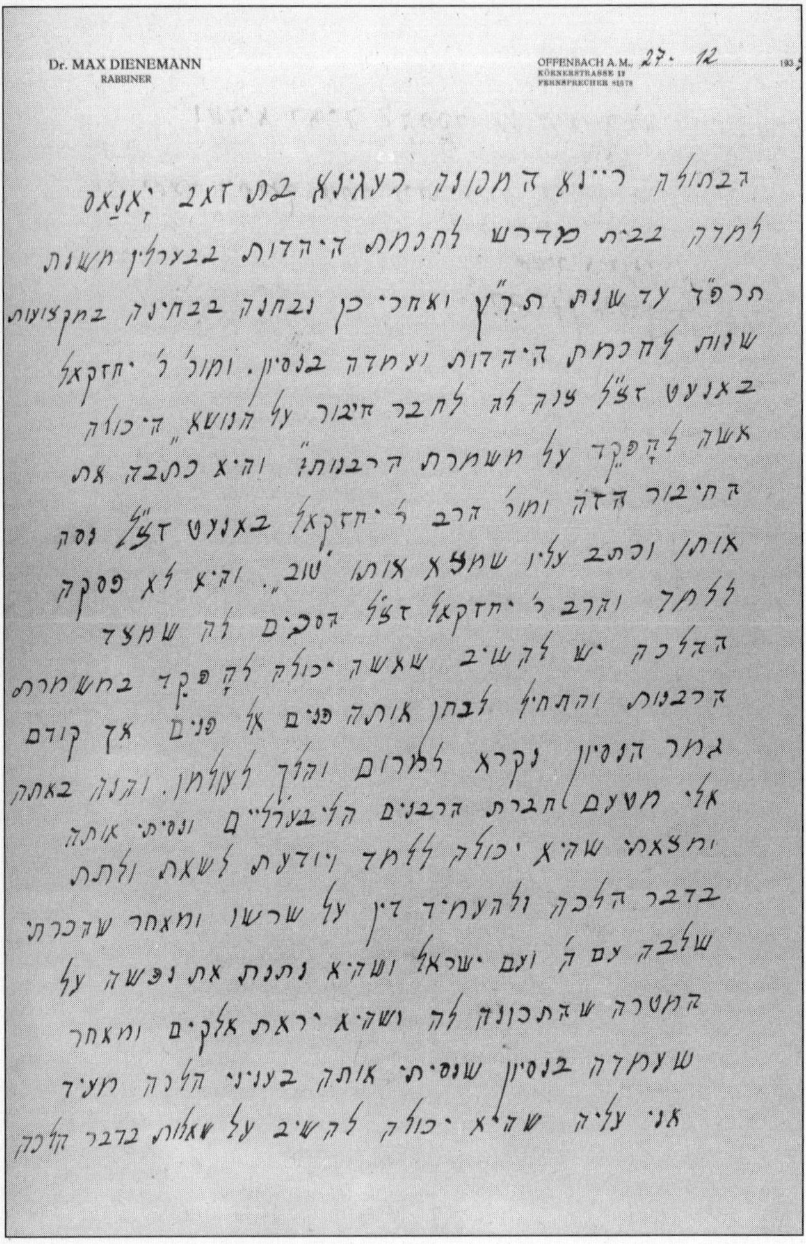

Dr. MAX DIENEMANN
RABBINER

OFFENBACH A.M., *27. 12* ....193_
KÖRNERSTRASSE 13
FERNSPRECHER 81578

[Handwritten Hebrew text of the ordination document]

Jonas's *smicha* [original ordination document] in Hebrew, page 1

*The original rabbinical diploma that Regina Jonas received
on December 27, 1935, from Max Dienemann.
Reproduction: Margit Billeb*

ושהיא ראוי' ה' להסמך על משמרת הרבנות

וה' יצבר וימסך אותה ויהי' עמה בכל דרכיה
יום א' טבת תרצ'
מאס ר' גאלדמן
רב דק"ק אפנבאך והגליל

Jonas's *smicha* in Hebrew, page 2

33

Dr.Max D i e n e m a n n   Offenbach a.M., den 27.12.1935
    Rabbiner   Körnerstr.12
                                       Fernsprecher: 81678

        Die Jungfrau R e i n e , die genannt wird R e g i n a ,
Tochter von Wolf J o n a s, hat an der Lehranstalt für die Wis-
senshhaft des Judentums in Berlin vom Jahre 5684 bis 5690 stu-
diert und nachher wurde sie in verschiedenen Fächern der Wissenschaft des Judentums geprüft, und sie bestand die Prüfung.
        Und der Lehrer, Rabbi Jecheskel B a n e t h - das
Andenken des Gerechten sei zum Segen - stellte ihr die Aufgabe,
eine Arbeit über das Thema "Kann die Frau das rabbinische Amt
bekleiden"? anzufertigen. Sie schrieb diese Arbeit, und Herr
Professor B a n e t h s.A. prüfte sie und schrieb, dass er sie
"gut" befinde. Und sie hörte nicht auf zu lernen, und Herr Prof.
Baneth s.A. stimmte zu, dass man seitens des Religionsgesetzes
antworten kann, dass eine Frau das rabbinische Amt bekleiden
kann. Er begann, ihr mündlich die Prüfung abzunehmen, jedoch vor
Beendigung der Prüfung wurde er in die Ewigkeit abberufen.
        Und nun kam sie zu mir im Auftrage des Liberalen
Rabbiner-Verbandes, und ich habe sie geprüft und gefunden, dass
sie lernen kann und versteht, das Für und Wider in einem reli-
gionsgesetzlichen Gegenstande zu behandeln, und dass sie eine
Religionsentscheidung auf ihre Quelle zurückführen kann.
        Da ich erkannt habe, dass ihr Herz mit G'tt und
Israel ist, und dass sie ihre Seele für das Ziel, das sie sich
gesetzt hat, hingibt, und dass sie gottesfürchtig ist, und da
sie die Prüfung bestanden hat, die ich ihr in religionsgesetz-
lichen Gegenständen abgenommen habe, bezeuge ich ihr, dass sie
fähig ist, Fragen des Religionsgesetzes (der Halacha) zu beant-
worten, und dass sie dazu geeignet ist, das rabbinische Amt zu
bekleiden.
        Und G'tt möge sie stützen und ihr beistehen und mit
ihr sein auf allen ihren Wegen.
1. Tebeth 5696.
                    gez.Meier D i e n e m a n n
                Rabbiner der heiligen Gemeinde Offenbach u.Umkreis.

Die Richtigkeit der Uebesetzung aus dem Hebräischen
wird hierdurch bescheinigt.
Berlin, den 25. November 1941

German translation of Jonas's *smicha*, signed by Leo Baeck

*A German translation of the rabbinical diploma certified by Leo Baeck
on November 25, 1941.
Reproduction: Margit Billeb*

An enthusiastic article in the *Jüdische Allgemeine Zeitung* in January 1936, in which the female writer hoped "to see the last bulwarks of prejudice fall away," since Regina Jonas was "born for the pulpit," nevertheless announced that additional obstacles were blocking recognition of Jonas's achievement.[18] In the course of this year, she learned that even with her rabbinical diploma she would not be immediately hired by the Jewish Community, let alone be sent as an official community rabbi to lead services and preach from the synagogue pulpits. Dienemann himself advised Jonas to be extremely careful, particularly in the use of her title: "under no circumstances should you call yourself rabbi. Allow Dr. Baeck to advise you on this."

Doubts were raised as to whether Jonas's rabbinical diploma was valid, because it was not a "private ordination" by a committee of three rabbis and bore only Dienemann's personal stamp, not the official stamp of the Liberal Rabbinic Association. Evidently, she was pressed to return her *Hatarah* [ordination]. "Though I can understand your suffering, I am unable to help you more than I already have," wrote Dienemann. "A 'Hatarah' once given can *not be declared invalid;* it remains in force. But I cannot interfere in the matter of the Berlin rabbis and in communal affairs."

Dienemann himself was an object of criticism. In the newspaper *Der Israelit* [The Israelite], Joseph Carlebach, one of the leading representatives of Orthodoxy, wrote a polemic article in which he ironically accused Dienemann of possessing a "charming chivalry towards women" that led him to "allow them to go first to the pulpit and make rabbinical decisions."[19] Repeatedly Dienemann exhorted Jonas to "be patient" and not to "underestimate the resistance out there." "If you take my advice, do not apply for any positions in Berlin, whether it be in the rabbinate or with individual rabbis; it will only provoke protest, because the majority is against you. Go your own way in peace; the board of the community will support you gradually; an oak does not fall with the first blow."

Meanwhile, a faction had emerged in the large Neue Synagoge, the symbol of German Jewry, which took up Jonas's cause. In April 1936 the synagogue's board received a letter from Max Brasch "on behalf of many members of the New Synagogue": "The *Rabbinerin* Miss Jonas delivered a sermon at the Senior Home in Berkaerstrasse, which was received with tremendous enthusiasm by the listeners. We, too, would like to hear Miss Jonas deliver a sermon in the New Synagogue, and since we members of

1 5

PROF. DR. H. TORCZYNER   פרופ' דר. נ. ה. טורטשינר

Jerusalem, Rehavia...............   9/1/36   ....ירושלים, רחביה.

Sehr geehrtes Fräulein Jonas:

Nun haben Sie Ihr Ziel also doch erreicht.
Ich selber habe ja G.s.D.solche heikle halachische Probleme nicht zu lösen und brau-
che meinerseits die Frage nicht zu beantwor-
ten,vor die Sie uns die ganzen Jahre gestell
hielten: Darf eine Frau Rabbiner sein.Nun
sind es.Und ich gratuliere Ihnen jedenfalls
herzlich zur Erreichung Ihres Wunsches.Hof-
fentlich bringt Ihnen dieser Erfolg und Ihr
Wirken die Befriedigung,die Sie sich durch
den langen Kampf verdient haben.Auch sonst
alles Gute.Ich benütze die Gelegenheit um
Sie im Namen von uns allen herzlichst zu
grüssen.

                Ihr,Ihnen sehr ergebener

                    ן. ה. טורטשינר

Letter of congratulation by Jonas's former teacher, Harry Torczyner,
January 9, 1936

Dear Fräulein Jonas:

So you have reached your goal at last. I myself do not have (thank G-d) such delicate halachic problems to solve and do not need myself to answer the question with which you confronted us for all those years: Can a woman be a rabbi? Now, you are one. And I congratulate you warmly on the fulfillment of your wishes. Hopefully this success and its results will bring the satisfaction that you have earned through this long struggle. Anyway, all the best wishes. I am taking this chance to greet you most warmly on behalf of all of us.

Your very devoted,

N. H. Torczyner

Letter of congratulation by Jonas's former teacher, Harry Torczyner, January 9, 1936 (translation)

בס"ד יום ב' ס' ... שלישי יפ..., תרצ"ו

לכבוד הרבנית מרת רבקה ממשפחת יונס

השמועה הטובה שמעתי ושמחתי על כל הטובה

שעשה ה' לכבודכן. חידוש ה'א מעשה

כזאת ולא נשמע כמהו בכל מדינתינו, וקדם...

שולח מעמקי לבי את ברכת מזל טוב שלי ונדמה

הדבר לי שיש "ניסים" גם בזמן הזה יהי רצון שתהא

המקרה הזה להגדיל תורה ולהאדירה

בשבת בעת צהרים אהיה בל"נ בביתי ואשמח לראותכן

בדרישת שלום גם בעד אמכן ורגשי כבוד

F. Singermann

Dr. F. Singermann
Absender:
Rabbiner
Bln. NO 43, Neue Königstr. 88

Postkarte
Nur deutsche
Telegramme nach Übersee
Fünf- und Sechsworte

BERLIN C.G   1.1.36.-21

Letter of congratulation by Berlin's Orthodox rabbi, Felix Singermann,
January 1, 1936

With God's Help.

Wednesday of the week which ends with the reading of the Torah portion "Vayigash elav Yehuda," in the year 5696 [Jan. 1, 1936]

To the honored *Rabbinerin Frau Rivka* of the family of Jonas.

   I heard the good news and have rejoiced over the good that the Eternal has done for you. This matter is an innovation, and nothing of the kind has ever been heard of in our entire country, and above all I send my deeply felt congratulations, and it strikes me as proof that there are also miracles in our times. The aim of this event should be to glorify and make great the Torah.
   On the Sabbath around midday I am sure to be home and would be delighted to see you.
   With greetings also for your mother and with great respect,

Dr. Singermann

Letter of congratulation from Berlin's Orthodox rabbi, Felix Singermann, January 1, 1936 (translation)

JÜDISCHE ALLGEMEINE ZEITUNG

Beilage
22. Januar 1936

Bekanntſchaft mit einer Rabbinerin

Wie Regina Jonas ihr Examen machte / Von FRIEDA VALLENTIN

Geschichtliche Gloſſen zur Tagesgeschichte

Glaubenstreue der Falaschas

Newspaper profile of Jonas (*Jüdische Allgemeine Zeitung*, January 22, 1936)

this modern synagogue have a liberal orientation, we count on the fulfillment of our wish in the near future."

Because no answer came, Max Brasch turned to the president of the
Jewish Community, Moritz Rosenthal, with an even more direct letter:

> We cannot understand why a woman as *Rabbinerin* with such ora-
> torical skills and deep knowledge should not preach to us from *the
> pulpit of the New Synagogue*. In the *Trausaal* [marriage hall] of the
> synagogue, *Frl. Rabbinerin Jonas* again spoke in an outstanding man-
> ner. In this case one definitely cannot speak of tradition, because in the
> course of our history women have played an outstanding role, such as
> Deborah etc. I believe if God, blessed be He, gave women prophetic
> abilities, so should people also not reject a woman who, through reli-
> gious conviction, has taken on the job of *Rabbinerin*. As the High
> Holy Days are close at hand, this should be the ideal moment to start
> implementing our suggestion with regard to *Rabbinerin Frl.* Jonas.

This letter, too, remained unanswered.

However, Karl Brotzen, a member of the New Synagogue's board, also
took Jonas's side. His son, Jack Brotzen, said Jonas would often phone
his father late in the evening to talk about her latest difficulties. He tended
to have a "sympathetic ear" for Jonas, particularly because his wife, Loni,
was a soprano in the New Synagogue choir and enjoyed discussing the
issue of why women could not also serve as cantors. A poster from 1938
announces a "second Havdalah service" (marking the end of Shabbat) on
February 2, at which Regina Jonas was accompanied by Loni Brotzen and
the famous German cantor Leo Goldberg-Gollanin, among others. It
seems the two women had formed an outright coalition. The fact that it
was a "second Havdalah service" can have various meanings, including
the possibility that the more traditional members preferred not to attend
Jonas's service, thus she was given only the second Havdalah service following the regular (perhaps better attended) first service.

At any rate, "It must be noted," Jack Brotzen admits, that Jonas "did
not suffer from shyness; on the contrary, she was by nature an assertive
person who knew exactly what she wanted."

Jack Brotzen's father, Karl, participated in organizing Shabbat sched-
ules for the various rabbis in the New Synagogue. It was he who made it
possible for Jonas to deliver several sermons and to co-officiate on special occasions such as Oneg-Shabbat (Friday evening Shabbat celebration)
in the wedding chapel off to the side of the main synagogue. In January
1936 members of the New Synagogue were invited to a "Lecture by
Fräulein Rabbiner Regina Jonas" with the title "Religious Customs in

Jewish Life." Karl Brotzen made sure to get announcements about Jonas's talks into the community newsletter and Jewish newspapers. In the community office, he organized the printing of notices to be posted in the synagogue lobby.

Jonas's conservative orientation sometimes contradicted the liberal practices of the New Synagogue, resulting occasionally in conflict between members. Evidently, Jonas preferred that the organ not be played during celebrations she led, in accordance with the "old rites." Brotzen, who absolutely respected her rabbinic authority, said he nevertheless could not fully share her opinion "that one should avoid organ music on Shabbat afternoon, although obviously your rabbinic decision should and must remain definitive. . . . King David played the psalter and harp for the glorification of God's name. That in fact is the reason why we also believe in using a technical instrument to support the singing on Sabbath. And if liberal religious regulations allow organ music during official services, it seems even more appropriate for a celebration of 'the joy of Shabbat.'"

It appears that the main pulpit of the New Synagogue remained off-limits to the very end for Jonas, with the possible exception that her previously mentioned havdalah service was held there. On this point, not even the board of the synagogue could bypass the decision of the board of Berlin's Jewish Community.

⁂

But other venues were opening. Increasingly, Jewish women's organizations claimed Regina Jonas as their own. She spoke for WIZO (Women's International Zionist Organization), the Jüdischer Frauenbund, and the sisterhoods of B'nai B'rith and other lodges. The titles of her talks ranged from "Women in the Bible and Talmud" and "Heroism and Destiny of Biblical Women" to general themes such as "Fundamentals of Judaism as Seen Through Our Holidays," "The Meaning of the Revelation on Mt. Sinai," and "Characters in the First Book of Moses—A Conversation with God."

A report in the Jewish Community newsletter about a "WIZO Afternoon" with Regina Jonas noted that *Fräulein Rabbiner* Regina Jonas explored the Midrash that there were already 70 peoples on earth before the establishment of the people of Israel—and that as the 71st nation Jewry has only one task, assigned by God: to create and maintain religious culture—and to point the way to faith through rituals and rites. She emphasized that it is the duty of women to be just like the female prophets, custodians and upholders of compassion and justice, of all that is good and right, of love and courtesy: 'Where women enter, hate and enmity must fall silent.'"[20]

In a contribution for Mala Laaser's survey, "What Do You Have to Say on the Theme of WOMAN?," in the *Central-Verein-Zeitung*—the "assimilationist" newspaper of the Central Association of German Citizens of Jewish Faith, which was the largest organization representing Jews who considered themselves as integrated in German society—Jonas wrote,

> I hope a time will come for all of us in which there will be no more questions on the subject of "woman": for as long as there are questions, something is wrong. But if I must say what drove me as a woman to become a rabbi, two elements come to mind: My belief in the godly calling and my love for people. God has placed abilities and callings in our hearts, without regard to gender. Thus each of us has the duty, whether man or woman, to realize those gifts God has given. If you look at things this way, one takes woman and man for what they are: human beings."[21]

In a portrait published by the Swiss women's newspaper *Berna,* Jonas protested that "For me it was never about being the first. I wish I had been the hundred thousandth!"[22] The woman who wrote the article determined that "although *Rabbiner* Jonas never belonged to or supported a particular movement, we may count her definitively as one of us, in consideration of her views on equality of the sexes, careers and education for women. Her goals contain everything that we, too, stand for; her ideals are ours."

For many of her former pupils, Jonas remained a lifelong role model. On Ilse Ehrlich's graduation diploma from the Auguste-Viktoria-Schule, she wrote: "With best wishes for your future! *Rabb.* R. Jonas." When the pupils of the Elisabeth-Schule in Berlin-Charlottenburg were about to enter middle school, Jonas asked them about their career goals and told them of the many hurdles she herself had overcome, "how everyone had advised her against [her choice to become a rabbi] and almost laughed at her because it was at that time very unusual and one assumed a woman rabbi had no future," as Lieselott Lilian Levy recalled. As a former pupil, she herself took courage from Jonas's words, confiding that she wanted to be an actress but that her parents had forbidden this. In a letter to Levy's parents, Jonas wrote that it would be an "inexcusable lapse" if their daughter's wish were not fulfilled. Thanks to this letter, Levy's parents permitted her to audition for Kurt Singer, director of the Jewish Kulturbund [the Jewish Cultural Union, an organization created by the Nazis as an umbrella group for Jewish cultural life]. Shortly afterward, however,

---

Gruppe Neue Synagoge im Synagogenverband Berlin.

**Sonnabend, den 25. Januar 1936 abends 8 Uhr
im Trausaal Oranienburger Str. 29**

Vortrag des Fräulein Rabbiner **Regina Jonas :**

Religiöse Gebräuche im jüdischen Leben.

Musikalische Umrahmung : Herr Oberkantor **Gollanin.**

Eintritt frei

Gäste willkommen   Der Vorstand.

Invitation card to a lecture by Rabbi Regina Jonas

*Announcement for one of the many lectures and speeches Regina Jonas delivered
in the Neue Synagoge [New Synagogue].
Reproduction: Margit Billeb*

Lieselott Lilian Levy and her parents emigrated to the United States, where she would not realize her dream of becoming an actress.

Margaret Collin, who sang in the choir of the New Synagogue and attended many Shabbat services with Jonas, recalled, "My uncle, professor Rabbi Dr. Leo Hohenstein, always held up *Rabbiner* Jonas as an example: 'If Regina Jonas can be a rabbi,' he would say, 'then you can be a cantor.'" Betty Zinvirt, granddaughter of Jonas's pupil Margot Kurzweg, always heard her grandmother say, "If you study hard, maybe you can also become a *Rabbinerin*, like *Frau Rabbiner* Jonas." And Jonas's former pupil Ruth Callman, who became first *Gabba'it* [member of the synagogue board who can take decisions on synagogue matters] of congregation B'nai Emunah in San Francisco, said: "I wish Regina Jonas could see me. She would be so proud of me. She always wanted to turn me into a good Jew—and she succeeded."

Neue Synagoge
Oranienburger Strasse 29

Sonnabend, den 19. Februar 1938
abends 8 Uhr

2. Hawdala-
Sabbat-Ausgangs-Feier

Es wirken mit:

Leo Goldberg-Gollanin
Loni Brotzen (Sopran)
Paul Lichtenstein (Orgel)
Dr. Bail (Cello)

Die Ansprache hält
Fräulein Rabbiner Jonas

Eintritt frei!

Vorstand
der Neuen Synagoge

Poster announcing a service led by Rabbi Regina Jonas
in the New Synagogue
*A poster displayed in the New Synagogue announcing a Havdalah service
at which Regina Jonas delivered a talk, February 19, 1938.
Reproduction: Margit Billeb*

34

Karl Brotzen

Fabrikation von Puderdosen, Lippenstiften und Kleinmetallwaren

---

Bank-Konto:
Dresdner Bank, Depositen-Kasse 20
Berlin S 59, Kottbusser Damm 79

Postscheck-Konto: Berlin Nr. 153626

Fernsprecher: F 6 Baerwald 7163

Telegramm-Adr.: Karl Brotzen Berlin

Berlin SW 29, 23.März 1936.
Urbanstraße 70a

Br/L.

Fräulein Regina Jonas
Berlin.W.24.
Krausnickstrasse 4.

Sehr geehrtes Fräulein Rabbiner!

Der Oneg Schabbat ist jetzt von mir definitiv für Schabbes hagedaul,also für den 4.April or,nachmittags 5 Uhr festgesetzt... Eine erste redaktionelle Notiz soll in Gemeindeblatt schon nächsten Freitag erscheinen,eine zweite fett gedruckte Kastennotiz soll in der Zeitung,die am 3.April herauskommt,eingerückt werden.Wegen dieser letz= teren Veröffentlichung spreche ich dieser Tage noch auf dem Gemeindebü= ro vor.Dass auch in den anderen jüdischen Zeitungen Ankündigungen heraus kommen,dafür sorge ich schon,ebenso,dass Sie als Leiterin überall angeg= ben werden.
Ferner hängt schon nächsten Sabbat ein Plakat in Vorraum der Synagoge aus.
Den Programmentwurf hätte ich gerne bald von Jhnen gehabt.Jch füge zu diesem Zweck eine Freimarke bei.Sollten Sie mich lieber telefonisch sprechen wollen,dann bitte nicht nach 9 Uhr abends.
Jch habe mir den Verlauf der Feier auch schon durch den Kopf gehen las= sen,kann mich indessen mit Jhrer Auffassung,dass man vom Orgelspiel am Sabbatnachmittag Abstand nehmen müsse,nicht ganz einverstanden er= klären,obwohl selbstverständlich Jhre rabbinische Entscheidung massge= bend bleiben soll und muss.Vielleicht befragen Sie darüber mal einen auteritativeh Kollegen.
König David hat zur Verherrlichung Gottes Psalter und Harfe gespielt. Das ist doch die Grundidee,warum wir glauben auch am Sabbat den Gesang durch ein technisches Jnstrument zu unterstützen.Wenn nun aber ,so sagt mir die Logik,das liberale Religionsgesetz, das Orgelspiel sogar am of= fiziellen Gottesdienst gestattet,warum nicht noch viel mehr≠ bei einer Feier"der Freude am Sabbat".
Jch hoffe hierüber noch von Jhnen zu hören,denn nur Jhre Entscheidung ist hier ausschlaggebend.
Beginnen werden wir mit einem Smiruagesang,dann können Sie beliebig lang sprechen,wir haben reichlich Zeit,30-45 Minuten.Eventuell vor und nach Jhrer Rede ein Sologesang,ebenso so schön wäre auch eine Rezitati= en eines Erwachsenen..Dann Verteilung von Theekuchen oder ähnlichem Gebäck.Wenn wir Gläser hätten,würde ich auch etwas zu trinken anbieten, aber Gläser fehlen einstweilen.Nach dieser Pause:Gemütliches Beisammer= sein.Jch werde bitten,um die Unterhaltung in Gang zu bringen≠Fragen zu stellen.Darüber vergeht viel Zeit.Schliesslich Ledewid Beruch und Hawdel loh.
Das ist im grossen und ganzen mein Gedankengang und hoffe ich nun von Jhnen zu hören.Der Sabbat dürfte etwa 7,20 Uhr aus sein.
Mit freundlichem Gruss
Jhr

Letter of support by Karl Brotzen, member of the New Synagogue board,
March 23, 1936

Letter from Karl Brotzen to Regina Jonas.
Reproduction: Margit Billeb

Dear *Fräulein Rabbiner*!

I have now definitely set the Oneg Shabbat for Shabbat *hagadol*, April 4, at 5 in the afternoon. . . . Next Friday, an initial notice will appear in the community newspaper, and a second bold-faced announcement will be in the paper that comes out on the 3rd of April. I will also mention this to the community office. I am already taking care of publicity in other Jewish newspapers, and also ensuring that you always are to be named as the director.

In addition, a poster will be hanging next Shabbat in the entrance of the synagogue.

I would appreciate your giving me a planned program soon. With that in mind, I am enclosing a postage stamp. If you prefer to talk to me on the telephone, then please not after 9 in the evening.

I have been thinking over the course of the event, and I have to say I am not completely in agreement with your view that one should avoid organ music on Shabbat afternoon, although obviously your rabbinical decision should and must remain definitive. Perhaps you should discuss it with an authoritative colleague.

King David played the psalter and harp for the glorification of God's name. That in fact is the reason why we also believe in using a technical instrument to support the singing on Shabbat. And if liberal religious regulations allow organ music during official services, it seems even more appropriate for a celebration of "the joy of Shabbat."

I hope to hear from you on this, for your decision alone is what counts.

We will begin with the singing of *zmirot* [Shabbat songs], and then you can speak as long as you wish, we have at least 30–45 minutes. Possibly before and after your talk there a soloist will sing, and it would also be nice to have one of the adults read aloud. Then we will distribute cakes or something similar. If we had glasses, I would also offer something to drink, but glasses are not available at present. After this intermission: a comfortable gathering. I would ask questions in order to get the conversation going. Time will pass quickly. Finally, Ledovid Boruch and Havdalah.

That is basically my line of thought, and now I hope to hear from you. Shabbat should be over at about 7:20.

Sincerely,
Your Karl Brotzen

Letter of support by Karl Brotzen, member of the New Synagogue board, March 23, 1936 (translation)

Apparently, Max Dienemann was right to assume that the board of the Berlin Jewish Community would support Jonas "gradually." Already in January 1936, she was permitted for the first time to deliver a sermon in the synagogue of the Jewish senior home on Iranische Strasse. In August 1937 the Jewish Community officially hired her. True, the contract referred to her only as a "religion teacher with academic qualifications." But she was also supposed "to provide rabbinic pastoral care in the social institutions of the community." Jonas was required to tend to the spiritual needs of patients in five public hospitals, in the Jewish Hospital on Iranische Strasse, and at the Hilfsverein für jüdische Taubstumme [Society for the Assistance of Jewish Deaf-Mutes]. On her own, she went to the trouble of gaining permission to counsel Jewish inmates in a women's prison.

⁂

In general, working with the ill and needy was considered less prestigious for rabbis than preaching in synagogues and teaching. But Jonas apparently did not share this view. Born and raised as she was in the Scheunenviertel, knowing from personal experience what it meant to be poor, Jonas identified the rabbinate with helping one's neighbor. Nearly every day she visited the elderly and ill, helping them get back on their spiritual feet.

Jonas's contract had a certain flexibility that allowed her, in the next few years, to work increasingly as a rabbi in synagogues. According to paragraph V, the board of the Jewish Community retained the right to "change her tasks according to her abilities and achievements"—giving her a back door that naturally could always be shut again. Jonas's first assignments were those that would be least likely to give offense—conducting services in the Jewish old age home and hospitals or at the conclusion of Shabbat, and delivering addresses for confirmation ceremonies or funerals—but she was not to deliver sermons in the larger synagogues, and had absolutely no role in delivering halachic (Jewish legal) decisions or executing weddings or divorces.

Günther Ruschin, son of the former cantor of the Levetzowstrasse Synagogue, where Jonas later served, said she wore a robe and cap during services but no tallit, the fringed prayer shawl worn in the morning prayer during Torah reading. On this point she respected traditional ideas: though she had demonstrated in her halachic treatise that women were just as eligible as men to be called to the Torah, Jonas considered being called up to the Torah simply an honor, and she was not oriented toward such honors.

School diploma signed by Rabbi Regina Jonas

Pupil Ilse Ehrlich's diploma from the Auguste-Viktoria School, 1937–1938.

Israel Alexander's father, Rabbi Siegfried Alexander, worked as a chaplain in the Jewish Hospital. His son was often present during Jonas's religious services there. "She wanted to deliver a talk or sermon during the prayer service, but whenever this one doctor [Dr. H. Hirsch] was there praying with them, he said to her: 'Do what you want, but during the prayers you go up with the women [in the gallery], and afterwards you come down.'"[23]

Similarly, Rabbi Alexander could not resist delivering an occasional dig at Jonas's expense. Rabbi Nathan Peter Levinson, who at the time was

Mala Laaser / *Frauenblatt* –
C.V.- Zeitung

Rabbiner Regina J o n a s :   60

Sehr geehrtes Fräulein Laaser,

nachdem ich mich nach Kräften dagegen gesträubt habe, Ihnen einen

Beitrag, das heisst etwas über mich selbst und den von mir ergriffenen

Rabbinerberuf (er hat mich eigentlich ergriffen, nicht ich ihn!) als

Frau zu schreiben, haben mich einige Ihrer Gründe schliesslich dennoch

bezwungen; welche, verrate ich nicht: Amtsgeheimnis! Zum ersten Mal

ergreife ich also die Feder, um mich zu der so oft an mich gestellten

Frage zu äussern, warum ich als Frau Rabbinerin geworden bin. Sie

stelle mich vor eine harte Aufgabe. Ich schreibe nicht gern; ausser-

dem müsste ich Ihnen von Mühlsal und Enttäuschung berichten, wer aber

tut das gern? Ferner müsste ich stets von m i r und m e i n e n Kämpfen

sprechen, da ich das Schicksal habe, die erste Frau in meinem Beruf zu

sein. Das liegt mir aber nicht. Jede romantische Umkränzung menschli-

cher Pflichterfüllung ist mir zuwider. In einer Predigt könnte ich als

Frau zu Frauen etwa sagen, was ich jetzt hier schreiben möchte. Ton,

Gebärde, Blick, Haltung beleben, was man künden will. Doch was ich

niederschreibe, dürfte im Versuch, mich auszudrücken, steckenbleiben.

Uebrigens will ich aber sagen, dass ich für uns alle eine Zeit erhoffe,

in der es Fragen um das Thema »Frau« nicht mehr geben wird: denn wo

Fragen sind, ist etwas krank. Wenn ich nun aber doch gestehen soll,

was mich, die Frau, dazu getrieben hat, Rabbiner zu werden, so fällt

mir zweierlei ein: mein Glaube an die göttliche Berufung und meine

Liebe zu den Menschen. Fähigkeiten und Berufungen hat Gott in unsere

Brust gesenkt und nicht nach dem Geschlecht gefragt. So hat ein jeder

die Pflicht, ob Mann oder Frau, nach d e n Gaben, die Gott ihm schenkte,

zu wirken und zu schaffen.- Wenn man die Dinge so betrachtet, nimmt

man Weib und Mann als das, was sie sind: als Menschen.

                          Mit den besten Grüssen

                          Ihre Rabbiner Regina Jonas

Article by Regina Jonas describing why she became a rabbi
(for the women's page of *Central-Verein-Zeitung*, June 23, 1938)
*Letter from Regina Jonas to Mala Laaser regarding the survey "What Do You
Have to Say on the Theme of WOMAN?" printed in the* Central-Verein-Zeitung
(June 23, 1938). Reproduction: Margit Billeb

Dear Fräulein Laaser,

After I struggled with all my might against writing something for you about myself and my chosen rabbinical career (actually, it chose me, not the reverse!), some of your reasons in the end won me over; I won't confess which they were: official secret! So for the first time I take up the pen to express myself on the question so often put to me: Why have I as a woman become a rabbi? You have given me a difficult task. I do not enjoy writing; and besides, I must report about hardship and disappointment, and who enjoys doing that? In addition, I have to speak about *myself* and *my* struggles, because it is my fate to be the first woman in this field. That is not my style. I find any romanticization of the human sense of duty to be repulsive. In speaking, I can more easily address myself to other women than in writing; for tone, gesture, expression, and posture enliven whatever I want to say. What I am writing gets stuck in my attempt to express myself. But what I was going to say is that I hope a time will come for all of us in which there will be no more questions on the subject of "woman": for as long as there are questions, something is wrong. But if I must say what drove me as a woman to become a rabbi, two elements come to mind: My belief in the godly calling and my love for people. God has placed abilities and callings in our hearts, without regard to gender. Thus each of us has the duty, whether man or woman, to realize those gifts God has given. If you look at things this way, one takes woman and man for what they are: human beings.

With best wishes,

Your Rabbiner Regina Jonas

Article by Regina Jonas describing why she became a rabbi (for the women's page of *Central-Verein-Zeitung*, June 23, 1938) (translation)

still studying at the Academy, said in his memoirs, "One day I was taking a walk with my teacher and friend Rabbi Hans Löwenthal, as well as with Rabbi Siegfried Alexander and *Frau Rabbiner* Jonas. Frau Jonas suddenly joked that the three of them actually formed a 'Bet Din' [a Jewish religious court consisting of three rabbis]. Alexander, her Orthodox colleague, looked at her wide-eyed and responded that Peter—meaning myself—still wasn't a rabbi. I couldn't see if she had turned red, but anyway she was the one who had provoked the reaction."[24] Among Orthodox Jews, Jonas's ordination remained extremely questionable. Marie Jalowicz often attended the Orthodox Heidereutergasse Synagogue (also known as the Old Synagogue, the oldest city synagogue in Berlin), to which Regina Jonas occasionally went, sitting with her mother during Shabbat services. Jalowicz remembered, "Everyone in the Old Synagogue knew she was a rabbi, and frequently members of the board referred to her as *Fräulein Rabbiner Jonas*. The word *Fräulein* was expressed in an unpleasant, I would almost say a bit snide manner. . . . As everyone knows, the tone makes the music. It was all about the way this word *Fräulein* was expressed—not always but sometimes in a somewhat mocking way."[25]

Nevertheless, there were also Orthodox rabbis such as Felix Singermann—one of the main figures in Berlin Orthodox circles—who supported Regina Jonas. Marie Jalowicz recorded that Singermann emphasized in his sermons that "it does a great damage to Judaism that women were not permitted to learn as men do. We also need women. It is neither correct according to law nor is it an expression of piety to reject this, rather it is absolutely false. One does not prove one's piety through false interpretations." Said Jalowicz, "He said this with great emphasis, aimed at a particular address."[26]

In his congratulations to Jonas upon the successful completion of her rabbinical exam, Singermann, writing in Hebrew, placed Jonas's case in an almost biblically miraculous context. Beginning his letter "With God's help. Wednesday of the week that ends with the reading of the Torah portion 'Vayigash elav Yehuda' in the year 5696—To the honored *Rabbinerin Frau* Rifka of the family of Jonas," Singermann continued, "I heard the good news and have rejoiced over the good that the Eternal has done for you. This matter is an innovation, and nothing of the kind has ever been heard of in our entire country, and above all I send my deeply felt congratulations, and it strikes me as proof that there are also miracles in our times. The aim of this event should be to glorify and make great the Torah."

The question remains as to whether the Berlin Jewish Community board was prepared to allow Jonas to work as a rabbi on a long-term basis, and what would have happened had there been no Shoah. Perhaps developments in the rabbinate would have been similar to those in the Protestant church, in which female vicars promoted in the absence of male priests during the war later had to give up their positions.[27] Some eyewitnesses suggested that Jonas was only permitted to work as a rabbi in Berlin because increasing numbers of her male colleagues had fled abroad or had been imprisoned by the Nazis. The lack of rabbis and the emergency situation of the Jewish Community were, say these eyewitnesses, "her chance." And in a sense, this certainly was the case.

In 1933, the year when the Nazi regime came to power, 180,000 Jews were living in Berlin. Immediately, numerous anti-Semitic actions were launched—including the nationwide boycott of shops and warehouses run by Jews, or the complete ban of Jewish lawyers from any juridical public bodies and associations. In 1935—the year of Jonas's ordination—the Nuremberg racial laws were enacted, implementing a complete ban against Jews in any public sphere. Such measures led Max Dienemann to emigrate to London; hundreds of rabbis in Germany left for other European countries or to America.

However, numerous other rabbis, such as Leo Baeck and Regina Jonas, consciously decided to stay despite the deteriorating situation. As German Jews they felt there was no other place for them to be than among their suffering people, who could still recall a time when Judaism was at its cultural peak in Germany. Despite the daily anti-Semitic pressures, the degrading defamations, and the continuous emigration from Germany of those clearheaded enough to leave the country early, German Jewry even experienced—paradoxically—a certain spiritual blossoming. For most Jews in Germany, the turning point was the Kristallnacht pogrom on the night of November 9–10, 1938. Until then, Jewish publications evidenced an amazing self-esteem. The Jewish publishing house Schocken, for example, brought out a series from 1933 through 1939 of the works of all major German-Jewish philosophers and religious thinkers, demonstrating for the last time the grandeur of the German-Jewish legacy.

As Jews were no longer permitted to teach or study at the universities; as theaters and concert halls were no longer open to Jews; as public life in general was "Aryanized," Jews flocked to the newly created Jewish cultural institutions. The well-established Academy for the Science of Judaism increasingly became a substitute university where newly jobless professors taught everything from chemistry to philosophy; Jewish students who no longer were allowed to attend universities came here instead. Drawing these disenfranchised students, the Academy became an oasis where the spiritual potential of German Jewry sent out new shoots.

While the ideology of the "Germanic superman" drove the non-Jewish populace deeper into a spiritual wasteland, at the Academy one could sit and listen to the lectures of Leo Baeck or Julius Guttmann. Many people for whom religion had long lost its meaning became interested again and took pride in this. The synagogues became important again, and their benches were no longer full only on Jewish holidays; every evening there were concerts and lectures. Many more people came to Shabbat services than in the pre-Hitler years. To go to the synagogue was also a way to demonstrate that human dignity remained unbroken. Members showed particular respect to their rabbis—bearers and teachers of Jewish knowledge. To be a rabbi also meant to take a stand, backed by an enduring moral standard, against the "Thousand-Year Reich" that the Nazis had proclaimed.

And it was precisely then, when rabbis received this kind of respect, that Regina Jonas was hired by the Jewish Community of Berlin. So the lack of rabbis was indeed her "chance," but in an ambivalent, double-edged way.

Never one to bow easily to pressure, she remained true to her belief that the Jewish people have a special God-given, ethical role in history, even as the Nazi regime took hold. After a Chanukah celebration in the Hermsdorf Synagogue in December 1937, a sixteen-year-old pupil reported (at that time) that "hundreds of people had gathered in the synagogue in order to hear the much loved, very lively speaker." In her talk, Jonas presented the figures from the First Book of Moses "as models for our deeds and actions." "But she did not stress victory or defeat in face of the evil inclination, but rather the struggle for good. And Jews in particular are chosen to fight for the good, in order to bring it to the people. Jews are the people of religion. Other people prefer to spread art and science, but the Jewish role in life is above all to plant the belief in God in all humanity."[28]

Jonas delivered speeches in Jewish institutions on religious, biblical, and talmudic themes. The Jewish newspapers published her rabbinical commentaries (alongside a notice of her office hours, 9:00–11:00 AM daily in her home at Krausnickstrasse 6), in which she referred to the sense and meaning of Jewish holidays, prayer, and customs, and always stressed that men and women shared the same rights *and* obligations.[29] In an article about Yom Kippur in October 1938, one month before the Kristallnacht pogrom, she cautioned the congregation not to leave the daylong Yom Kippur service before it was finished; she criticized women for skipping out on important prayers "to go home and prepare coffee and cake," and men for not staying through the ten-minute evening Ma'ariv service, instead running home to break the fast, so that by the end of Yom Kippur "only the minyan [required quorum of ten men]" would be left in the synagogue.[30]

A month later, those Jews who had fooled themselves into thinking Jewish life in Germany would still be possible—even under ghetto conditions of centuries past—were brutally disillusioned. On the night of November 9–10, 1938, the Nazi regime revealed its murderous ambitions. Kristallnacht saw the sanctioned destruction of most German synagogues, set afire and vandalized by government order. In a foreshadowing of what the Nazi regime had in store for the Jews, SA storm troopers looted Jewish homes and businesses, and ten thousand Jewish men were taken to concentration camps.

Six months after Kristallnacht, Jonas wrote a rabbinical commentary about the Yizkor memorial service for the departed—in German, "Über die Seelen-Feier"—which not only referred to the shock of the pogrom but also portrayed Jonas's view, that once again time had put the Jews to the test:

> We are living today in a time of trial by fire, testing the strength of our love for children, gratitude, the mutual support of family and friends in these alien conditions. Many people wanted, in spite of all obstacles, to preserve a true sense of Jewish family and peoplehood. Our sages say that the Torah was only given to Israel when the people presented guarantees, and only after they offered their children as guarantees to God. If worry and despondency seek our undoing, then we should think about Yizkor in such a way that we identify ourselves as *"are-vim tovim"* [good guarantees], standing up for Israel, carrying on the work of our ancestors from Sinai; in that we today are truly their children, and in that we are the parents of the future generations, then the chain does not break and we gain the strength to carry out nobly these historical responsibilities, and to thank God sincerely that *Yizkor has become the celebration of our own souls.*[31]

Numerous people urged Jonas to leave Germany. After all, they said, in America or elsewhere she could have had a career as the first female rabbi in the world. But apparently she rejected all thoughts of this kind. "She wanted to stay where her people were, just like Leo Baeck," observed Gad Beck, author of the autobiography *An Underground Life*, who had worked in the same factory with Jonas as a slave laborer. Her former pupil Rita Nagler recalled, "One sensed that for her it meant more

Über die Seelen-Feier

Von Rabbiner Regina Sara Jonas

Wenn jüdische Menschen zum ersten Male im Jahre wieder eine Festtagsfeier begehen, sprechen sie die Brochoch, „Schehechejomi", wir danken dir, o Gott, daß du uns wieder die Festeszeit erleben ließest." — Wenn Gott dem menschlichen Leben ein „genug jetzt" entgegenruft, dem Sterblichen die Seele nimmt, sprechen Juden das Kaddischgebet, „geheiligt werde sein Name."

Es ist kein Geringes, wenn viermal im Jahr, am Peßach, Schowuaus, Schmini-Azeres und Jaum Kippur, am Ende der Feste, die Haskoraus - N'schomaus - Seelenfeier für unsere Dahingeschiedenen in unseren Gotteshäusern stattfindet. Manch einer wird sagen: Zum ernsten Jaum Kippur paßt „Seelenfeier", aber zu den drei Wallfahrtsfesten, die doch durchaus freudigen Charakter haben, da soll die Festesfreude durch den Gedanken an Tod und Trauer unterbrochen werden? Gerade in der Freude will jüdische Seelenhaltung sich klar machen, daß nur die Freude Bestand hat vor dem Blicke der Ewigkeit, und den Namen Festesfreude verdient, die nicht mit Oberflächlichkeit und Ausgelassenheit verwechselt wird, sondern ein Dank an Gott ist, das heißt Freude in der Familie und im Volke, geadelt durch Opfer- und Liebestaten für sie.

Es hat sich aber nun leider im Laufe der Zeit ein sehr unangenehmer Uebelstand entwickelt. Kaum beginnt die Seelenfeier, so verlassen Jugendliche (nicht nur Kinder) und auch Aeltere, die noch das große Glück besitzen, ihre Eltern an ihrer Seite zu haben, das Gotteshaus, und „draußen" oder auf dem Hofe wird Müßiges geschwätzt. Während an heiliger Stätte tiefernster Gottesdienst abgehalten wird, schließen sich Menschen aus einem falschen Empfinden heraus von diesem wahrlich eindrucksvollen Teile unserer Festandacht aus. Diesen unreligiösen Brauch müssen wir einmal durch ernstes Ueberlegen zu beseitigen suchen. Teilnehmen an einem Gottesdienst heißt, Weihe und Würde empfangen und geben, sich seelisch bereichern. Ein Schwatzen bei der Andacht oder früheres Verlassen des Gotteshauses heißt sich selbst ärmer machen, am Wesen des Gottesdienstes vorbeigehen. Wer aber selbst nicht so viel Disziplin aufbringen kann, der Andacht bis zum Schluß zu folgen, der soll wissen, daß sein „Auszieh'n" aus dem Gottesdienst die wirklich Andächtigen stört. Außerdem ist es sinnlos. Erstens kann man an jedem Gottesdienst teilnehmen, auch wenn das direkte Betroffensein nicht zutrifft. Ferner aber erstreckt sich die Seelenfeier nicht nur auf die Eltern, sondern auf alle Menschen, denen der andere zu Dank und Gedenken verpflichtet ist, somit Verwandten weiteren Grades, Lehrern in Israel. Wer aber wirklich glaubt, gar keinen Zugang zu diesem würdigen Teil unserer Andacht finden zu können, der respektiere das Leid, das Gedenken der anderen, bleibe ehrfurchtsvoll an seinem Platze und lausche Tönen und Worten. Er selbst unterläßt eben dann nur das spezielle Seelengebet.

Wir leben jetzt in einer Zeit der Feuerprobe, ob Kindesliebe und Dankbarkeit, Verwandten- und Freundestreue sich in der Fremde bewähren, viele Menschen wollten allen Hindernissen zum Trotz wahren jüdischen Familien- und Volkssinnus unter Beweis stellen. Schowunus zeigt als Lektüre auf — früher im Gotteshaus, jetzt privat — das Büchlein Ruth, das „Hohelied" der Familien-

treue und -liebe. All dies tiefernst religiöse Empfinden kann nur ausgelöst werden, wenn die ganze Gemeinde Israel im Gotteshause weilt, wie einst ganz Israel, Männer, Frauen und Kinder, am Sinai die Tora empfingen. Die Tora, sagen unsere Weisen, wurde Israel erst dann gegeben, als Israel Bürgen stellte und erst dann, als es seine Kinder als Bürgen Gott anbot. Wenn Sorge und Kleinmut sich unserer bemächtigen wollen, dann wollen wir an das Seelenfeiererlebnis denken, uns als „trewiin tauwiin", „gute Bürgen" für Israels Bestand zu fühlen, das Werk unserer Voreltern vom Sinai fortzusetzen; sind wir heute doch im Hinblick auf sie, ihre Kinder, und wir, für folgende Geschlechter, die Eltern, so reiße die Kette nicht ab und gebe uns diese geschichtliche Verantwortung Kraft zu edlen Leistungen, auch im Ernste Gott zu danken, daß die Seelenfeier zur Feier unserer Seele werde, „Sauweach Taudoh j'chabdoni", „wer mir Dank opfert, ehrt mich" (Ps. 50,23).

Erez Israel in einer Aggada des Midrasch rabba

R. Levi sagte: Mosche führte Klage bei dem Heiligen, gelobt sei Er: Herr der Welt! Die Leiche des Josef ist in Erez Jisrael bestattet worden, aber ich darf nicht in das Land der Verheißung kommen und darf dort nicht meine letzte Ruhestätte finden. Der Heilige, gelobt sei Er, ließ diesen Vorwurf nicht gelten und sprach: Der Patriarchensohn ist in Erez Jisrael beigesetzt worden, weil er sich ausdrücklich zu Erez Jisrael bekannte, er sprach zu dem Mundschenk, dessen Traum er gedeutet hatte: „Ich bin gestohlen worden aus dem Lande der Hebräer." (1. Buch Mosche 40, 15). Aber du sollst nicht nach Erez Jisrael kommen und auch nicht dort begraben werden, wenn du dein irdisches Leben vollendet haben wirst, weil du das Land der Verheißung einmal verleugnet hast. Denn du hattest, als die Töchter Jthros sagten: „Ein ägyptischer Mann hat uns gerettet" (2. Buch Mosche 2, 19) nichts darauf erwidert und jene Bemerkung nicht richtiggestellt. (Dwarim rabba 2).

Diese Aggada (sie ist auch aus diesem Grunde beachtenswert, weil wir aus ihr ersehen, daß ein Aggadist, R. Levi, der mit größter Verehrung zu Mosche aufblickt, dessenungeachtet an seiner Haltung tadelnd Kritik zu üben wagt) prägt uns sehr überzeugend den Gedanken ein: Wer sich zu Erez Jisrael bekennt und es wie jener Patriarchensohn nicht verleugnet, darf zur Alija kommen und ist würdig, den Boden Erez Jisraels zu betreten.

Die Aktualität dieser Aggada ist leicht zu erkennen. Gerade heute, da so viele, die auswandern wollen, ihre Blicke nach Erez Jisrael richten, sollte man nicht vergessen: Die Immigration nach Palästina ist wesensverschieden von der nach anderen Ländern. Bei dieser müssen besonders Voraussetzungen äußerlicher Art erfüllt werden, z. B. die Sprache, die im Einwanderungsland gesprochen wird, muß erlernt werden, bei der Alija aber haben vor allem seelische Tatsachen, besonders innerlichste Verbundenheit mit dem Lande, größte Bedeutung.

Rabbiner Dr. Ernst Israel Steckelmacher

(Weitere Festaufsätze Seite 10)

Article by Regina Jonas about the Yizkor service ("Seelen-Feier," *Jüdisches Nachrichtenblatt*, May 24, 1939)

Regina Jonas's exposition of the Yizkor theme in the Jüdisches Nachrichtenblatt *[Jewish Newsletter] of May 24, 1939.*

to serve those who trusted in her than to save herself." To all those who spoke with her about the last chances to flee, Jonas responded that she could not leave her mother.

By this time, of the 180,000 Jews in Berlin before Hitler came to power, about seventy thousand were still left—mostly older people with neither the money nor the strength to start a new life in another country. As the deprivation of their rights accelerated, these Jews fell victim to increasing destitution; many were reduced to dependence on welfare organizations, soup kitchens, and "Winter Help" of the Jewish Community. Jonas helped support numerous people. Her files contain letters of thanks from across Europe as well as from China and North America, from Jews who were grateful for what she did for their elderly relatives, mostly parents. Jonas applied to the American Joint Distribution Committee to pressure one German immigrant in New York to send regular help to his suffering mother. In one letter to the committee, she included the address of Lily Montagu, founder of the liberal Jewish movement in Great Britain, who—like Bertha Pappenheim in Germany—had founded important social institutions in England. Through the Jewish Winter Help and "clothing drop," Jonas organized the collecting of underwear for elderly people, gifts for a Chanukah party in the hospital, and books for the patients there. She also continued her weekly visits to her teacher and colleague Max Weyl, in order to study halachic literature with him. Since the Nazis had banned Jewish religious education in Berlin schools, Jonas invited the girls to study in her apartment.

♪ ♪ ♪

Another likely reason why Regina Jonas did not want to leave Germany was her love relationship with Rabbi Dr. Joseph Norden of Hamburg, which began in the summer of 1939. The two met in July, at his sixty-ninth birthday celebration. At their first meeting, Jonas invited Norden to address her with the familiar *"Du"* instead of the polite, more distant *"Sie."* On Jonas's thirty-seventh birthday, barely two weeks later, he sent her mother a card of congratulations "on your marvelous daughter." Norden—whose wife had died nine years before—visited Jonas in the winter of 1939 in Berlin and invited her in June 1940 to his apartment in Hamburg. In August 1940 he wrote to her: "From the hour that I met you last summer, I fell in love with you. It is a shame that I am a man of 70. Because if I were 30 years younger, I would have wanted you as my wife, and married you."

Jonas's feelings for a man thirty-two years her senior exemplified a recurring pattern in her life: her apparent attraction to father figures who

Rabbi Joseph Norden (left), sitting next to Rabbi Zwi Carlebach
Rabbi Max Plaut took the photo on December 6, 1939, at a Chanukah party
in the Jewish Orphanage for Girls in Hamburg.
Reproduction: Margit Billeb

were able to recognize her as an equal. Jonas's mentor of many years, Rabbi Weyl, considered her an esteemed colleague and had extra respect for Jonas's struggles as a woman fighting her way into the rabbinate. He and Norden delivered the same kind of professional recognition to their younger female colleague.

For Jonas, whose rabbinical identity placed a high moral value on modesty, this unexpected love for a man—who in his first letters called her "Madonna Regina"—must have led to a conflict of conscience. It is hard to know how far the relationship went. Norden regularly wrote love poems for Jonas. One poem bore the title "Praise for the Hanse City Hamburg—dedicated to my beloved, beautiful and noble colleague Regina

Jonas on New Year's Eve 1939." After four stanzas describing Hamburg—and between the lines, Jonas's visit there—the fifth stanza concluded with

> *O Elbe Du, o Alster! Ihr habt mirs angetan,*
> *Ihr habt mich schier verzaubert, erkennt es selber nur.*
> *Und weil Hamburg liegt an diesen beiden Flüssen,*
> *Musst' ich Reginalein umarmen süss und küssen.*
> [Oh you Elbe, Oh Alster, you have captivated me,
> You have simply bewitched me, just accept it.
> And because Hamburg lies at these two rivers,
> I had to embrace my little Regina sweetly and kiss her.]

Jonas often wrote brief comments on Norden's letters. Under this last stanza, she wrote: "No, poetic license; it never came to that."

Reading the remaining 116 letters from Norden to Jonas in chronological order, it becomes clear that there must have been several attempts to separate after Jonas unsuccessfully urged Norden to marry her. At first, Norden had rejected these proposals, and even defended himself after an outing on the Alster River in Hamburg: "How could I have known that you would grant wishes such as those I have expressed (to kiss, etc.), to only one man, the one who marries you?"

In a letter from 1941, during another period of separation, Norden wrote angrily

> Your use of the term "seduction" sounds comical to me: A woman of 38 years letting herself be seduced like a teenager. But you expect that I will change my attitude. I can only beg you once more: Stop the debating. It is useless, in written form as much as in oral form—if there will be a chance for another opportunity. With the kind of *ahavah* [love] as you wanted it, it is over. I don't want to have another wife, just as I don't want a *ke'eyn*-wife [as-if-wife]. The *ke'eyn*-game is over! For two years we have courted each other. You wanted to force me morally into marriage. For two years I couldn't emerge from unrest and excitement. For two years a nightmare has lasted. Now the nightmare is over and will not come back. Despite malnutrition and the much too heavy workload for my age, I feel much better than I have in years, because my soul feels liberated from the pressure you had put on me.

Despite such unresolved issues, Jonas visited him at least four times up to the end of 1941, usually spending the summer break with him in his apartment.

Like Jonas, Norden tended to mix traditional with modern views. He had studied at Berlin's Orthodox Rabbinical Seminary and later became one of Germany's leading liberal rabbis. Norden was even considered a "radical" liberal; he had participated in all the conferences of the World Union for Progressive Judaism since its founding in 1926. His son, Albert Norden, who survived the Nazi period in exile in the United States and later joined the Politburo of Communist East Germany, defined his father's political philosophy before World War I as "liberalism—but under a monarchy that of course should not rule according to the mercy of God but according to a constitution."

Norden's own publications vouch for this interpretation. In 1915 he dedicated a booklet to Kaiser Wilhelm II with the title *Unser Kaiser* [Our Emperor]. It contained fifteen birthday speeches he had written in honor of the kaiser. At the same time, Norden translated the works of the English Jewish religious reformer Claude Montefiore into German and in 1918 published *Grundsätze und Ziele des religiösen liberalen Judentums* [Foundations and Goals of Religious Liberal Judaism].

Born in Hamburg, Norden had spent several decades as rabbi of the Elberfeld Synagogue (today in Wuppertal). He retired in 1935, two years after the Nazis came to power and the same year that Regina Jonas received her ordination. After the pogrom of November 9–10, 1938, when the rabbi of the Hamburg Jewish Community, Bruno Italiener, was forced to emigrate abroad, Norden made himself available to the congregation of the Israelitischer Tempel in Hamburg, the city of his birth. The synagogue had been closed after the pogrom, but services were held in a theater of a building that belonged to the Jewish Community.

As with Jonas and Weyl, joint study of rabbinical texts played an important role in the relationship between Jonas and Norden. Norden's letters contained interpretations of biblical quotes that he wished to use in his upcoming sermons; poems by Goethe, Schiller, Heine, or Uhland; and many love poems in which Norden repeatedly expressed how proud he was of Jonas's rabbinical accomplishments.

When Jonas shared with Norden her halachic treatise on whether women can become rabbis, he reacted, quoting their friend Weyl: "You 'extremely ambitious Lady!'" Delighted with her "knowledge of and familiarity with talmudic writings" as well as her courage to express a "divergent view," Norden advised Jonas on the "possible publication" of the text. He also sent her words of praise—including notes from other respected personalities whom he had urged to write, and whose letters he then marked with the official seal of the Rabbinate of the Israelitischer Tempel Hamburg. Furthermore, Norden officially invited his lover and friend to attend sermons in his community. However, he found Jonas not at all radical; rather, he agreed with a friend who described her as "nice, smart, very beautiful, in other words not the usual type of female combatant for emancipation but actually quite feminine."

Norden's children, who had fled abroad, first heard about their father's alliance with Regina Jonas in November 1940. The family still has letters Norden wrote to his daughter Bertha and her husband, Werner Bohnstedt (who by then lived in Alliance, Ohio), as well as to his youngest daughter, Hanna, and her husband, Josef Hochfeld, who had fled together to Tientsin in northern China. In his letter of November 28, 1940, Norden wrote to Bertha and Werner Bohnstedt:

> Have I ever mentioned my young colleague Fräulein Rabbiner Jonas, with whom I have been friendly since July of last year? She is one of a kind, at least here in Germany. Last summer she spent her vacation in Hamburg, and we were able to get to know each other. She was enrolled at the Berlin Academy for seven [sic] years and received a rabbinical diploma. Her path was not without obstacles, but she possesses the necessary energy and intelligence. In addition, she has a wonderful gift of rhetoric and a sonorous voice. On my birthday she came especially from Berlin and spoke at the official reception in my home, beautiful words for the younger generation of rabbis, and she spoke likewise on Friday night after services at the evening meal among the inner circle (the board of the community and of the Temple). We have spent some hours together, diligently exploring biblical territory, and as I recently took a five-day break in Berlin, we picked up where we left off. When your mother died, I promised myself never to marry again. I tell myself one should not remarry, after thirty-four years of marriage, of sharing one's joys and sorrows. Otherwise, a woman such as this colleague, with her physical, spiritual and psychological advantages, would have been a good companion for me. In the meantime I am an old man and she is a young woman of thirty-eight.

In the same letter, Norden asked about possible jobs for Jonas in the United States: "But it would interest me to know if the USA has female rabbis, or if [Jews there] would be receptive toward them. Because ultimately, she, too, must be anxious to find a new home. I would be happy if it were possible to find out something more specific on this score, perhaps through the Hebrew Union College in Cincinnati. Hopefully my request doesn't put you to too much trouble." The inherent apology in the last sentence was typical of letters many Jews wrote to relatives outside Germany.

On May 27, 1941, Norden reported about a visit to his former community in Elberfeld and mentioned just at the end of his letter that he stopped in Berlin on the return trip from Elberfeld to Hamburg, where he spent two days with Regina Jonas and visited Leo Baeck with her.

It appears that Norden's children also greeted Regina Jonas in their letters to him. Norden even referred to a letter Jonas had received from his daughter Bertha. In July 1941 Jonas spent three weeks with Norden in Hamburg. In Norden's letter to Hanna and Josef Hochfeld, in which he described his outing with Jonas at Blankensee and on the Elbe and Alster rivers, Jonas—who must have been about the same age as they were— added a humorous line herself: "My dear young friends! I allow myself to address you as such, for I am a 'dignified old lady' compared to you." In addition to sending good wishes, she asked for a photo of Norden's children and promised to send one of herself: "Don't worry, not in my clerical robe!"

In hindsight, many of Norden's letters seem strangely removed from the worsening conditions for Jews in Germany. They testify to the tendency of most Jews who had stayed there to repress this reality and pretend a kind of "normality." But Norden and Jonas's correspondence also reveals a certain strength: despite the ever-present Nazi terror, they went on with their daily existence. Today, the mere word *resistance* usually brings up heroic fantasies. But under the Nazi regime, it was an act of resistance, too, to persevere and live life with all its ups and downs; to carry on with one's love in all its aspects, sometimes exciting, sometimes banal; to take the train to Hamburg, to take a seat in the wooden third-class rows assigned to Jews, and to spend one's vacation in Joseph Norden's apartment—that was indeed an act of resistance too.

Though Norden had insisted, to his children as well as in his earlier letters to Jonas, that he did not want to remarry, ultimately, it appears the two became engaged. After Jonas's stay with Norden in the summer of 1940, he addressed her in his letters as "my sweet little bride Reginalein!" and concluded with "your little groom Josilein." In one letter dated June 27, 1940, Norden wrote to Jonas, "I am happy, more than happy, that we now have fully reached an understanding, that peace now prevails between us completely." The same letter also appears to deal with Jonas's possible wedding gown, and Norden's words are tinged with evidence of the poverty now afflicting all the Jews in Germany alike: "Norden cannot obtain the fabric for his charming bride; where should he procure this? I cannot ask for this, but try yourself; see if there is a source in Berlin. I would gladly contribute toward it as a birthday gift for you."

By the winter of 1940–1941, Jonas had been forced by the Nazis to move out of her apartment on Krausnickstrasse. Berlin, unlike cities such as Warsaw, had no Jewish ghetto; instead it had so-called *Judenhäuser* [Jews' houses], where several families were placed in an apartment, each family sharing one room. Jonas now shared a room with her mother in such a *Judenhaus* on Spandauer Brücke 15 in Berlin-Mitte.

That winter, Jonas received an additional work assignment. The Reichsvereinigung der Juden in Deutschland—the Nazi-instituted umbrella organization for Jews in Germany, to which all Jews were forced to belong from its inception in July 1939—hired Jonas to visit Jewish communities whose rabbi had immigrated or been imprisoned. She traveled through Germany and preached in Pommern, Braunschweig, Göttingen, Frankfurt on Oder, Wolfenbüttel, and Bremen.

The *Jüdisches Nachrichtenblatt* [Jewish Newsletter] was the only Jewish newspaper that still existed in Germany; its task—defined by the Nazis—was mainly to announce new anti-Semitic laws and regulations limiting Jewish life. During this period, it sometimes published articles about Jonas's prayer services, such as this one following a visit to the city of Stendal:

> Recently, the members of our Jewish Community met for a program. Whereas our membership before 1933 was about 70, it now has dropped to 12. So we were able to fit comfortably in the living room of one of our community members. Fräulein Rabbiner Jonas of Berlin soon won our hearts with her excellent remarks. She and the community department of the Reich's Association receive our most sincere thanks for looking after even such a small Jewish community as ours.[32]

The more clearly disaster loomed for European Jewry, the more feverishly Jonas and Norden plunged into their rabbinical duties. Norden's work quota took on a superhuman measure—visits, discussions, preparations for sermons, bar mitzvah lessons—"one task chases after the next," he wrote to Jonas. In one letter he suggested that she "Please read Psalm 74; I can and will say no more about yesterday, at least not in writing." The Psalm includes the following verse:

> Lift up Your steps because of the perpetual ruins,
> Even all the evil that the enemy has done in the sanctuary.
> Your adversaries have roared in the midst of Your meeting-place;
> They have set up their own signs for signs.

It seemed as when men wield upwards
Axes in a thicket of trees.
And now all the carved work thereof together
They strike down with hatchet and hammers.
They have set Your sanctuary on fire;
They have profaned the dwelling place of Your name even to the
ground.
They said in their heart: "Let us make havoc of them altogether";
They have burned up all the meeting-places of God in the land.

For both of them, their deepening relationship apparently became an important sustaining force. As had Jonas, so had Norden turned down all invitations to leave Germany. His son, Albert Norden, wrote in his auto-biography: "In view of the persecution of Jews in the Hitler period, numerous influential English personalities whose religious philosophical texts he had translated and published in Germany offered him [Joseph Norden] a visa and a position in Great Britain. [But] he rejected both with the explanation that he had stayed with his community in good times and now wanted to hold out through the terrible conditions."[33]

His daughter Hanna Hochfeld wrote in a letter from San Francisco to Kurt Schnöring in Wuppertal (September 5, 1980): "We tried even before war broke out in 1939 to bring my father out of Germany. But he refused, because he did not want to leave his community in Hamburg in the lurch."[34]

Increasingly Norden's letters contained references to the "evacuations" (the official term for deportations)—"declarations of property" that all the Jews of Hamburg were forced to deliver, members of the community who "had to leave" (who were deported), and the "depressed mood" of those remaining.

In one letter Norden tried to comfort Jonas: she should "not cry so much," there is "absolutely no use in crying, it doesn't help anyone and only has a negative effect on you, especially your beautiful, sweet eyes." Another letter concluded with the advice to "do well, be an advocate and a support for our depressed people." Norden even reminded Jonas to eat properly: "In these difficult times you may truly close an eye to the laws of *kashrut* [the ritual laws related to food]."

Of some of Norden's many letters to Jonas, all that remains are torn fragments—usually the conclusions. It is likely that Norden wrote much more about the deportations. By the fall of 1941, three months before the Wannsee Conference, where the so-called "Final Solution of the Jewish question" was laid out, thousands of German Jews already had been "transferred to the east," to their deaths. For a Jew to possess such information in writing was virtually fatal. On some of the reverse sides of the letter fragments, however, one can read in half sentences that Norden was making ready for his own likely transfer and had prepared a list "of the very least that one can bring along, so the packing will go quickly."

Jonas, too, was deeply troubled by her own likely deportation. From Norden's words in the above-mentioned fragment one can deduce that Jonas worried about what would happen to the documents testifying to her rabbinical work. In one fragment of a letter, Norden wrote: "I have not yet heard that one cannot bring documents along. Just in case, I advise you to somehow . . ."—the page was torn at this point. On another fragment appears Norden's question "What does Baeck actually want from you, in asking you to come to him?"

Perhaps Jonas and Baeck discussed her documents. Baeck knew about the murder of the Jews in ghettos and concentration camps, but did not speak of it. This was a point on which many survivors criticized him sharply after the war. It could have been that, fearing Jonas's possible death, Baeck—who more than anyone understood the historical value of her documents—might have recommended that she leave them behind in Berlin.

⁂

Regina Jonas and her family did not escape the fate awaiting most of the fifty-five thousand Jews still in Berlin in 1941. As of March that year, all Berlin Jews over the age of fourteen had to work in the armaments industry and other war-related enterprises. A "receipt" issued on May 5, 1942, by the packaging material factory Epeco in Berlin-Lichtenberg reports that "Frau Regina Sara Jonas, living in Berlin C.2, Spandauer Brücke 15, is working here from 7 AM to 5 PM. She therefore cannot do her shopping in the time set aside for Jews."

Soon after her arrival at the factory, Jonas became known as "the *Rabbinerin*." Even the guard, a former member of the SA (Nazi storm troopers), supposedly respected her, recalled Gad Beck. Jonas's job was to rivet and stack covers. But because she had "two left hands," said Beck, "one couldn't let her near the machinery.

In the factory, conditions were relatively bearable for Jews. Beck attributed this to the fact that one of the three factory owners was not anti-Semitic and regularly greeted the Jewish slave laborers when making the rounds through the shop. In addition, the Jewish-administered Employment

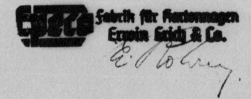

Bescheinigung.   21

    Frau Regina Sara J o n a s , wohnhaft in
Berlin C.2, an der Spandauer Brücke 15, ist bei uns
von 7 Uhr bis 17 Uhr beschäftigt. Sie kann daher ihre
Einkäufe in der für Juden vorgeschriebenen Zeit nicht
besorgen.

    Berlin, am 5.Mai 1942.

Certificate of Jonas's forced labor
*Certificate from the factory in which Regina Jonas was forced to work
as a slave laborer, May 5, 1942.*
Reproduction: Margit Billeb

Office for the Jews had certain discretion to decide about the assignment of
forced labor, so there were more intellectual and artistic people working at
this factory, including several well-known Jewish personalities such as the
poet Gertrud Kolmar.

Regina Jonas talked with many other laborers and made a generally
upbeat impression. It appears she was not demoralized by the daily chi-
canery and humiliations practiced against the Jews; rather, her commitment to her rabbinical calling grew stronger. "Her synagogue was
everywhere," said Gad Beck. She even taught the guard about God and
the world from the Jewish standpoint. For her this was a time in which
Jews "must prove their mettle." It even seems she had no fear. One day
she announced to the guard that she had to go home earlier because her
mother was ill. When he replied that it was forbidden for Jews to leave
the factory early, she responded indignantly, as Beck recalled: "I cannot

stay today. You would also take care of your mother, if she were ill." She left, and apparently there were no repercussions.

༄ ༄ ༄

Jonas continued to work as a rabbi and, even under the anti-Semitic terror, she extended to her full pastoral potential. Because the forced laborers no longer were able to attend the weekday and Shabbat services, the Jewish Community set up special early evening prayers, at which Jonas also officiated as rabbi.

The Nazis had left a few synagogues untouched in the November 1938 pogrom, because they were located in the inner courtyards and any fire would have endangered neighboring buildings. The New Synagogue on Oranienburger Strasse was never set afire, thanks to the courageous intervention of the police chief, Wilhelm Krützfeld, who drove out the SA with his pistol drawn. The synagogues at Levetzowstrasse and Lützowstrasse suffered only minor damage and a few months later were used again for services. In addition, there were still some improvised prayer rooms such as the auditorium of the Jewish School in Kaiserstrasse or the gym of the Joseph-Lehmann-School in Joachimstaler Strasse, where the Reform Community now held services.

When Jonas preached in these places, she tried to encourage the people and turn their thoughts to the timeless, spiritual basis of Judaism in order to boost their vitality.[35] Meanwhile, the Nazis were deporting some thousand Jews from Berlin each day, mostly to Theresienstadt but also to the Jewish ghettos of Lodz and Riga. Increasingly, they were sent straight to Auschwitz. Many who attended Jonas's prayer services wrote grateful letters that are preserved in her legacy. In one, Ruth Cronheim, a young, pregnant woman who heard Jonas's sermon on April 8, 1942, at the Haskarat Neschamot (Yizkor service on the last day of Passover), wrote to her that she had felt it would be irresponsible in these difficult times to bring a child into the world. But Jonas's words reassured her that she and her husband had made the right decision and that life itself, despite "forced labor and worse," remained a gift.

On October 3, according to a report in the *Jüdisches Nachrichtenblatt*, Jonas delivered a sermon in the Jewish Community boardroom in the New Synagogue, which the community now used as a chapel.[36] In addition, she was assigned to give an "honorary" talk (the Jewish Community no longer could afford to pay her) during the Shabbat service on October 10, 1942, in the synagogue at Schönhauser Allee 162. This was likely her last sermon in Berlin.

Last letter from Joseph Norden to Regina Jonas, July 13, 1942

On November 3 Sara and Regina Jonas had to fill out the infamous "declaration of property," a clear prelude to deportation. Their property, consisting of a few pieces of furniture and a gramophone, was confiscated for the "benefit of the Third Reich" and auctioned for 142 reichsmark. Two days later, mother and daughter were to appear in a *Sammellager*, the former Jewish senior home in Grosse Hamburger Strasse, which the Nazis had turned into an assembly center. Joseph Norden already had been deported to Theresienstadt on July 15 from Hamburg and Max Weyl on August 24 from Berlin; both died there some months after arriving. Regina's brother, Abraham, was taken with the second Berlin transport to the "East," which arrived in the Lodz ghetto on October 24, 1941; he

Dear Regina,

All at once, fate has caught up with me and most of the community. There is no time to think about it calmly and to pack one's stuff. We have to show up tomorrow (Tuesday) in order to be sent to Theresienstadt on Wednesday.

I am writing in the midst of chaos. The time has come to say goodbye. There are also people from Elberfeld and Cologne coming to Theresienstadt. Maybe Berliners will be sent, too. In that case perhaps there will be a chance for us to see each other again, if Berliners also have to go.

So, dear Regina, live well! God be with you and with all of us and with all Israel.

Your Joseph

Last letter from Joseph Norden to Regina Jonas, July 13, 1942 (translation)

did not return. On November 6, 1942, Sara and Regina Jonas also left Berlin, in the seventy-third *Alterstransport* (the official term for deportations of the elderly) to Theresienstadt.

Theresienstadt, located in today's Czech Republic, was different from other concentration and extermination camps in that the Nazis pretended it was a "Jewish town" with a Jewish self-administration. Encircled by barbed wire, the original fortress city, together with its nearby prison, had the character of a ghetto and concentration camp at the same time. A large percentage of German Jewry—especially the elderly but also many prominent Jews such as Leo Baeck—were deported to Theresienstadt. Nutrition and labor conditions in Theresienstadt were just as bad as in other concentration camps. However, the ghetto was established as a model with which the Nazis tried to fool the world, especially the International Red Cross, whose delegations regularly were allowed to visit the ghetto and see with their own eyes the "privileged" conditions under which the Jews lived. Because the *Ältestenrat* [council of elders] had to "run" the camp, provide the daily slave laborers, and ensure the smooth functioning of the camp, there was a certain kind of autonomy. Theresienstadt, for example, had a cultural department that organized lectures featuring its many imprisoned scholars.

Even in Theresienstadt, Jonas continued to function as a preacher and minister. She worked in the so-called Department for Psychological Hygiene, another section of the ghetto's self-administration led by the famous psychoanalyst Viktor Frankl from Vienna. Frankl, who later was sent to Auschwitz, wrote numerous books after the war in which he developed his own approach to psychoanalysis based on his experiences in both camps. His most famous work is *Man's Search for Meaning* (first published as *Ein Psychologe erlebt das Konzentrationslager* [A Psychologist Experiences the Concentration Camp], 1946). In a telephone interview in 1991 with the German-American theologian Katharina von Kellenbach, Frankl remembered his former colleague. He said he had appointed Jonas to his staff because "she was a gifted preacher and speaker," and aside from that she was a "personality with energy" on whom one could depend.

Jonas's job was to receive new transports from the *Altreich*—prewar Germany—at the train station and to reduce their first shock upon arrival. The fortress city Theresienstadt was built to accommodate about seven thousand soldiers, but now crammed together fifty-eight thousand Jewish prisoners. Jonas led the people to the *Ubiquation* [the living quarters], where two dozen people shared a room, sleeping on straw, and tried to calm them. Once she delivered a talk to Frankl's staff that deeply impressed him. She explained that, according to Jewish tradition, those who were mentally handicapped or senile had no less integrity than any other human beings. As an analogy she used the story of Exodus, in which Moses received the tablets with the Ten Commandments. The tablets were carried by all the people of Israel in the journey through the desert, including the old and the ill. Thus, the elderly are just as valued as any other community member.[37]

In Theresienstadt, Jonas again ran into stumbling blocks as a female rabbi. A survivor remembered that the "Head Rabbi" of Theresienstadt refused to recognize her rabbinical authority in any way. But that did not stop her from going to the women's quarters and talking about Jewish history, holidays, and customs. The women always were pleased to see the *Rabbinerin*. Often they gave her a crust of bread as thanks, which Jonas always then gave to her mother.[38]

Jonas left a list in the so-called Administration for Spiritual and Leisure Activity in Theresienstadt, with the title "Lectures by the Only Female Rabbi: Regina Jonas."[39] The lectures were part of the series of cultural programs permitted at the self-administrated ghetto. The document today is in the Memorial Archive of Theresienstadt. The list names twenty-four biblical, talmudic, and religious themes about which Jonas spoke, and in addition there are notes about one sermon focusing on the story of Balaam, who tried to curse the people of Israel but ended up blessing them. Jonas cited the verse in Numbers 22:12, in which God said to Balaam, "Do not go with them, also do not curse this people, as they are blessed."

Jonas's notes once more drew upon her fundamental religious philosophy:

> Our J. people has been planted by God in history as being blessed. To be "blessed" by God means to bless, to do good and be loyal to others wherever one goes, in every situation. Humility before God; selfless devoted love to his creatures, preserve the world. It is the task of all Israel to build these foundations for the world—man and woman, woman and man are obligated as Jews to carry out this duty in equal measure. This ideal is served by our grave work at Theresienstadt, which puts us to the test as servants of God, and as such we turn from the earthly to the celestial sphere—May all our work be for the blessing of the future of Israel (and of humanity). . . . Upright "J. men" and "brave noble women" were always the pillars of our people. May we be found worthy by God to be counted in the circle of these women and men.
>
> Rabbinerin Regina Jonas—formerly of Berlin.

As the Red Army approached and the end of the Third Reich seemed inevitable, the Nazis accelerated their effort to complete the so-called Final Solution. Starting in September 1944, many trains left Theresienstadt for Auschwitz-Birkenau. One of the last transports, on October 12, 1944, brought the forty-two-year-old Regina Jonas and her sixty-eight-year-old mother to the extermination camp, where—most likely right after their arrival—they were murdered.

❧ ❧ ❧

As the biographer of Regina Jonas, I could stop here. But I don't wish to do so. As a Jew in Germany, I grew up with many stories of people who ended in the black hole of the Shoah, leaving no way to bridge the abyss. Being committed to Jewish life and not Jewish death, I have become sensitive to a literary dramaticism that puts wartime Jewish biographies into a scenario that causes the reader to feel awe for the murderous Nazi system of persecution and extermination. Regina Jonas herself would not have liked her biography to be read with this kind of morbid fascination, but rather would have wanted it to be seen as a chronicle of her professional accomplishments as a rabbi. She did not choose the time in which she lived. It was not her wish that her fight for women in the rabbinate would coincide with the destruction of European Jewry. Her life was dedicated to the renewal of Judaism. And it was precisely this aspect of her struggle that did not perish in Auschwitz. Jonas left enough traces of the foundation she had laid to enable the next generation to build bridges to the future.

Many Jews took their most important documents with them in the deportation trains to the death camps. Viktor Frankl described how he had managed to save an unpublished manuscript of a research project as the last piece of evidence of his previous life, up to his further deportation to Auschwitz-Birkenau, and how it was torn from him immediately upon his arrival there.[40]

Regina Jonas had not taken her documents with her; she had left them in Berlin, most probably handing them over to the Jewish Community for safekeeping. One can assume that the Community soon passed this legacy on to the Gesamtarchiv der deutschen Juden [the Central Archive of German Jewry]. As with the Jewish Museum of Prague, this archive was not destroyed by the Nazis, who planned to use it to document the "vanished Jewish race" in Europe.

Did Jonas, when she gave her documents to the Jewish Community, suspect that she would not return alive, or did she expect someday to retrieve them? Her intentions in leaving her "estate" with the Jewish Community remain unknown. But the result is that hundreds of writings were preserved—certificates, manuscripts, letters, postcards, newspaper clippings, and several articles, as well as announcements and official notices of the Jewish Community of Berlin.[41] Alongside her treatise, "Can Women Serve as Rabbis?", the legacy contains two photos of Jonas as rabbi. In both, she is wearing her ankle-length clerical robe and cap and is holding a book, probably the Bible, in her hand. One photo appears to have been taken shortly after her ordination. On the back it says, "Feb. 18th 1936, Iranische Str. 3, Jewish Senior Home, Rosenberg" and scribbled in Hebrew from the book of Exodus (3:14), "I shall be who I shall be." The other photo may have been taken later. Jonas's rubber stamp on

Lectures by Jonas in the Theresienstadt concentration camp
List of themes on which Regina Jonas spoke in Theresienstadt,
after being deported from Berlin on November 6, 1942.
Reproduction: Margit Billeb

**Cover sheet for Berlin to Theresienstadt deportation list,
November 1942 to February 1943**
*Regina Jonas and her mother were deported from Berlin to the Theresienstadt
concentraion camp on November 6, 1942.*

```
77. Berliner Transport                                    6.11.1942.
I/77

Lfd.  Name           Beruf   Geb.    Letzte          Kennkar-  Kennzei-
No.   Vorhame                Dat.    Adresse         tennr.    chennr.
-----------------------------------------------------------------------
9690  Jonas          ohne    3.8.    Bln.,Spandauer  A0425 3   010594a
      Regina S.              1902    Brücke 15

9691  Sachs 24.8.42.F ohne   4.12.   NW. 87, den/              010822
      Alice S.               1879    Tile Wayburgerstr.26a

9682  Joseph Dr.1662F2 ohne  9.12.   Charlbg.                  010894
      Karl Isr.              1871    Giesebrechtstr.20

9693  Joseph           ohne  8.9.    dto. 1663Ea     A368138   010895
      Betty S.               1886

9694  Stern Samuel    ohne   14.2.   Grwd.,          A438452   011463
      Richard Isr.           1871    Jagowstr,21a

9695  Stern 42.43.F    ohne  14.6.   dto.                      011464
      Elsa S.

9696  Tebrich          ohne  29.12.  Kaiserallee 73  A514860   011549
      Max Isr.               1872

9697  Tebrich          ohne  4.3.    dto. 1664Eas    A514861   011550
      Martha S.              1887

9698  Kary 10.11.42.F  ohne  3.10.   W.62,           A 523463  011561
      Fritze S.              1859    Keithstr,6

9699  Lewin  Elias    ohne   6.2.    Holzmarktstr.11           011899
      Emil Isr.              1875

9700  Lewin            ohne  17.2.   dto.                      011900
      Rosa S.                1873

9701  Bril 25.5.43.F   ohne  24.3.   Mommsenstr.2    A358745   011947
      Franziska S.           1870

9702  Sommerfeld 21.2.43 ohne 27.6.  Sächsischestr.  A011966   011966
      Clare S.               1876    57

9703  Schwarzweiss Dr. ohne  14.8.   W 30,           A500955   012332
      Leo Isr.               1873    Heilbronnerstr.2

9704  Schwarzweiss     ohne  30.11.  dto.                      012333
      Else S.                1864

9705  Glück Lea Brane  ohne  26.8.   NO 55,                    012597n
      Lea Branje             1878    Weissenburgerstr.20

9706  Philippstein     ohne  4.5.    SO. 36,         A365381   012625
      Willy Isr.             1879    Graetzerstr.4

9707  Gurewitsch 14.1.43F ohne 2.3.  NO. 18,                   012635
      Jakeb Isr.             1866    Georgenkirchstr.56

9708  Gurewitsch       ohne  25.5.   dto.            Fr.P.H.   012636
      Sara                   1875                    57L38

9709  Tartakowsky      ohne  15.9.   W 30,           Fr.P.     012678
```

Berlin to Theresienstadt deportation list, page with Jonas's name
(second from the top)

Equ

12. 10. 1944

Cover sheet for Theresienstadt to Auschwitz deportation list,
October 12, 1944

ansport Equ				12.10.1944.	
721	Lubasch Helga	3.4.1928	Jugendl.	9639-I/76	
722	Jonas Regina	3. 8.1902	Rabbinerin	9690-I/77	
723	Less Max	7. 7.1888	Kaufmann	11577-I/90	
724	Less Hertha	24.12.1891	Stenotyp.	11578-I/90	
,5	Weissblum Kathe	14. 2.1890	Krankschw.	12909-I/95	
726	Geissmar Elisabeth	13. 3.1880	Haushalt	493-II/10	
727	Perlmutter Luise	28. 2.1880	Haushalt	679-II/14	
728	Steinheimer Sophie	4. 3.1881	Haushalt	813-II/17	
72^	Frank Meta	9. 1.1885	Haushalt	117-II/26	
730	Schäler Fanny	1. 4.1881	Haushalt	560-II/26	
731	Cahn Eduard	29. 3.1889	Hilfsarb.	680-III/2	
732	Cahn Ella	1.11.1896	Haushalt	681-III/2	
733	Engelbert Abraham	14.10.1886	Hilfsarb.	108-V/3	
734	Stillschweig Gertrud	24. 5.1907	Arbeiterin	46-VI/5	
735	Emmel Thea	22.10.1903	Arbeiterin	391-VII/2	
736	Borower Edgar Artur	22. 2.1887	Krankpfleg.	72-IX/3	
737	Borower Edith Rosalie	8. 9.1929	Jugendl.	654-IX/3	
,38	Biel Gertrud	25. 2.1887	Krankschw.	8-IX/4	
73y	Hochheimer Erich	8. 1.1891	Beamter	106-IX/4	
740	Hochheimer Gertrud	14.11.1889	Haushalt	107-IX/4	
741	Sandberg Arthur	1. 8.1881	Hilfsarb.	207-IX/4	
742	Sandberg Frieda	11.10.1892	Haushalt	208-IX/4	
743	Weissenberg Karl	18. 6.1883	Hilfsarb.	251-IX/4	
744	Weissenberg Selma	19. 2.1893	Haushalt	252-IX/4	
745	Breitbarth Margarete	27.12.1898	Haushalt	19-IX/5	
746	Weinberg Rosa	20.11.1886	Haushalt	891-XI/1	
747	Meyer Therese	14.12.1890	Haushalt	27-XI/2	
748	Falkenstein Bertha	29. 9.1883	Haushalt	10 58-XII/2	
749	Falkenstein Edgar	3.10.1929	Jugendl.	1059-XII/2	
750	Bondi Franziska	25. 5.1899	Haushalt	132-XII/3	

Theresienstadt to Auschwitz deportation list, page with Jonas's name
(second from the top)

the back already includes the name *Sara,* which all Jewish women officially had to add after 1939: "*Rabbiner* Regina Sara Jonas."

Among the documents is the previously mentioned profile that appeared in the Swiss women's magazine *Berna* in February 1939, two months after the Kristallnacht pogrom, in which Regina Jonas said, "I came to my work out of the religious belief that God is not an oppressor, therefore man does not control woman, nor does he hold spiritual supremacy over her. I came to this from the belief in the absolute and complete spiritual, psychological, moral equality of the sexes, created by a just and kind God."[42]

⅗ ⅗ ⅗

It was not until 1972, with the ordination of Sally Priesand at Hebrew Union College in Cincinnati, that another woman reached the position of rabbi. In Europe, the first to follow Jonas was Jacqueline Tabick, who received her rabbinical diploma in 1976 at the Leo Baeck College in London. In 1984 the Jewish Theological Seminary in New York ordained Amy Eilberg.

By then Jonas had completely fallen into oblivion. The 1970s and 1980s saw intensive debates at rabbinical seminaries of the Reform and liberal-conservative movements over whether Judaism could admit women to the rabbinate.[43] The halachic arguments laid out in testimonials and responsa were similar to those of Regina Jonas in "Can Women Serve as Rabbis?" but barely go beyond. Jonas's treatise not only was unprecedented but remains one of the most comprehensive attempts ever to justify the female rabbinate on the basis of Halacha—Jewish law.

Still, the theme of women's ordination faded from Germany's Jewish communities for decades. The few survivors of the Shoah often were deeply shaken in their beliefs and clung to traditional ways. New ideas were rejected reflexively. This led to an internally rigid religious-spiritual life, which even today has not been fully overcome. When Daniela Thau— the second woman from Berlin to become a rabbi after Regina Jonas— concluded her studies at the Leo Baeck College in London in the 1980s, she had no chance of being hired as a communal rabbi in Germany and therefore chose to remain in England. By the time Rabbi Bea Wyler, born in Switzerland and ordained at the Jewish Theological Seminary in New York, was hired in Oldenburg in 1995—in a decision that broke taboos and met great resistance from the Jewish establishment in Germany—the theme of female rabbis could no longer be suppressed.

⁂

In Berlin in May 1999, the first Bet Debora conference took place—a historic, first-ever gathering of European female rabbis, cantors, scholars, and other spiritually interested Jewish women and men.[44] The name *Regina Jonas* was mentioned in virtually every lecture and discussion held in the Centrum Judaicum's Great Hall, in the former women's gallery of the New Synagogue. Retroactively, the first female rabbi in the world took her place as a pioneer. As Rabbi Sybil Sheridan of Leo Baeck College told the nearly two hundred participants, "We are her future. May we live up to her ideals and prove ourselves worthy of the aspirations she did not live to fulfill."

Regina Jonas had answered the question of whether a woman can be a rabbi with "Yes." The participants in the conference asked what the consequences might be if Jewish women were to have an equal impact on the direction of religious life. Themes such as women's rituals, new interpretations of Bible and Talmud, changes in liturgy, or lesbians in the rabbinate certainly were not part of the constellation of issues with which Rabbi Regina Jonas was concerned.

Yet she may have seen herself reflected in the experiences of her modern-day colleagues. Many described themselves as "outsiders"; Daniela Thau called herself a "rabbi on the margin." At the same time, female rabbis from central and eastern Europe, including Katalin Kelemen of Budapest and Nelly Shulman of Minsk, said their communities were driven primarily by the engagement and energy of women. The same was true for the progressive Jewish communities in Vienna and London or the "egalitarian" prayer groups in Berlin, Frankfurt, and Amsterdam. It was exactly this inspiration that led Regina Jonas to urge the inclusion of women in the rabbinate as a "necessity." Though her ideal of chastity and her view that a female rabbi should not marry stand in an outdated social context, she managed to create a new image of the rabbinical role—as a woman alone—that revolutionized the patriarchal standard.

In the world today there are hundreds of female rabbis in Jewish communities, mostly in the United States. By now, some forty European women have been ordained; the majority live and work in Great Britain. Each of these women has had to vie for recognition. Each one can recognize herself in Regina Jonas. And in each of them, Regina Jonas's legacy lives on.

NOTES

1. Compared to the American system of congregations, which are characterized by their different denominations, Germany's Jewry had and has a very different organizational system. Dominant is the so-called *Einheitsgemeinde* [unified community], in which Jews of all denominations, and even secular, cultural, or atheist Jews, unite under one umbrella. It has the juridical status of a *Körperschaft des öffentlichen Rechts* [corporation of public law], which is financed by the national "church tax" for German citizens, and whose members elect their community parliament and board every four years. Each town had one such large community, which could, as in the case of Berlin before the Nazi era, comprise more than one hundred thousand members and run dozens of synagogues, varying from liberal to Orthodox, as well as kindergartens, schools, social institutions, and the like. Although there have also been Orthodox and Reform breakaway communities, the system of one big unified community per town still prevails. Until the fall of the Wall in 1989, Berlin's Jewish Community counted six thousand members; the number doubled after the Jewish immigration from the former Soviet Union.

2. Marion A. Kaplan, *The Jewish Feminist Movement in Germany: The Campaigns of the Jewish Women's Organization, 1904–1938* (Westport, Conn., and London: Greenwood Press, 1979).

3. Marianne Brentzel, *Anna O., Bertha Pappenheim, Biographie* (Göttingen: Wallstein Verlag, 2002). Another fascinating view of how Bertha Pappenheim cured herself by becoming a militant Jewish feminist is provided by Daniel Boyarin, *Unheroic Conduct: The Rise of Heterosexuality and the Invention of the Jewish Man* (Berkeley, Los Angeles, and London: University of California Press, 1997), 313–359.

4. For example, in 1935, one year before her death, Pappenheim wrote, "For a small fraction of Jews, Palestine may be spatially important—for the spirit of Judaism, however, the world is just big enough" ("Denkzettel," September 15, 1935, Archive Leo Baeck Institute, New York).

5. *Bertha Pappenheim: Gebete/Prayers* [in German with an English translation], ed. Elisa Klapheck and Lara Dämmig (Teetz, Germany: Hentrich & Hentrich, 2003). See also Britta Konz, "Bertha Pappenheims neuer Familienbegriff—Bertha Pappenheim, Anruf" [Bertha Pappenheim: A New Look at the Concept of the Family], *Bet Debora*, 1991, *2*, 20 (http://bet-debora.de). Konz describes Pappenheim's revolutionary religious-political thoughts about the relationship between women, God, state, and society.

6. Leonard Baker, *Days of Sorrow and Pain: Leo Baeck and the Berlin Jews* (New York: Macmillan, 1978), 102.

7. All statements in Irene Kaufmann, "Die Hochschule für die Wissenschaft des Judentums 1872–1942: Die Institution and ihre Personen" [The Academy for the Science of Judaism, 1872–1942: The Institution and Its People], a master's degree thesis, Academy for Jewish Studies, Heidelberg, 1992, 73–75; and "Regina Jonas war die erste deutsche Rabbinerin" [Regina Jonas Was the First German Female Rabbi], in the German weekly Jewish newspaper *Allgemeine Jüdische Wochenzeitung*, Sept. 1994; in addition, see Esther Seidel, *Women Pioneers of Jewish Learning: Ruth Liebrecht and Her Companions at the Hochschule für die Wissenschaft des Judentums [Academy for the Science of Judaism] in Berlin 1930–1934* (Berlin: Jüdische Verlagsanstalt Berlin, 2002).

8. See also: Abraham Geiger, "Die Stellung des weiblichen Geschlechtes in dem Judenthume unserer Zeit" [The Position of the Female Sex in Judaism Today], *Wissenschaftl. Zeitschrift für Jüdische Theologie* [Scientific Journal of Jewish Theology], 1837, *3*, 13–14.

9. Pamela Nadell offers a comprehensive presentation in *Women Who Would Be Rabbis: A History of Women's Ordination, 1889–1985* (Boston: Beacon Press, 1998); in addition, see Elizabeth Sarah's contribution "Rabbi Regina Jonas 1902–1944: Missing Link in a Broken Chain," in *Hear Our Voice: Women Rabbis Tell Their Stories,* ed. Sybil Sheridan (London: SCM Press, 1994), 4; and Michael M. Meyer, *Responses to Modernity: History of the Reform Movement in Judaism* (New York: Oxford University Press, 1988), 379.

10. The full text of Lily Montagu's speech is reproduced in "Mitteilungen der Jüdischen Reformgemeinde zu Berlin" [Reports of the Jewish Reform Congregation of Berlin], Sept. 1928. The speech was devoted to "private religion," the central concept of Lily Montagu's religious view of the world and humanity. See also Ellen M. Umansky, "Lily Montagu and the Advancement of Liberal Judaism: From Vision to Vocation," *Studies in Women and Religion,* vol. 12 (New York and Toronto: Edwin Mellen Press, 1983); and Simone Ladwig-Winters, *Freiheit und Bindung: Zur Geschichte der Jüdischen Reformgemeinde zu Berlin von den Anfängen bis zu ihrem Ende 1939* [Freedom and Commitment: On the History of the Jewish Reform Community of Berlin from Its Beginnings to Its End in 1939], ed. Peter Galliner (Teetz: Hentrich & Hentrich, 2004), 162–163.

11. Shoshana Ronen, "We Didn't Aspire to the Rabbinate" [in German], *Bet Debora,* 2000, *1;* see also www.bet-debora.de.

12. Assessments by Hans Hirschberg, *Leo Baeck College News 1993,* cited in Sarah, 1994.

13. "Uns fällt auf . . ." [We Noticed . . .] *Israelitisches Familienblatt* [Israelite Family Bulletin], June 4, 1931.

14. "Können Frauen Rabbiner werden?" [Could Women Become Rabbis?], *Israelitisches Familienblatt* [Israelite Family Bulletin], November 5, 1931.

15. Copy of a typewritten manuscript in Jonas's legacy, now in the archives of the Stiftung Neue Synagoge Berlin—Centrum Judaicum. I found no indication of whether or where it might have been published.

16. Letter in the framework of a survey by Mala Laaser in the *Central-Verein-Zeitung* [Newspaper of the Central Association of German Citizens of Jewish Faith], "Was haben Sie zum Thema FRAU zu sagen?" [What Do You Have to Say on the Theme of WOMAN?], published June 23, 1938.

17. Memorial Archive of Theresienstadt, Památnik Terezín, Ustredni Kartoteka, collection of Karl Hermann.

18. Frieda Valentin, "Bekanntschaft mit einer Rabbinerin: Wie Regina Jonas ihr Examen machte" [Acquaintance with a Female Rabbi: How Regina Jonas Passed Her Exam], in the German Jewish newspaper *Jüdische Allgemeine Zeitung,* supplement of January 22, 1936.

19. Joseph Carlebach, "Nachbrocho," *Der Israelit: Ein Centralorgan für das orthodoxe Judentum* [The Israelite: A Central Organ for Orthodox Jewry], February 20, 1936.

20. "Ein Wizo-Nachmittag" [A WIZO Afternoon], *Jüdisches Gemeindeblatt für Berlin* [Jewish Community Newspaper for Berlin], June 26, 1938.

21. Laaser, 1938.

22. Annette, "Die Rabbinerin" [The Female Rabbi] in the Swiss magazine *Berna,* an organ of the Women's Association of Bern, February 10, 1939.

23. Cited in *Zerstörte Fortschritte: Das Jüdische Krankenhaus in Berlin* [Destroyed Progress: The Jewish Hospital in Berlin], ed. Dagmar Hartung-von Doetinchem and Rolf Wienau (Berlin: Edition Hentrich, 1989), 143.

24. Nathan Peter Levinson, *Ein Ort ist, mit wem du bist: Lebensstationen eines Rabbiners* [A Place Is Who You're With: The Stations in the Life of a Rabbi] (Berlin: Edition Hentrich, 1996), 39.

25. Marie Simon (née Jalowicz), in a conversation about Regina Jonas with Hermann Simon on July 30, 1998.

26. Report by Marie Simon, November 23, 1994, quoted in the book accompanying the permanent exhibit by the Stiftung Neue Synagoge Berlin—Centrum Judaicum: Hermann Simon (ed.), *Tuet auf die Pforten: Die Neue Synagoge 1866–1995* [Open the Gates: The New Synagogue 1866–1995] (Berlin: Museum Educational Service, 1995), 25. See also the essay by Maren Krüger in the same book, "Regina Jonas: Die erste Rabbinerin in Deutschland 1935–1942" [Regina Jonas: The First Female Rabbi in Germany 1935–1942].

27. Katharina von Kellenbach undertook a comparison between Regina Jonas's position as *Rabbinerin* and the position of Jonas's contemporaries, the Protestant female vicars in Germany, in "Denial and Defiance in the Work of Rabbi Regina Jonas," in *In God's Name: Genocide and Religion in the Twentieth Century,* ed. Phyllis Mack and Omar Bartov (Oxford and New York: Berghahn, 2000). Kellenbach also wrote a series of research papers on Regina Jonas, among them "Fräulein Rabbiner Regina Jonas: Eine religiöse Feministin vor ihrer Zeit" [Miss Rabbi Regina Jonas: A Religious Feminist Before Her Time], *Schlangenbrut,* August 1992; "Jonas, Regina—Rabbinerin," *Jüdische Frauen im 19. and 20. Jahrhundert: Lexikon zu Leben and Werk* [Jewish Women in the Nineteenth and Twentieth Centuries: An Encyclopedia of Lives and Work], ed. Jutta Dick and Marina Sassenberg (Reinbeck bei Hamburg: Rowohlt, 1993); "Forgotten Voices: German Women's Ordination and the Holocaust," in *Proceedings of the Second Biennial Conference on Christianity and the Holocaust,* vol. 2 (Rider College, 1992); " . . . die Majorität ist gegen Sie: Der Leidensweg der Regina Jonas. Rabbinerin in Nazi-Deutschland" [The Majority Is Against You: The Ordeal of Regina Jonas, Female Rabbi in Nazi Germany], *Aufbau,* 1993, 59(6), March 12; "God Does Not Oppress Any Human Being: The Life and Thought of Rabbi Regina Jonas," in *Leo Baeck Institute: Yearbook XXXIX* (New York: Secker & Warburg, 1994), 213–225; "Fräulein Rabbiner Regina Jonas (1902–1945): Lehrerin, Seelsorgerin, Predigerin" [Miss Regina Jonas (1902–1944): Teacher, Minister, Preacher], in *Yearbook of the European Society of Women in Theological Research* (Kampen: Kok Pharos, 1994); and "Reproduction and Resistance During the Holocaust," in *Women and the Holocaust,* ed. Esther Fuchs (Lanham, Md.: University Press of America, 1998).

28. Manuscript by an unnamed sixteen-year-old pupil, "Gemeindeabend in der Synagoge Hermsdorf" [Community Evening in the Hermsdorf synagogue], December 4, 1937; from Jonas's legacy.

29. "Gemeindeabend in der Synagoge Hermsdorf."

30. Regina Jonas, "Eine Jom-Kippur-Mahnung" [A Yom Kippur Warning], *Jüdisches Gemeindeblatt für Berlin* [Jewish Community Newspaper for Berlin], October 2, 1938; see also "Häusliche Gebräuche" [Domestic Customs], *Jüdisches Nachrichtenblatt* [Jewish Newsletter], March 3, 1939.

31. Regina Jonas, "Über die Seelen-Feier" [On the Yizkor Service], *Jüdisches Nachrichtenblatt* [Jewish Newsletter], May 24, 1939.

32. Item in column titled "Reports of Communities" in *Jüdisches Nachrichtenblatt* [Jewish Newsletter], January 28, 1941.

33. Albert Norden, *Ereignisse und Erlebtes* [Events and Experiences] (Berlin: Dietz Verlag, 1981).

34. Hanna Hochfeld, living in San Francisco, wrote this in a letter to Kurt Schnöring in Wuppertal, September 5, 1980.

35. Nathan Peter Levinson and Wolfgang Hamburger, then-rabbinical students, remember that Jonas served in the synagogues on Lützowstrasse and Joachimstaler Strasse; see Kaufmann, 1992, 76; Günther Ruschin heard Jonas speak at Levetzowstrasse; see in addition the announcement of lectures and sermons in the *Jüdisches Nachrichtenblatt* [Jewish Newsletter] as well as in Kaiserstrasse (December 26, 1941) or Joachimstaler Strasse (July 10, 1942).

36. *Jüdisches Nachrichtenblatt* [Jewish Newsletter], October 2, 1942.

37. Viktor Frankl in a telephone conversation with Katharina von Kellenbach, June 10, 1991.

38. Frantisek Ehrmann, *Terezín* (Prague: Council of Jewish Communities in the Czech Lands, 1965).

39. Memorial Archive of Theresienstadt, Památník Terezín, Ustredni Kartoteka, collection of Karl Hermann.

40. Viktor E. Frankl, *Ein Psychologe erlebt das Konzentrationslager* [A Psychologist Experiences the Concentration Camp] (Vienna: Verlag für Jugend und Volk, 1946).

41. The legacy is now in the archives of the Stiftung Neue Synagoge Berlin—Centrum Judaicum, cataloged as signature CJA, 1, 75 D Jo 1.

42. Annette, 1939.

43. For more on the debates, see Nadell, 1998; Pnina Navè-Levinson, "Eva und ihre Schwestern: Perspektiven einer jüdisch-feministischen Theologie" [Eve and Her Sisters: Perspectives of a Jewish-Feminist Theology] (Gütersloh: Gütersloher Verlagshaus, Gerd Mohn, 1992), 168–174; Sheridan (ed.), 1994; Simon Greenberg (ed.), *The Ordination of Women as Rabbis: Studies and Responsa* (New York: Jewish Theological Seminary of America, 1988); Susan Weidman Schneider, *Jewish and Female: Choices and Changes in Our Lives Today* (New York: Simon and Schuster, 1984); and Simon Schwarzfuchs, *A Concise History of the Rabbinate* (Oxford and Cambridge, Mass.: Blackwell, 1993).

44. Bet Debora was organized by Lara Dämmig, Rachel Monika Herweg, and Elisa Klapheck. Lara Dämmig is a cofounder of the Egalitarian Minyan of Berlin. She has written various essays on Jewish female personalities in Berlin, among them Bertha Falkenberg, the first member of Berlin's Jewish Community parliament (in *Leben mit der Erinnerung: Jüdisches Leben in Prenzlauer Berg* [Living with the Memory: Jewish Life in Prenzlauer Berg], ed. Kulturamt Prenzlauer Berg [Berlin: Edition Hentrich, 1997]). Rachel

Monika Herweg is the author of *Die jüdische Mutter: Das verborgene Matriarchat* [The Jewish Mother: The Hidden Matriarchy] (Darmstadt: Wissenschaftliche Buchgesellschaft, 1994), as well as of various articles about Regina Jonas, among them: "Mein Name ist Frau Regina Jonas. Ich bin nicht die Frau eines Rabbiners. Ich bin Rabbinerin. Was kann ich für Sie tun?" [My Name Is Regina Jonas. I Am Not the Wife of a Rabbi. I Am a Rabbi Myself. What Can I Do for You?], in Elke Kleinau (ed.), *Frauen in pädagogischen Berufen* [Women in Pedagogic Professions] (Bad Heilbrunn: Klinkhardt, 1966), and "Regina Jonas (1902–1944)" in Hans Erler, Ernst Ludwig Ehrlich, and Ludger Heid (eds.), *Meinetwegen ist die Welt erschaffen: Das intellektuelle Vermächtnis des deutschsprachigen Judentums, 58 Porträts* [The World Was Created for My Sake: The Intellectual Legacy of the German-Speaking Jewry, Fifty-Eight Portraits] (Frankfurt am Main and New York: Campus Verlag, 1997).

Since 1999 Bet Debora has organized three conferences for European female rabbis, cantors, scholars and other spiritually interested Jewish women and men. See documentation in volumes 1 to 3 of the journal *Bet Debora* (2000, 2001, and forthcoming), as well as on the Internet at www.bet-debora.de.

PART TWO

Rabbiner Regina Sara Jonas

H a l a c h i s c h e   A r b e i t.   1
_____

Kann die Frau das rabbinische Amt bekleiden ?

Die Frage, ob die Frau das rabbinische Amt bekleiden kann,
oder - um den neuen Namen für diesen Beruf zu gebrauchen - ob die
jüdische Frau Rabbinerin werden kann, ist ein so umfangreiches
Problem, dass es hier, im Rahmen einer halachischen Abschlussarbeit,
nicht e r s c h ö p f e n d behandelt werden kann. Der Grund hier-
für leigt darin, dass die gesamte Einstellung zu dem Problem der
jüdischen Frau, wie sie in unserem gesamten jüdischen Schrifttum
zum Ausdruck kommt, behandelt werden müsste. Ich musste mich daher beschränken, nur die wichtigsten Punkte herauszugreifen.
Ausserdem lässt sich nicht für jeden Zweig dieses Berufes, der in
der Arbeit behandelt werden soll, halachisches Material finden.
Damit kommt man zu der Hauptschwierigkeit, nämlich der, dass der
Begriff "Rabbinerin" ja noch in unseren Tagen ein neuartiger ist
und um wieviel mehr in der Zeit unseres jüdischen Schrifttums.

Da ich aber persönlich diesen Beruf liebe, und ihn, wenn es
einmal möglich wird, sehr gern ausüben möchte, und mein sehr ver-
ehrter Lehrer, Herr Professor Dr.E.Baneth, mir dieses Thema auch
als halachische Abschlussarbeit an unserer "Hochschule für die Wissenschaft des Judentums" gab, will ich versuchen, nach meinen be-
scheidenen Kräften die Frage etwas zu beleuchten.

Um diesem Problem näher zu kommen, ist es erstens einmal
nötig zu sehen, weshalb man nichts über den Beruf Rabbinerin im
jüdischen Schrifttum findet. - Um das zu können, muss man untersu-
chen, was sich über den Rabbinerberuf findet und zwar in der Weise,
dass man die Aufgaben des Rabbiners feststellt und dann sieht, ob
es halachisch und im Sinne des jüdischen Schrifttums und der jüdischen Vergangenheit möglich ist, dass auch die Frau das rabbinische Amt mit diesen Aufgaben erfüllen kann. Ferner ist es nötig
zu sehen, wie die Tätigkeit der jüdischen Frau in Bibel, Talmud

---

First page of Jonas's treatise "Can Women Serve as Rabbis?"

PRELIMINARY NOTES

ON THE HALACHIC TREATISE OF REGINA JONAS

THE TYPED MANUSCRIPT of the treatise "Can Women Serve as Rabbis?, which according to Regina Jonas's own account is eighty-eight pages long, actually extends to ninety-five pages with the addition of extra sheets. On the first page, directly over the title and in the margin, are two indelible, purple stamps that catch the eye: "Rabbi Regina Sara Jonas" and *"Berlin C2—An der Spandauer Brücke 15—Tel. 42 02 96"*—two seals marking her life's work. As of 1939 the Nazis required all Jewish women to take on the additional name of *Sara,* and the address is the last place that Jonas lived in Berlin.

The document that was found with her papers actually is not the original, but a copy that Jonas made with blue, and occasionally black, carbon paper. One notices upon first perusal the many handwritten notes on the pages. Some are located in the text itself, others on the margin. Many were made with fountain pen—in black ink, using the old German script; most are additions to the text. In addition, the pages bear virtually countless other remarks: commentary, hints, terms, and criticism—some written in the old German script and others in Latin script; some made with an indelible marker, others with pencil or red marker.

In all, there are five recurring handwritings. I assume that they are all Regina Jonas's, as she apparently used the manuscript at different times as a basis for lectures. Penmanship was not Jonas's strongest point. On her diploma from the Oberlyzeum Weissensee she received the grade of "inadequate" for handwriting. Her oddly chaotic, often even sloppy script produced different styles of writing, which however only at first glance seem to be of different origin.

On the other hand, it might be possible that this document is not the version that Jonas handed in to the Hochschule für die Wissenschaft des Judentums [Academy for the Science of Judaism] in 1930. On the last page, she wrote that she had contacted "knowledgeable acquaintances" for advice on unclear points. Perhaps the work is only a draft that she presented to her acquaintances for their critical review, so that she could rework it once again. Yet this does not seem plausible to me, as there are no letters among Jonas's remaining documents in which these "styles" of writing can be found—neither are they comparable with the handwriting of Rabbi Max Weyl, who certainly was among Jonas's "knowledgeable acquaintances," nor with that of her Talmud professor Eduard Baneth, nor with any of the many other rabbis with whom Jonas was in contact, and for whom we have writing samples.

Another problem in editing Jonas's treatise was presented by the numerous Hebrew terms and citations from the Bible and rabbinical writings. In her own transcription of the Hebrew, Jonas swung between the centuries-old Ashkenazi pronunciation common to German Jews and the modern Sephardic Hebrew. Thus, she might call a Talmud tractate *Shabbos* or *Shabbat,* or even *Sabbat.* Neither did she follow a single format for citing biblical and rabbinical sources. Often Jonas did not include entire quotes, but rather only the first words; probably she assumed her readers would be familiar enough with the rabbinical writings to recognize the text. At any rate, it must have been a challenge for her to add the many Hebrew passages, written from right to left, into the primarily German text. She left the necessary spaces free, and later inserted the Hebrew citations.

The original German version of this book is a critical edition, which retains Jonas's pagination and contains all handwritten annotations, distinguishing between the different writing styles. It also reproduces all Hebrew quotes, with translations and comments only in the footnotes.

However, to enhance legibility, it was decided that this English-language version should be one continuous flowing text. Therefore, this edition does not include Jonas's handwritten annotations. In addition, all longer Hebrew quotes are presented here directly in their English translation. When necessary, I completed partial citations and explained them within the context of the relevant rabbinical discussion.[1] Every editorial addition is in square brackets [ ]. When I explained Jonas's quotes from rabbinic literature within their wider frame, which might be unfamiliar to the nonrabbinic reader, I announced it with the word *context.* When Jonas quoted only some words or a part of a quotation, I occasionally provided the rest to help the reader; such additions follow the word *continued.* Rabbinic codification literature has developed its own style of quoting.

Expressions like "end of citation" or "up to here the quote" serve as quotation marks. To maintain the "rabbinic" tone of Jonas's writing style, I kept all the technical Hebrew terms that she used in her manuscript, followed by their English translation in square brackets (for example: *Torah shebichtav* [Written Torah] and *Torah sheba'al peh* [Oral Torah]). To avoid confusion, I also worked the extra pages Jonas inserted into her manuscript into the present English-language version so that they form part of the text flow. In keeping with the style of her day, Jonas used extra spaces and underscoring to highlight passages or words; this edition respects her emphases by use of italics.

In naming sources and reproducing Hebrew words, I held to the Sephardic pronunciation common in Israel today, seeing as Jonas herself was inconsistent in use of the Ashkenazi pronunciation. To avoid redundancy, I have not repeated explanations of general Jewish terms and great halachic works that Jonas regularly cited. They are described in the Glossary. There, too, I held to the Sephardic pronunciation.

Beyond that, the manuscript is unchanged.

E. K.

NOTE

1. For biblical and talmudic citations, the translator of this edition relied on the *Artscroll Series: Talmud* (New York: Schottenstein Edition, Mesorah Publications, 1991); *The Talmud: The Steinsaltz Edition* (New York: Random House, 1989); and *The Holy Scriptures, According to the Masoretic Text* (Philadelphia: Jewish Publication Society of America, 1955).

HALACHIC TREATISE

CAN WOMEN SERVE AS RABBIS?

Rabbi Regina Sara Jonas
Berlin C2
An der Spandauer Brücke 15
Tel. 42 02 96

THE QUESTION OF WHETHER women can serve as rabbis, or—to adopt
the new term for this position—whether a Jewish woman can serve as a
Rabbinerin—is such a hefty problem that it cannot be handled exhaus-
tively within the framework of this halachic treatise. This is because one
would then have to deal with the overall approach to the depiction of the
Jewish woman in our entire Jewish literature. I therefore must limit myself
to taking on the most important points. It also is not possible to find
halachic material on every branch of the profession that will be dealt with
in this treatise. This brings one to the main difficulty, namely, that if the
term *Rabbinerin* is a novelty today, how much more so when relating it
to the time of our Jewish sacred texts!

But because I personally love this profession and would love to practice it if it were ever possible, and because my very honored teacher, Professor Dr. E. Baneth,[1] gave me this topic for a final paper on halachic
matters at our Academy for the Science of Judaism, I will attempt to illuminate the theme using my modest abilities.

In approaching the subject, it is essential first of all to understand why
one finds no mention of the female rabbi in Jewish sacred texts. To accom-

plish this task, one must investigate what has been written about the *rab-binic profession*[2] in general, so as to ascertain the tasks of a rabbi, and then see whether it is possible, halachically and in the sense of Jewish texts and Jewish history, for women to fulfill these rabbinic requirements as well.

Furthermore, it is important to see how the actions of Jewish women in the Bible, the Talmud, and history have been depicted and how our Sages of blessed memory and authorities relate to them. Once theory and practice have been considered, it is quite permissible to seek through these inferences an answer to the question of whether a female rabbinate is acceptable; that is, if a woman is permitted to enter it.

It is certainly fitting within this framework to point out that not only is the female rabbinate not mentioned in our holy texts, but—with very few exceptions, which will be discussed later—there is virtually no discussion of female *public* roles. This is because, first of all, the basic spiritual founda-tions for such roles were, according to my understanding, less available to the woman, in that the spiritual education of Jewish youth was almost exclusively theological and intended only for Jewish boys, as we later will see. A second important reason seems to me to be that the woman's soci-etal and economic position was completely different from what it is today, so that there was no need for her to take on a self-affirming profession. However, some light is shed from within the private sphere of women's occupations illuminating our special question of female rabbis.

For the time being, it should be noted that the job of a rabbi as such, according to today's understanding of the role as communal servant, also is not found clearly in biblical, talmudic, and post-talmudic texts. The heads of communities were *gedolim* [great scholars] in knowledge and in character; they studied and taught after receiving their *smicha* [rabbinical ordination] from their teacher and they cared for those who put their trust in them. Today, however, the duties of the rabbi have grown significantly.

What then are the demands placed on the modern rabbi? To fully elu-cidate my theme, I am now going to list all the possible tasks he must ful-fill, although it is not possible to treat each of them with the same degree of thoroughness for all the aforementioned reasons.

1. The rabbi must be well versed in the most important Jewish writ-ings of both a spiritual and secular nature, particularly the *Torah shebichtav* [Written Torah] and *Torah sheba'al peh* [Oral Torah].

2. He must teach others, both children and adults.

3. He must be active as a preacher in the synagogue and in addition must deliver religious addresses for funerals, weddings, and bar mitzvah.

4. He must fulfill actively the requirements for marriages and for the *get* [divorce decree], *chalitzah* [taking off the shoe],[3] and the acceptance of *gerim* [converts].

5. He must make halachic decisions, *pasken*.[4]

6. He should deliver talks outside the synagogue to arouse interest in Jewish subjects among the Jewish Community.

7. He should be available to help congregants with personal matters related to any distress of their soul.

8. He must work for social welfare, for youth welfare, and for general communal welfare, as well as arbitrate in conflicts between members.

9. And last but not least, obviously, he must lead an appropriate lifestyle by following the religious teachings of Judaism and fulfilling the tasks given him as leader of the community.

These listed tasks apply to the male rabbi and therefore to the female rabbi as well.

Concerning the work of a female rabbi in a house of worship, it also must be considered, regarding the separation of the sexes during public prayer services, that the access to the pulpit is designed in a way that prevents the chances of their meeting. In our synagogues, this is usually the case anyway, for the rabbi most often has his own entrance to the pulpit.[5] Finally, the matter of being called to the Torah should be mentioned, although it is not really necessary because this is only a *kavod* [honor], which can be ignored. (Although BT *Megillah* 23a indicates that women were allowed to be called to the Torah: "The Rabbis taught: Everyone is permitted to be one of the seven called up to the Torah, even a minor and even a woman; but the Sages said that a woman may not read the Torah out of respect for the community." [It would shed a bad light on the spiritual level of the community if women were better Torah readers than men.])

In order to better understand what we will later encounter, we now examine a basic term of Judaism related to women and men, the term *zniut* [practicing restraint, in the sense of modesty, chastity, humility], which will be dealt with later in greater detail. It is not always expressly stated in some stories of the Bible and Talmud and decrees of our Sages of blessed memory because it was so vivid in the consciousness of the Jewish people. Yet we do find it occasionally in the Talmud. See BT *Sukkah* 51b:

The Rabbis taught: At first, women sat within [the women's courtyard in the Temple] and the men outside; but when it came to frivolities, it was ordered that the women should sit outside and the men within. But since the frivolities continued, it was ordered that women sit above and the men below. [The "frivolities" came about while one group passed by the other.]

Further, BT *Shabbat* 113b:

He [Boas] perceived a manner of modesty about her [Ruth]. The standing ears of corn she gleaned standing; the fallen ears she gleaned sitting. [Ruth's chastity was expressed in that she did not bend forward, so as to avoid putting her clothing behind her in disorder.]

and BT *Bava Metziah* 87a:

And they said to him: "Where is Sarah your wife?" And he said: "Behold, in the tent." To inform [us] that Sarah our mother was modest. [According to the talmudic rabbis, on that day Sarah got her monthly period. Sexual relations between a man and a menstruating woman is a great sin according to Jewish religious law. Sarah thus prevented the danger of sexual relations during menstruation by staying behind in the tent.]

In addition, some of what is said in the Torah appears to be related to *zniut*, for example in the First Book of Moses, 24:65:

And Rebecca said to the servant: "What man is this that walks in the field to meet us?" And the servant said: "It is my master." And she took her veil, and covered herself.

It becomes evident that the woman practiced chastity and modesty even with respect to her own husband. See also Rashi on the First Book of Moses, 12:11, where we confront the term *zniut* on the part of the husband in relation to his wife.

"See, now I recognize," the agadic Midrash says, up to now he [Abraham] had not known her because both were chaste, now he recognizes her by the course of events [as the Pharaoh is likely to desire Sarah because of her beauty].

If such modesty were required toward one's own husband, how much more so when it comes to a stranger! It therefore seems to me that this might have been another reason why the woman in those days refrained

from public activity. Perhaps the later customary veiling of the woman
had played a role here; for in earlier times, as we see from the First Book
of Moses, 12:14, our matriarch Sarah freely went unveiled with *Abraham*
and was seen by strangers.

. . . when Abram came into Egypt, the Egyptians beheld the woman that she was very fair.

We will not yet begin with the theoretical section, as it will occupy a
prominent place in our treatment; therefore the first presentation is a
description of the woman through her appearance and actions in the
Bible. Afterward, the appearance of the woman in the Talmud will be handled, and her role in both talmudic and later times. One often thinks of
the beautiful words of Psalm 45:14: "All glorious is the royal daughter
within. . . ." noting that in biblical times our women all led their lives in
the background.[6]

This applied to the majority of women, but a few towered above the
rest through some major historical feat that bears witness to the knowledge, abilities, skills, and intelligence with which they worked *for* the
entire community, and also sometimes *in* and *with* the *entire* community—though not in the sense of a profession as would be defined today.
The Bible delivers manifold examples of this to the attentive reader.

It is not really necessary to point out the silent impact of our matri-
archs as loyal, caring wives and teachers of children. Our Jewish mothers do break out of their seclusion, not literally but figuratively. Both men
and women had gathered to receive the Torah at the fundamental event
of our Jewish people, the *Matan Torah* [giving of the Torah] on Mount
Sinai; see the Second Book of Moses, chapters 19 and 20, and see Rashi
on 19:3:

"So you should speak," with these words and in this order—Mechilta—"to the house of
Jacob," those are the women; speak gently to them [*continued:* "and announce to the
children of Israel" the penalties and exact regulations, proclaim the words to the men,
bitter as wormwood.] [Rashi refers to the doubling in the passage "Thus you shall say
to the *house of Jacob* and tell *the children of Israel*" (emphasis of editor). The former are
the women, the latter, men. "Speaking"—as the more sensitive act—is oriented toward
the women; "announcing"—as the stricter—toward the men.]

That experience in all its sacred grandeur also is embraced by the daughters of Israel, who feel duty-bound as servants of G-d, alongside the men,
in the realm of "Priests", as part of the "Holy People."

Let us examine in detail the lives and deeds of our Jewish women with reference to the Bible. Miriam (Second Book of Moses, 15:20) sings with the women, inspiring both them and G-d, just as the men had done before them, to thank G-d for his miraculous rescue.

And Miriam the prophetess, the sister of Aaron, took a timbrel, etc. [The scene occurs right after the drowning of Pharaoh's soldiers in the Sea of Reeds.]

The modest, but intelligent and remarkable request of the daughters of Zelophehad in the Torah is well known. See the Fourth Book of Moses, 27:1 ff:

Then drew near the daughters of Zelophehad, etc. [Upon the death of their father, the daughters demand a part of his inheritance, which the law originally did not guarantee them. After they recited their demand, God spoke: "If someone dies and had no son, then his inheritance shall be turned over to his daughter."]

BT *Bava Batra* 119b:

Zelophehad's daughters were wise, well-informed and pious in their deduction. They were wise, because they spoke at the proper time. . . . they were well-informed in their deduction, for they said: If he had had a son, we would not have spoken. [They knew how to justify their claim.]

Just as the man is permitted to bring his sacrifice, so is she permitted to do so at particular times. See the Third Book of Moses, 12:6:

And when the days of her purification are fulfilled, for a son, or for a daughter, she shall bring a lamb of the first year for a burnt-offering, and a young pigeon, or a turtle-dove, for a sin-offering, to the door of the tent of meeting, to the priest.

The fact that G-d told Moses to call upon both men and women to come together and he taught the biblical laws at the end of every seven-year period, at the time of Sukkot, is seen in *Hakhel* [God's command: "Assemble!"] in the Fifth Book of Moses, 31:10 ff.

[The decisive sentence is Deuteronomy 31:12 ff.] Assemble the people, the men and the women and the little ones, and your stranger that is within your gates, that they may hear, and that they may learn, and fear the Eternal your God, and observe to do all the words of this law. [Commentary of Rashi on Deuteronomy 31:12: "The men are there to learn; the women, to hear."]

Naturally, a thorough discussion on these points will follow in the the-
oretical-halachic section. This mutual teaching of men and women also is
described in the Book of Nehemiah, 8:1–9.

And Ezra the priest brought the Law before the congregation, both men and women,
and all that could hear with understanding, upon the first day of the seventh month.
[The passage describes the first Jewish New Year festival after the return of the Jews
from exile in Babylon; it is the only biblical passage that closely describes such an
"assembly" of men and women, as commanded in Deuteronomy 31:12 and the lines
that follow.]

It is hardly necessary to illuminate more closely the courageous acts of
Judith, the valor and readiness to sacrifice of women like Hannah,
Samuel's mother (see the First Book of Samuel, chapter 1) and of Han-
nah, known to us through the Chanukah story (BT *Gittin* 57b):

And R. Yehudah said: This verse is illustrated by an incident concerning a woman and
her seven sons. [It deals with a mother who sacrificed seven sons to the Emperor, who
killed them because they refused to pray to an idol.]

as well as of Esther (see the Book of Esther, BT *Megillah* 4a Tosafot
"Nashim"):

Because also they [women] participated in this miracle. [Thus women are obligated
to read the Megillat Esther.]

Who could be unaware of the visionary work of the prophetess Huldah, from the Second Book of Kings, chapter 22:14, and the following:

Then the priests went to the *prophetess* Huldah, wife of Shallum, etc.

With extraordinary courage, energy, and intelligence, the political heroine Deborah lifted herself above the ranks of her contemporaries (see
Book of Judges, chapter 4:4):

And Deborah, the *prophetess,* wife of Lappidot, *judged* Israel at this time.

And a great disaster was avoided through the sensible intelligence and daring decisiveness of Abigail, vis-à-vis a man who later became king (see
First Book of Samuel, 25:23 ff.):

Now when Abigail saw David, she hurried [*continued*: to dismount from the donkey and to fall on her knees in front of David].

It already has been noted here that the BT *Megillah* 14a freely and gladly elevated seven women to the rank of prophetess; in some cases they are even mentioned [as such—as "prophetess"] in the Tanach [Hebrew Bible].

The rabbis taught: Forty-eight prophets and *seven prophetesses* preached to Israel. . . . Who were these seven prophetesses? Sarah, Miriam, Deborah, Hannah, Abigail, Huldah and Esther.

In this connection, it also is to be noted that, just as Deborah is a political heroine for biblical times, so were post-biblical times blessed by the political actions of a Jewish queen—the pious Queen Salome Alexandra;[7] see [Simon] Dubnow's *Die Weltgeschichte des Jüdischen Volkes* [The World History of the Jewish People], 1925, volume 2, §30, pages 165–167:[8] Page 167 reads: "This epoch of national-religious restoration was portrayed in the legend of the Pharisees as an unspoiled, happy period. 'Under Simon ben Shetach and Queen Salome (Salma, Salminun), rain fell on the eve of the Sabbath, just as the work in the fields drew to a close; wheat kernels were as large as kidneys, the barley seeds like olive seeds and the lentils like golden dinars. . . . Their policies were based solely on protection of the land." See also Heinrich Graetz's *History of the Jews*, third volume, fifth edition,[9] note 13, p. 706: "Later, they named the period after the Queen and Simon ben Shetach." See BT *Taanith* 23a with regard to her name:

At the time of Simon ben Shetach, it rained every Wednesday night and Sabbath eve, until the wheat kernels were as large as kidneys.

Also see Tosafot "De'amar" on BT *Shabbat* 16b:

R. Yehudah told the story of Queen Shel Zion/Shlomzion. [*Context:* R. Yehudah said in the name of Rav: Once the Queen Shel Zion prepared a festival meal for her son and all her pots became unclean; Tosafot: R. Yehudah told the story of Queen Shel Zion. He brought a proof. In the days of Simon ben Shetach a law was enacted about the impurity of metal crockery, according to which broken items that are newly smelted return to the original state of impurity.]

Furthermore, Graetz spoke of her in the seventh chapter of the third volume of the *History of the Jews*, page 135—"It was fortunate for the

Jewish people that a woman of gentle temperament and sincerity led the state, at a time after a man's impetuosity had caused the state's downfall," (fifth edition, Leipzig, 1906)—referring to her "righteousness and wisdom and gentle nature."[10]

Enough with biblical and post-biblical examples. They demonstrate, I believe, that in any era, when women *wished* to and were *able* to express themselves, no obstacle was placed in their way as long as their work was valuable and carried out in a solid [true] way. One does not encounter religious immaturity, excessive seclusion, and false timidity, or carelessness, frivolity, and ignorance on the part of these women; rather they are graced with salvation, bravery, kindness, and gentleness. Naturally they also made mistakes, but did not King David also commit sins?! This is due to *human* weakness in both men and women.

Let us see what the Talmud says *in general* about women, since it reports in its objective, incisive, and fair manner about both men *and* women. The Talmud attributes to women an understanding of human nature, an essential ability for the profession under discussion, almost as important as keen intellect and kindheartedness.

See BT *Brachot* 10b:

A woman recognizes the qualities of her guests better than a man.

In addition see BT *Niddah* 45b:

It says: and the Eternal built the rib; this teaches that the Holy one, blessed be He, gave the woman more understanding than the man. [The Hebrew word *bina*—understanding, insight—is derived from *bana*—to build.]

In addition see BT *Megillah* 14b:

Because women are more compassionate.

However, it is more difficult to understand the verse in BT *Nedarim* 20b, which traverses the marital sphere and touches on another aspect that does not completely belong here. Still, it should be noted that possibly such comments and similar ones were misinterpreted by the "masses" of readers, who have seen this as an expression of a lower estimation of the woman.

It says in the aforementioned verse [BT *Nedarim* 20b]:

. . . rather, one could do whatever one pleases with his wife [during sexual relations]

We are led into a related sphere by BT *Ketubot* 59b:

A woman is only for beauty: a woman is only for children. And R. Chiya taught: A woman is only for a woman's ornaments. [*Context:* The Mishna determines the following tasks that the woman must perform for the man: grinding grain, baking, washing, cooking, suckling her child, making the bed for him, and working with wool. The sentence then continues: "Our Mishna does not represent the view of R. Chiya, for R. Chiya taught:" followed by the citation.]

Certainly, the woman believed that self-decoration and beauty were the most important matters, because the overarching philosophy of life considered beauty, marriage, and motherhood to be her main sphere of activity. Unfortunately, it turned out that there is too much emphasis placed on appearance and beauty, and such an interpretation of the woman's life in this regard must clearly lead to superficiality with no room for serious spiritual work. From there, the view elucidated in BT *Shabbat* 33b and BT *Kiddushin* 80b may be expressed in the well-known phrase, *nashim da'atan kalah aleyhen* [women are light-headed].

Moreover, the Talmud is too accepting of her artificial beautification. See BT *Mo'ed Katan* 9b:

The Rabbis taught: The following are the woman's beauty items: she may decorate her eyes, do her hair and anoint her face.

And see also BT *Ketubot* 66b:

What is the basket? Rav Ashi said: The basket of perfumes. [*Context:* Both partners in a marriage are obligated to bring certain items of value to the marriage. The groom is obligated to contribute ten dinars to finance the bride's "basket" for beauty products.]

As work primarily intended for the woman, the following is mentioned in BT *Ketubot* 59b:

Mishna: And these are the tasks that a wife performs for her husband: She grinds, and bakes, and launders, [and] cooks, and nurses her child, [and] makes his bed, and works with wool, etc.

(See also Proverbs Solomon 31:10 ff.)[11] Those were the activities seen by the Talmud as ideal for the married woman, because it was easy for them to marry and fulfill their beautiful profession of being housewives. However, today many women are denied this role, because in some countries there are not enough men available; aside from that, a woman today is not simply married off, but rather approves of the match or chooses her husband herself. In addition, the modern, unmarried woman has a considerable number of other opportunities within the sphere of public professions.

The comment in Talmud BT *Kiddushin* 82b seems rather mysterious:

The world cannot exist without men or without women; but fortunate are those whose children are male, and woe to those whose children are female.

Whether this view refers to some physical changes of the woman through giving birth and through *niddah* [impurity of the woman during menstruation] or to the difficulties in amassing a dowry or even to the influences of other cultures (or to the inability to fulfill the *mitzvot* [commandments]) is not clear; it can also come from the unfortunate experience of the teacher who made this statement.

Consideration also is due to the passage in BT *Shabbat* 62a:

Women are a nation unto themselves [*context:* Ula is of the view that what is suitable for a man is not suitable for a woman, and what is suitable for a woman is not suitable for a man. Rather, said R. Yosef, Ula holds that women are viewed as a nation unto themselves],

which unfortunately also is interpreted to the disadvantage of the woman. It would be just as sad if the comment from BT *Shabbat* 152a were to come very much into play:

A woman is like a leather jug full of excretions, whose opening is full of blood. Yet in spite of this everyone chases after her!

For the fact that G-d created human beings as man and woman, according to the Torah, First Book of Moses 1:27, is said beautifully in BT *Yevamot* 63a:

Any man who does not have a wife is not a complete human being [*continued:* as it says: He created them male and female. . . . and he called their name Adam (human being)].

There still are many passages that testify as to the high esteem in which the woman was held, particularly in the roles of wife and mother. But to list them all here first of all would be too much, and secondly it would stray too far from the subject at hand.

A sentence frequently cited to the detriment of the woman is found in BT *Kiddushin* 49b.

Ten *kab* [a measure] of talkativeness came down into the world, and women received nine of them, etc.

But one can still declare it to be either *lignay* [for shame] or *lish'vach* [for praise],[12] because just as any positive attribute can be turned into its opposite, so can speech be either talkativeness or eloquence capable of moving the heart; the latter is an attribute not to be underestimated in the professional work of the female rabbi.

In BT *Kiddushin* 49b, it is referred to as

Ten kab of talkativeness came down into the world, and women received nine of them.[13]

In conclusion, among all these general examples, there is still one that testifies to the good and positive qualities of the woman; see BT *Brachot* 17a:

The promise that the Holy one, blessed be he, gave to the woman is greater than that which he gave to men, for it says [Isaiah 32:9]: "Rise up, carefree women, listen to my voice; you confident daughters, listen to my speech." Rav spoke to R. Chiya: How do women make themselves deserving?—By allowing *their children to study in the* house of prayer, by allowing their husbands to study in the school of the rabbis and by *waiting for their husbands* until they come home from the school."

Rashi: "Waiting for their husbands"—that is, they wait for their husbands, give them permission to go to another city and study Torah there.

We see from these words that her seriousness, her respect for our holy teachings, and her ability to sublimate her ego are given due recognition. (For the last point, see particularly the Rashi statement mentioned earlier.)

There is a serious reason why we have spent a relatively long time with these general talmudic statements about the woman, though they are *not directly* part of the *actual* theme of the work. It is clear from these few examples, and naturally there are many more available, that the Talmud contains *pros* and *cons* related to the woman; but definitely not *only* cons. Because for one thing, one must protect oneself against granting these statements too much influence. Such statements are to be expected as merely bald *opinions* of our Sages of blessed memory that, however, have infiltrated the public consciousness. And often, unfortunately, only the negative and doubting statements are impressed upon the memory. For example, the words *nashim da'atan kalah aleyhen* [women are light-headed] are used way too often as a weapon against women's ways, although, as I will attempt to demonstrate, much is said praising her *seriousness* and her profound character.

Who would ever, to move into a different field, seek a serious guiding principle in the rather harsh words of Mishna *Kiddushin* 82a:

Even the best of the doctors should be destined to Hell!

Even Rashi tries to give this a milder interpretation. It is likely that this word only emerges from the unfortunate experience of the teacher involved. It is comparable to the disparaging views of women. We see that the Talmud, in its integrity, not *only* mentions the less flattering aspects of women in general and of particularly important women (see Beruria, as will be explained), but also those of the great men, teachers in Israel.

The rich spiritual strength and erudition with which a Beruria[14] was blessed—there will be more to say about her—is well known. Nevertheless she often is presented as an example of how women are light-headed, and that, despite their knowledge, they would rather look condescendingly upon our teachings than approach them with the respect they are due. As Rashi says on BT *Avodah Zarah* 18b:

And some say because of the story of Beruria, who once made fun of the Sages, who said that women are light-headed. He said to her: "By your life, in the end you will agree with their words," and assigned one of his students to seduce her, and he put pressure on her for several days until she gave in, and when this became known about her, she strangled herself, and R. Meir fled because of the scandal.

Poor Beruria, who after a long moral conflict ultimately fell victim to trickery! No one today would abuse this highly esteemed personality of a woman—who despite everything remains a guiding light for all maidens and mothers of Israel—by using her as an example of how women's studies have to result in *havai* [nonsense] and reveal superficiality and ignorance! With equal openness the Talmud tells us how three great male scholars, including even the esteemed husband of this heroic woman Beruria, also almost surrendered to seduction; and the tragedy could have been complete had it not been for a higher power that stepped in, so they could control themselves.

See BT *Kiddushin* 81a, which reports about these three scholars, who were almost brought down by the *yetzer harah* [evil inclination, sex drive], and among them was, as mentioned, Rabbi Meir, *furthermore* R. Amram and R. Akiva:

1. It happened one time that captured [women] were brought to Nehardea [a city in Babylonia in which there was a great Talmud Academy] there they were put up [in the second story] of the home of Rav Amram the pious one . . . [*continued:* and he removed the ladder before them (that would connect the upper and lower floors). When one of them passed by and a beam of light fell into the room through a hatch, R. Amram (who found her beautiful) took the ladder and climbed up. Ten people could not have carried it, but he carried it alone. When he was halfway up the ladder, he stood and called out in a loud voice: Fire in the house of Amram! The rabbis came in (but saw there was no fire). They spoke to him: You have shamed us. But he replied: It is better that you be shamed in the house of Amram in this world, than that you be ashamed of him in the world to come. Whereupon he cried out (to drive out the evil inclination) and it flew out of him like a pillar of fire. Then he spoke to it: See, you are fire and I am flesh, but I am stronger than you.]

2. R. Meir was accustomed to scoffing at sinners. One day, Satan appeared to him as a woman on the other side of the river, and as there was no ferry to take him over, he grasped the rope [that stretched across the span] and crossed. When he was halfway across, Satan released him, saying "Had they not said in Heaven that one should be careful of R. Meir and his Torah knowledge. . . ." [*Continued:* "I would have made your life worth two Ma'ah" (two copper coins that are worth little).]

3. R. Akiva was accustomed to scoffing at sinners. One day, Satan appeared to him as a woman at the top of a palm tree. . . . [*Continued:* He grabbed the palm and began to climb. As he reached the halfway point, Satan released him, saying, "Had they not said in Heaven that one should be careful of R. Akiva and his Torah learning, I would have made your life worth two Ma'ah."]

Different and more difficult are the issues, if we look *generally* at the religious duties of a woman, related to her religious majority with regard to permitting her to be taught, to her participation in the religious services, in short with regard to everything that falls within the religious sphere in the broadest sense.

Regarding "prohibitions" [negative commandments], the woman is equal to the man, see BT *Pesachim* 43a:

"When a man or woman shall commit any of the sins of the human being . . ." [Numbers 5:6]. The Torah here has equated a man to a woman regarding all punishments and relevant prohibitions in the Torah.

And BT *Yevamot* 84b:

Raba responded: If he is forbidden, she also is forbidden, and if it is not forbidden to him it also is not forbidden to her. Is it to be deduced that this is actually from a teaching of

R. Yehudah in the name of Rav!? R. Yehudah said in the name of Rav, and it was also taught in the school of R. Yishmael: If a man or a woman has committed any human sin; scriptures place the woman on an equal level with the man regarding prohibitions.

When it comes to the fulfillment of "positive commandments," she is similarly obligated, with the exception of the small, well-known group of regulations that are "time bound," from which she is freed. See BT *Brachot* 20b:

. . . women are exempt from all positive commandments, which are time bound.

She is required to fulfill three obligations; see BT *Brachot* 20a below,

Mishna: Women, slaves, and minors are exempt from reciting the Shema, and from donning Tefillin. But they are *obligated* in prayer, and in the command to affix a Mezuzah, and in reciting Birkat Hamazon.

In relation to religious maturity, she stands on the same level as slaves. See BT *Chagigah* 4a:

. . . for every commandment to which a woman is obligated, the slave is also obligated, and for every commandment to which the woman is not obligated, the slave is also not obligated.

But it is interesting to note that one Mrs. Brune Mainz wore a *Talit Katan* [garment with fringes *(tzitzit)*, worn under the clothing]. (See [Leopold] Zunz, *Zur Geschichte und Literatur* [On History and Literature], page 173.) He quotes the treatise of the Maharil on the customs of the fringes. It is stated there

Regulations related to the *Tzitzit* and *Tefillin*: If there is a man in a place who knows how to repair the fringes, the woman should not repair them. He said, it is not clear to him why there are women who have taken on the obligation to wear the fringes. One asked him: Why does he not protest because of the *Rebbetzin, Mrs. Brune,* in his city? She *always* wore a shirt with fringes. He answered: Perhaps she does not listen to him [her husband]—in such a case it is better if one remains [unwittingly] in error, than that one becomes [willingly] malicious.

If she had infringed on an *issur* [prohibition], it would have been necessary to stop her from doing so. Therefore "she shouldn't do it," but if she ends up doing it, nothing terrible has happened.

Also, by the way, as regards tefillin [phylacteries], an essential reason why she should not put them on, according to BT *Eruvin* 96a, Tosafot "Michal," is the term *guf naki* [clean body]. It states that for tefillin a clean body is required, and women are not good at taking care of this.

But if she does pay attention to cleanliness, could she not put on tefillin?! BT *Eruvin* 96a tells of a woman who also put on tefillin and was not prevented from doing so:

Michal, the daughter of the Kushite [another name for King Saul] used to put on tefillin, and the Sages did not protest against her.

See also BT *Rosh Hashanah* 33a Tosafot "Ha."

Mishna: One does not stop children from blowing the shofar, the ram's horn, for the New Year festival, rather one should practice with them until they learn how to do it.

Gemara: Thus one hinders women, and [in contrast] it is taught that one hinders neither women nor children when they blow shofar on the holiday!?

As already has been stressed, the terms *zniut* and to some extent *prizut* [unchaste, licentious behavior] play a major role in the Talmud, and some decrees came about in relation to them.

See Rambam, *Mishneh Torah*, Regulations for Blessings, Chapter 5, Halacha 6:

To prevent licentiousness, women, slaves and minors should not assemble together . . .

Regarding how our sensitivities have changed in relation to *zniut* and *prizut*, see Rambam *Mishneh Torah*, Regulations for Marriage, Chapter 24, Halacha 12:

What is the law applied to the Jewish woman? *Demureness,* which was a custom of the daughters of Israel. Through the following things, of which she does one, she transgresses the law incumbent upon Jewish woman. . . . if she spins in the marketplace thereby revealing *her upper arm* to the people, or if she *flirts* with *young men.*

And Halacha 11:

. . . if she goes to the market with uncovered head.

Furthermore, it says in BT *Brachot* 24a:

The voice of a woman is shame. . . . The hair of a woman is shame.

Also in this regard, again particularly dealing with the covering of a woman's hair, today's attitude is different, as practice shows. Neither does the hearing of a woman's singing voice provoke impurity in most cases. Considering what is to come in this work, the term of *yichud* [private proximity of a man and woman who are not married] must be mentioned; see Mishna BT *Kiddushin* 82a:

Anyone whose business is with women may not be *alone* with women.

But there will be more to say about this later. One notes here the section of BT *Megillah* 23a, which calmly states that a woman, strictly speaking, can be called to the Torah; but as I see it, only *zniut* prevents this.

How else would one explain the expression *mipney kavod zibur* [out of respect for the dignity of the community], which stands as the reason for preventing her from being called up. It says there that

Everybody can be part of the seven who are called to the Torah reading, even a minor *and even a woman;* however, the Sages said that a woman may not read from the Torah, out of respect for the dignity of the community.

because it would be a *fallacy* to suggest that one might consider it shameful for women to be called up instead of men, since her being called up does preclude his being called up, as is similarly reasoned in BT *Sukkah* 38a, as we soon will see.

But as to being called up to the Torah, it actually is said that she has to be called up from the center. Yes, she can even recite the *brachot* [blessings] although she is not required to do the *talmud torah* [Torah study], because when one is called to the Torah one does not pronounce the *brachot* over the *talmud torah,* just as the *Levi* [member of the priestly tribe] if necessary, is called up instead of the *Cohen* [member of the priestly family] and thus does the *brachah* [blessing] twice.[15] See here First Tosafot "Ha" in BT *Rosh Hashanah* 33a:

R. Yossi, son of Yehudah, brings a proof. How does one know that a woman should perform the blessing over all the commandments that are time-bound? (*Megillah* 23a:) Everyone is permitted among the seven who read from the Torah, even the *woman,* even the minor—and this is so even though the woman is not obligated to occupy herself with Torah study, as it is said in the first chapter of *Kiddushin* (34a) and at the beginning of the chapter "Bechol Me'arvin" (*Eruvin* 27a); R. Tam says: That is neither a proof for the blessing before and after, nor for the *study of the Torah*. Because even when the blessing "Make beautiful the words of the Torah" was already said, or the blessing "With great love" was said, he [the man] repeats and blesses. Know, in a place where there is no Levi, the Cohen reads in place of the Levi and blesses, although he already gave a blessing at the first reading, and it is also possible to say that a woman comes up for the Torah reading, that means to the center because it was not common to make the blessing, as it is written in the chapter "Hakoreh Omed," BT *Megillah* 21a. [In other words: Because throughout a service many "unnecessary" repetitions of blessings are made on the same theme, for example in the prayers "Make beautiful the words of the Torah" or "With great love," which contain a similar content to the blessing over Torah study, and because the Cohen may repeat the same blessing twice on the Torah study if there is no Levi available, then a woman may also say the blessing over Torah study, also if it is "senseless" because she is not required to study Torah. In addition, in earlier times it was not common to make a blessing of the Cohen and Levi, thus she in this case would not be embarrassed.]

According to Rashi, as previously noted, BT *Sukkah* 38a in the Mishna shows that she can read Hallel [hymn of praise, collection of psalms read on the Jewish holidays of Pesach, Shavuot, Sukkot, Chanukah, and Rosh Chodesh] aloud to him. But this is not looked upon favorably. Not because the woman is "unsuitable," but rather here her reading in itself, as it were, bars him from reading, and that is shameful, indicating he had learned nothing or somehow wants to escape his obligations. In the text itself [BT *Sukka* 38a], it says:

Mishna: If a slave, a woman or a minor reads aloud the Hallel for someone, that person must repeat what has been read aloud, and he is cursed!

Rashi: Because he did not learn how to read (or that he needs such readers).

Just as *zniut* justifies not being called up to the Torah, so does it support the regulations for covering a woman's hair, as we already saw in BT *Brachot* 24a; it is thoroughly discussed in BT *Ketubot* 72a Mishna and Gemara as well. So whoever steps across that line treads on "Jewish Law." Have not many of us who take Halacha seriously found that in most cases the "Daughters of Israel" received no legal sanctions when they went out into the public with their own hair visible? [BT *Ketubot* 72a:]

Mishna: And these [divorced wives] go out without [their] money to be returned in case of a divorce, fixed in the *ketubah* [marriage contract]: She who violates the law of Moses or Jewish custom . . . And who is she [who violates] Jewish custom? [She who] goes out with her head uncovered or spins in the market place, or talks with everybody.

Gemara: [But surely] an uncovered head is [forbidden] by Torah law, for it is written: "And he shall uncover the woman's head." And [a Sage] of the Academy of Rabbi
Yishmael taught: "[This is] a warning to the daughters of Israel that they should not go
out with an uncovered head." Then the uncovering of the head is [a prohibition] from
the Torah!? To be precise (Numbers 5:18)—he uncovered the woman's head, and in
the school of Yishmael it was taught that this amounted to a prohibition, that the
daughters of Israel not go out with uncovered head.

Rashi: It is written that he [the priest] would uncover her hair, thus it was uncom-
mon in this time that she was uncovered, in other words, it is not the custom of the
daughters of Israel to go out with *uncovered head* and wild hair. . . . [See Numbers 5:18:
"And he shall present the wife before the Eternal one, and loosen her hair"; one derives
from this that Jewish women did not go out with their hair loose.]

It is undeniable, be it said in all modesty, that despite loyalty to our
holy and beautiful laws nevertheless there has been a development in public sentiments as a natural result of present circumstances that also has
left its mark on Judaism. In later comments we will find this confirmed
often. It should be mentioned at this point that it is the *yichud* with regard
to the teaching position of the woman.

The abundance of material and the depth of the problem attached to
my chosen theme unfortunately make it impossible to cover every aspect
with exhaustive thoroughness, so that much that was already said at the
outset can only be dealt with briefly.

Another proof that her religious majority—essential for the career in
question—in and of itself is *not* denied emerges from the following. See
BT *Brachot* 20b:

Rav Adda bar Ahavah said: *Women* are obligated *by Torah law to recite the* consecration
of the day, for example the blessing at the onset of Shabbat day or the blessing for the
holiday before the meal. . . . Rather, answered Raba, [Exodus 20:8 says] "Remember,"
and [Deuteronomy 5:12 says] "Observe": whoever is required to observe is also
required to remember, and because women are required to observe the laws of the
Shabbat, as they are subject to all the prohibitions, they also are required to remember. [*Context:* The Shabbat commandment, which is the fourth in the list of the Ten
Commandments, begins differently in each of its two references in the Torah: Once
with *"Zachor"*—"Remember!" (Exodus 20:8) and once with *"Shamor"*—"Observe!"
(Deuteronomy 5:12). The Rabbis conclude from this: Women are required to follow
the prohibition (*"lo ta'asse"*—"Do not!"), whether or not they are bound to time—and
this includes "observe." If the women are required both through the commands
"shamor" and *"zachor,"* this must likewise include the commandment (*"asseh"*—"Do!")
and with it the consecration of the day.]

See in addition Tosafot "Ha" in BT *Rosh Hashanah* 33a. Even if the *Gemara* in *Brachot* and later the *poskim* [decisors of halachic law] are of different minds as to whether she can be *motzi* [to enable others to fulfill their obligations][16]—the citations provide a strong foundation for religious majority, which will no longer be explored here in depth. At any rate, it is generally decided according to Halacha that she is *chayevet* [obligated] to do *Kiddush* [blessing over wine]; it is only questionable regarding Havdalah [prayer at conclusion of Shabbat], which, however, also belongs to this *inyan* [theme]. According to the opinion of the Taz, she can be *motzi* for others at Kiddush. The original Hebrew text provides evidence that the woman is required to make Kiddush and even to be *motzi* for *others*:

Shulchan Aruch, Orach Chayim, cipher 271, paragraph 2—Taz: On the citation ". . . and they [grammatically: women] were *motzi* for men," etc. Although it was laid down in cipher 689 in the *Shulchan Aruch* that in that case women during the reading of the *Megillah* [the Megillat Esther] are *not "motzi"* for men, although they are *required* to read, this is not to be compared with the case at hand. Because as far as the theme of *Megillah* is concerned, there are a views that women should not bless "on the reading of the Megillat Esther," but rather, "on the hearing of the Megillat Esther," as it is written there in the Bet Yosef [commentary on Tur]. Therefore it is certainly not correct that she should ideally be *"motzi"* for other men [in the care of *Megillah*]. But this is not the case here where *everyone agrees that there is absolutely no difference between men and women, thus it is correct that they [women] are "motzi" for men.* And Rashil [R. Solomon Luria, also known as "Maharshal"] and Moch ["my father-in-law"; Joel Sirkes, born in Lublin, sixteenth century] of blessed memory also *decided here that they [women] are not "Motzi"* in the same way as with the Megillat Esther, *and that case doesn't force you* [to decide the same way in this one].

Despite *zniut*, the Talmud presents us with cases in which women were religiously active in the community, and our Sages of blessed memory did not hinder them. One woman joins the journey at the *Shalosh Regalim* [three pilgrimage festivals]; another, as mentioned, puts on tefillin; and another participates in the *smicha* [leaning on the animal][17] during the sacrifice. See BT *Eruvin* 96a:

Michal, the daughter of the Kushite [a name for King Saul] used to put on Tefillin, *and the Sages did not hinder her,* and the wife of Yonah the Prophet used to ascend to Jerusalem on the pilgrimage festivals of Pesach, Shavuot and Sukkot and the Sages did not hinder her.

Having said that, Rashi notes:

So they were of the opinion that it is not one of the time-bound commandments.

He says it *would* be as the Tosafot say, but this is not the case.

In addition to the open participation of a woman in the three pilgrimage festivals, we find the religious activities of a woman, as already mentioned above, extensively reported in BT *Chagigah* 16b regarding sacrifice, where the reason also is given for why the woman ultimately is allowed such things, namely *kedey la'asot nachat ruach* [to give satisfaction to them]; although in this situation there still is, to be sure, the danger of committing an act of profanation of the act of sacrificing the animal, because of the unnecessary "leaning."

One objected: [Leviticus 1:2, 4] "Speak to the sons of Israel" etc., "He should lean" [place the hands on the sacrificial animal]; only the sons of Israel should lean but not the *daughters of Israel*; R. Yossi and R. Shimon say the daughters of Israel have the option to perform *smicha* if they wish. R. Yossi said: Abba Elazar told me that they once had a calf as a holy offering and it was *brought* past the women's courtyard [of the Temple], where *the women leaned* their hands on it; not because the leaning by the woman was required, but to *give satisfaction to the women*.

Nevertheless Tosafot BT *Chagigah* 16b says

"To give satisfaction to the women"—final chapter, BT *Rosh Hashanah*, page 33, commentary of R. Yitzhak ben Shmuel: If the women about whom we are speaking come to perform a commandment that is time bound, and wish to make a *blessing*, one should *not bar them* from this, although they are not obligated to do it; it also does not count as an *invalid blessing*; one can learn from it: I have set out more on this in the tractate *Rosh Hashanah* and have expressed myself in depth on this.

We see that, according to Tosafot, the nonfulfillment of time-bound commandments is relative, based on whether women absolutely *want* to fulfill them. Such a lenient interpretation would not have been permissible were there a prohibition in the strictest sense on this point, or principal opposition to her religious activity. They actually never could have been allowed to make a *brachah* [blessing] over something that stands under the *issur* [prohibition]. See on this point also Tosafot "Dilma" in BT *Eruvin* 96a, where it simply is accepted that Michal, the daughter of Kush, made a *brachah*.

Women are permitted to make a *blessing* over all commandments that are time bound, although she is *not obligated to do so*, like *Michal, the daughter of Saul, who probably similarly blessed.* [If Michal put on tefillin, say the rabbis, she most likely also said the blessing over them beforehand.]

Review also the oft-repeated passage of Tosafot "Ha" in BT *Rosh Hashanah* 33a. The final illustration of the general talmudic approach to women's religious activities and majority status to be included here is the oft-mentioned BT *Megillah* 4a and 19b in the same tractate:

4a: In addition, R. Yehoshua b. Levi said: Women are *obligated* to read the Megillat Esther, because they, too, took part in this miracle.

19b: Mishna: *Everyone* is permitted to read aloud the Megillat Esther. . . .

In comparison, it should be mentioned how Rambam and his commentary on Hilchot Megillah, Perek 1, Halacha 1 view her religious activities, through which she appears as a majority member in the religious sense.

It is a positive mitzvah decreed by the rabbis to read the Megillah at the appointed time. . . . all are required to read it, men and *women,* converts and freed slaves.

Further evidence of the religious majority of the woman now will be presented, as already shown in connection with Megillat Esther:

Rambam, *Mishneh Torah,* Regulations on the Megillat Esther, Chapter 1, Halacha 1: It is a positive mitzvah ordained by the rabbis to read the Megillah at the appointed time. . . . all are required to read it, men and *women,* converts and freed slaves.

Maggid Mishneh: All are required to read the Megillat Esther, and we say, this includes women, as according to the Ribal [R. Josef ben Levi], who said, *women* are *required* to read the Megillat Esther, as they also took part in the miracle.

In the *Shulchan Aruch,* Orach Chayim, cipher 689, paragraph 2, it says, "And there are some who say *that the women are not* 'motzi' *for other men.*" So it was written in the name of the author of "Halachot Gedolot" [by Shimon Kajara, ninth-century Babylonia], and also in [the book titled] *Mordechai* [by Mordechai ben Hillel Ashkenazi, thirteenth century] and in the name of the "Raviah" [R. Eliezer ben Joel Halevi of Bonn, twelfth to thirteenth century].

If it says here that "*some*" believe she cannot be *motzi* for others, then "most" *must* be of the opinion that she certainly can be *motzi* for others. Her religious majority with regard to *Kiddush* according to the Taz already has been emphasized. Her religious majority likewise includes that she is allowed, if there is no man present, to carry out the *Brit Milah* [circumcision], a point on which the Kesef Mishneh [Joseph Karo] provides a more detailed explanation.

Rambam *Mishneh Torah,* Regulations for Circumcision, Chapter 2, Halacha 1: *All are suitable to perform circumcision,* even one who is not circumcised, a servant, and *a woman* and a minor; they do the circumcision in a place where there is no man." [If there are men, women should not do the circumcision; in general however it is permitted for women to do it.]

    BT *Avodah Zarah* 27a: Rather, there is a difference in opinion between them regarding a woman. According to the one, who derives it from: "But you should keep my covenant" [God, who spoke to Abraham; the covenant is expressed in circumcision] *it is not permissible*; for a woman is not suitable to do circumcisions [as the argument goes] he who has been circumcised, shall also circumcise—and according to those who derive it from: "the circumciser should be circumcised!" [the Hebrew word *circumcised* is said in *infinitivus absolutus,* a grammatical form of an absolute command, addressed to men and women alike] *it is permissible* that a woman is to be regarded as circumcised. If someone should say that a woman is not suitable, it is written [Exodus 4:25] "Zipporah took a sharp stone!?" Read: She had someone take it. But it says: "and circumcised"!? Read: and had someone circumcise; she said it to someone and he did it. But if you want, I say: She began it, and then Moses came and completed it.

Even if Tosafot "Nashim" weakens the argument, saying she cannot be *motzi* for others and saying that the *chiyuv* [obligation] is reduced to "hearing," it is quite interesting to note the presentation of the logical reasons why she should be *chayav lemikrah megillah* [obligated to read the Megillat Esther]. The reason is surely that first of all she, too, was in danger, and secondly she contributed to the rescue. Therefore she was given the right to religious activity as shown above in *Megillah* 4a. As we mentioned in the introduction, it emerges clearly from the following Tosafot "She'af" BT *Megillah* 4a that women accomplished great deeds in the public arena and did not only wile away their days as "the rulers of their kitchens":

The Rashbam [R. Samuel ben Meir, ca. 1080–1158, son of Rashi's daughter Yocheved and brother of R. Tam] said: The main part of the miracle took place because of them, in the case of Purim, it was through Esther; on Chanukah it was through Judith, and on Pesach it was in the merit of the righteous women of that generation [that we were redeemed].

See also BT *Sotah* 11b:

R. Avira reported: Through the service of pious women of that age the Israelites were released from Egypt.

The material makes it obvious that, as stated in the Talmud, women eagerly assumed religious responsibility and were active alongside men in public religious life, despite the wonderful and ever-true Jewish term *zniut*, and the serious demeanor of women meant that *zniut* never was disrespected by them. How wonderful it would be if today's women still wished to keep the values of *zniut* as already shown by the quote of Rambam, Hilchot Ishut, Perek 24, Halacha 12, which hints at contact between boys and girls and discusses modest fashion, according to which it was improper to reveal body parts. Here, too, the sensibilities of Jewry apparently have changed, unfortunately to the disadvantage of Jewish ideals. Unfortunately, in strict, halachically observant circles, when these bounds in particular are overstepped it is not seen as a transgression against the law, though the transgression is stated clearly.

But when it comes to a relaxing of the religious ban in the loosest sense of the word, in which the justification of *zniut* is given, as regarding the religious activity of a woman in the service, whereas certainly seriousness, good manners, and pure motivation are guiding her, because most women long for this, *it nevertheless* is looked upon as a "destruction" of Judaism. How beneficial it could be to have a woman in the rabbinic role to reclaim the lost meaning of *zniut* by example and through teaching.

In spite of everything, in dealing with the theme at hand one must, as is often repeated here, take both the changing times and the sensibilities of earlier times into account. In previous days, the decrees of our Sages of blessed memory, which restricted women from certain religious responsibilities and actions, were quite fitting and earn the highest respect—however, today, where the woman clearly is present in public life and accomplishes practical tasks in cooperation with men, contact has become casual. As a result, her presence among men, even in a House of God, is no longer sexually stimulating to men and certainly not to women. Many decrees of our Sages therefore were withdrawn, as we earlier have seen; particularly concerning this kind of *zniut*, they lose much of their severity.

In support of my modest opinion it may be permissible to cite the following book, Derech Pikudeycha [*The Path of Your Command*], by Zvi Elimelech Shapira, published 5634 (1874):

Regarding the prohibition against having sexual relations with a married woman—Halacha 35: In this warning it is also advised against further enjoyment with women, as our Sages of blessed memory, warned: "Do not speak too much with a woman," with "one's own wife" they said, inferring from the light to the heavy, etc.—that is, if not with "one's own wife," then so much the more "with the wife of your friend" [quote from "Teaching of the Sages" 1:5]. But here there is no longer anyone who *fears this*. I found in the book of Levush on the theme of customs, that it would likely no

longer be warned today, because women *are accustomed to be among us,* among men—
that is in the trades, in the crafts, in the shops and so on, without it coming to sinful
fantasies. Her appearance to us is like that of the "white geese" [an Aramaic expression for "without any erotic attractiveness"] because of adaptation. And so the sins
are "threshed like wheat" [Aramaic expression]. End of citation. But it must be said
that during the time when the *"Keren Yisrael"* [cornucopia of Israel] was in its proper
place [that is when all was well in Yisrael], and the economic situation of Israel was
excellent, one saw no woman outside the house, because *they were not involved in trade.*
If a man had an opportunity to see a woman, it was something special, it seized his
thoughts and his heart with fantasies—*which does not happen any more; today* under the
burden of life in the Diaspora and the difficulties of earning a living, *women work in the
trades.* It is *nothing special* to see women, it is a *matter of being accustomed,* it *does not excite*
the fantasies of a man. If this is the case, then this also corresponds with our theme
of the increased speaking with a woman. It must be seen in this way, for the view of
the woman does not excite the man and he does not slip into fantasies because of
adaptation, because she, the woman, is regularly among us.

These words provide the strongest proof yet that, as already mentioned,
much that was decreed in particular times and economic social circumstances was aimed at preserving the beautiful characteristics of the people of Israel. Frankly, it was rare to see a woman in public at all, because
in those days it was not necessary for her to leave the security of hearth
and home. But if it was important to do so, then—as we have seen—she
became openly active, without inflicting damage on her self-image or that
of society. Why should it then be impossible today, when rabbinic service
performed by women gradually becomes a necessity!

As can be seen from experience, women have led beneficially in all
careers. In societal and economic relations one is accustomed to seeing
her, so that, as is often noted, even in a male environment her presence is
not sexually stimulating. The view that she is incapable of leading or less
able to lead a life in the spiritual realm no longer is held today, as the
modern woman has delivered evidence as to her capability in this realm,
too. Earlier, unfortunately, another view was held; see BT *Yomah* 66b:

The wisdom of the woman is only in the spinning wheel.

The wheel of time turns, moving our world of Jewish thought, and with
the general development of humanity and our world, attitudes toward the
woman also have developed and changed. Many religious decrees of an
exclusionary nature for women have a *ta'am* [reason]. This changes with
the other circumstances and often becomes obsolete, as we will see in the

next section; but there also is evidence available from the book mentioned above. Even if *al tarbeh sichah im ha'ishah* ["Do not speak too much with a woman" Teachings of the Sages, 1:5] is a less stringent prohibition, it still is considered incorrect behavior. One who wishes to be true to himself will—must—admit that almost no religious Jew today has pangs of conscience in the religious sense if he talks "too much" with a woman. In fact, he barely notices whether it is too much or too little; he simply speaks with her because it is just not possible to avoid doing so. In this connection see also the *zniut* regulations mentioned in *Shulchan Aruch, Even Ha'ezer*, Regulations on Marriage, cipher 21 as

A man should keep his distance from women

almost none of which are observed any more, even in Halacha-observant circles.

However, it must be clear to us that such matters have led to a profound isolation of the woman in Judaism, particularly in areas of ritual and religion. Many falsely believe that, G-d forbid, should one wish to ease her situation, Judaism would be "destroyed," particularly if she leads the religious service.

It seems as if other non-Jewish ideologies also have had an influence on Judaism in this sense; one thinks of the old phrase *mulier taceat in ecclesia* ["The woman should remain silent in the community" (Paul, Corinthians 14:34)]. It is undeniably true, historically speaking, that women in almost all ancient cultures had to stay out of public life because the man held the leading role in this realm. If this were so in even earlier days, when matriarchy and the sad reality of polyandry dominated, in contrast, among us Jews the woman always played a leading role as mother and wife; but one also must stress that she generally was kept far from spiritual and religious ritual activity, even if praiseworthy exceptions illuminate the darkness.

Following this more general discussion, I now will attempt to demonstrate the stand of the Talmud, Rambam, Tur, and *Shulchan Aruch* on specific rabbinical functions that the woman as rabbi, just as the man, would have to fulfill. This should begin with the first point in the list of rabbinical obligations, namely *learning*, followed by *teaching*. We start therefore with a woman's learning, as it prepares the ground for this profession.

As mentioned in the introduction, the learning of our holy literature was only intended for male youth. For girls, the first contentious issue is whether they should be allowed to study at all, and second, if they are allowed, it is furthermore to be asked whether they may be taught only

Written Torah or only Oral Torah. It is already clear now that this point is debated, but *under no circumstances* is a *direct ban* in the sense of an *issur* presented. Furthermore there is *absolutely no* underlying doubt that she may teach *herself*. But let us here allow the sources to speak.

The basic source providing insight into arguments for and against women's learning is the well-known passage of Mishna BT *Sotah* 20a. Here, the question is posed, whether one is *chayav* [required] to or *patur* [exempted] from studying with her; that is, whether a father or teacher must learn with her or is not obligated to do so, or if it is not at all permitted to learn with her.

I. From this Ben Azay concluded that one is required to teach his daughter Torah, so that if she must drink the water of bitterness she will know that her merits will support her.

II. R. Eliezer said: Whoever teaches his daughter Torah, teaches her *frivolity*.

III. R. Yehoshua said: A woman prefers one *kab* [measure] of wantonness to nine *kab* of abstinence. He used to say: A dumb, overly pious man, a cunning villain, an overly pious woman and the degradations of a Pharisee, these are the ones who destroy the world. [*Context*: It relates to the water of bitterness that the suspected adulteress must drink— Numbers 5:26 ff. "It says: If she has merit, the fatal effect of the water is withheld, that is the effect is not immediate; some merit holds back for a year, sometimes two and even three years. Ben Azay concludes from this . . ."—the three citations follow.]

On the same point, Tosafot BT *Sotah* 21b remarks

Ben Azay concluded that one is required, etc.

Ben Azay did not agree with R. Elazar ben Asarya in the Talmud Yerushalmi. The latter interpreted (in *Chagigah* 3a): "Assemble the people, the men, the *women,* the children"—the men come to study, the *women* to *listen*. The result of his explanation is a commandment for women to listen so that they know how one carries out the commandment, but not for the reason that their merit will support them. [Only hearing, but no deep learning.] A certain matron asked R. Elazar: Why did three different forms of death follow from the sin of the creation of the golden calf? He responded to her: the wisdom of the woman is only in the spinning wheel. His son Hyrkan spoke to him: By not answering her with a word of Torah, every year I lose 300 *kur* [a measure] of grain. [The father had allowed the earnings to be lost because he did not want to give the correct answer.] He responded to him [father to son]: The grain should be burnt, but one should not deliver a single word of Torah to women.

Another talmudic passage that speaks against the teaching of women is BT *Kiddushin* 29b:

From where do we know [that a father is obligated to teach his son Torah]. For it is written [Deuteronomy 11:19] "You shall teach it [the Torah] to your sons." And how do we know that a mother is not obligated to do so? It is written: "And you shall teach," and one can also read it as: "You shall study." Anyone who is commanded to study Torah is likewise commanded to teach Torah, and whoever is not commanded to study is not commanded to teach. And how does one know that [a woman] is not obligated to teach herself [Torah]? For it is written, "You shall teach," which can also be read as "You shall study." One whom others are commanded to teach also is commanded to teach oneself; and one whom others are not commanded to teach is not commanded to teach oneself. And how do we know that others do not have to teach her? The scripture says: "You shall teach it to your sons and *not your daughters." [Context: Mishna BT Kiddushin 29a: "With regard to all the father's obligations related to the son, men are obligated and women are exempt. With regard to all obligations of the son to the father, both men and women are obligated. Regarding all the positive commandments bound to time, men are obligated and women exempt. But regarding positive commandments that are not time bound, both men and women are obligated. With respect to all negative commandments, whether time bound or not, both men and women are obligated to keep them.]

One should note that, in *opposition* to not teaching the daughter in Talmud Yerushalmi, *Brachot*, Perek 3, Halacha 4, I found the following essentially different view.

Impure and ill men and *impure, ill women, those who are menstruating and giving birth,* can read *Torah, learn Midrash, Halachot and Agadot* [interpretations, laws, and stories], but all this is forbidden to the man who had an accidental emission of sperm.

This text suggests an apparently limitless study for the woman, because it presupposes that someone must have studied Midrash, Halacha, and so on with her and that she then can continue to learn on her own, if one wishes to interpret this passage in this way, so that it speaks of self-education. At any rate, similar evidence for learning *Mikrah* [Bible] with her is found in BT *Nedarim* 35b.

In the same way he [another person] may teach him Midrash, Halacha and Agadah. But not the Scripture; but he may teach his sons *and daughters* the Scripture.

It certainly seems that the Talmud already had assumed this to be permissible. It is also interesting in this connection to read what Tosafot says elsewhere. See BT *Gittin* 2b Tosafot "Ed Echad":

She has the ability to learn how to slaughter.

If she can learn the *dinim* [laws] for the *shechitah* [ritual slaughter], someone has to explain these things to her; how could she correctly grasp it on her own, since learning—properly speaking—was not common for her? The *dinim* should not be taken so lightly that one might think she could learn them herself. In this connection it is interesting to note, and therefore it is already now mentioned, that in later times a written *kabalah* [certificate permitting kosher slaughter] in the responsa of Isaac b. Emanuel Lattas to two women have reached us. But that will be explored in greater depth later.

First, we will pause to consider the talmudic regulations before examining other halachic sources, so that clarity is not lost. Given what has been discussed previously, the following image speaks for itself.

Evidently, one teacher favors her studying, even saying one is *chayav* [required] to do it; one opposes it and sees it as a *tiflut* [frivolity]; and the third considers that she is not serious enough for such undertakings. Therefore it is said that one should not learn with her, but this is only meant as an *etzah tovah* [good advice]; a halachic ban however is not discernable. In the Torah, it is clear through *Hakhel* ["Assemble!"] that women were taught. However, it was said that learning should be limited to mere "listening" in order to fulfill the *mitzvah* [commandment]. But is mere listening enough for this purpose?! Is not every skill a kind of learning; for listening without understanding makes no sense? Things that are heard and not understood must be explained through questions. The result is once again the act of being taught. If one argues that women can instruct each other, it may be acceptable for all other branches of learning; but when it concerns religious study, in order to fulfill religious duties, then everything must be studied *exactly*, down to the smallest detail. Such study can only take place with *beki'im* [experts], and in those days there were not so many women among the experts; today it would already be different, since in fact women do learn nowadays. The passage BT *Kiddushin* 29b only deals with the issue that one is not *metzuveh* [commanded] to teach her. Because one who is obligated to learn also is obligated to teach; one who is not obligated to learn is also not required to teach; whoever is required to teach others must also learn. All of this does not apply to her, but she can learn *voluntarily*, because all of this is not *geserah* [law whose logic is unclear] without *ta'am* [reason], as with *shatnes* [the forbidden blend of wool and linen]. It was only recommended not to do it because of a particular estimation of the woman's mental orientation. So she is not prevented from voluntarily taking on those tasks that were barred, just as the Talmud shows that the idea of learning with her gradually took hold.

But who needs theories, when in fact talmudic examples testify eloquently for the fact that women learned from men, even *Torah sheba'al peh* [Oral Torah]. One even drew her objections into the discussion and did not always reject her so energetically as in the case of the matron in the aforementioned Tosafot. See also BT *Chullin* 109b:

Yalta [the *wife* of R. *Nachman*] spoke to R. Nachman: Mark the compassionate God, for all that God has forbidden us, he has correspondingly allowed something equal. . . . [*Continued:* He permitted us the liver instead of the forbidden blood; the blood of purity (sexual relations with the woman during the days of purity after giving birth) instead of menstruation (menstruation is considered to be postponed, even if she notices blood; see Leviticus 12:4); fat of wild animals instead of the fat from cattle; the brain of the Sibuta (a kind of fish) instead of the pig; the tongue of the fish instead of the Giruta (a forbidden bird); the divorced woman during the lifetime of her husband, instead of a married woman—etc.]

Even the justifiable anger of Yalta was handled in a talmudic report. See BT *Brachot* 51b:

Ula visited the house of R. Nachman, and after he had eaten, he spoke the *birkat hamazon* and gave R. Nachman the wine cup of blessing. Then R. Nachman spoke to him: "Let the master send the cup of blessing to Yalta" [his wife]. [Ula] responded: "R. Yochanan said that the fruit of a woman's belly is blessed only through the fruit of the husband's belly, as it says [Deuteronomy 7:13] and He will bless the fruit of your belly. It does not say the fruit of her belly, rather it says the fruit of *your* belly. It was also taught that R. Nathan said: How do you know that the fruit of a woman's belly is blessed only through the fruit of the husband's belly? It is stated: and he will bless the fruit of your belly. It does not say the fruit of her belly, rather *your* belly." When Yalta heard this, she stood up angrily, went into the wine storage room and broke four hundred barrels of wine. Then R. Nachman said to him: The master should send up another cup to her. And he [Ula] sent her the cup with a message, "All this wine in the barrel belongs to the cup of blessing." She sent back a message: "From loafers comes nonsense, from rags come vermin."

Who is not familiar with the knowledge of Beruria, wife of Rabbi Meir, the intelligent application of her abilities, combined with such good-heartedness and showing no *tiflut* [frivolity] or *divrey hevel* [trivial words], as is so often said in later discussions about the intelligence of women? See BT *Pesachim* 62b:

Now if *Beruria,* the wife of R. Meir and the daughter of Chananya ben Teradyon, *who would learn in a day three hundred rulings* from three hundred myriad rulings, nevertheless did not succeed in learning it in three years, do you say that you want to finish it in three months! [Angry response of R. Yochanan to a "young disciple."]

Also see BT *Eruvin* 53b, where she applied her teachings to life.

1. R. Yose the Galilean was going down a road when he met Beruria. He asked her, "Which is the road we take to Lod?" She said to him, "Foolish Galilean, did not the Sages say: Do not speak too much with a woman. You should have said, 'Which to Lod?'"
2. Beruria encountered a certain student who was reviewing his studies quietly. She kicked him. She said to him: "Is the following not written in Scripture: [2 Samuel 23:5] Arranged and all secure? If your learning is arranged in all your two hundred and forty-eight limbs, then it is secure and will not be forgotten; but if not, it is not secure and will be forgotten."

Beruria's talmudic agility and the delicacy of her soul become apparent in BT *Brachot* 10a:

In the neighborhood of R. Meir there lived some boors, who tormented him greatly, and R. Meir pleaded against them that they should die. Then his wife Beruria spoke to him: "You are supporting yourself on the scripture [Psalms 104:35] 'Let sins cease,' but that does not mean the sinners, only the sins. Furthermore note the end of the verse: 'and let the wicked ones be no longer there;' if the sins are eradicated, then there are no more evildoers. You should rather pray for mercy for them, so that they will repent." From then on he pleaded for mercy for them, and they repented.

Similarly to Rabbi Abahu, she, too, was consulted as an authority; see *Brachot* 10a:

A Sadducee spoke to *Beruria*: . . . [*Continued:* It is written (Isaiah 54:1): "Sing out, you who are barren, who have not given birth." Should she sing because she has not given birth!? She said to him: "Fool, see the conclusion of the verse, where it says, 'For the children of the desolate are more numerous than the children of the inhabited, said the Eternal.' The phrase 'barren, who have not given birth,' can also be so understood: Rejoice, people of Israel, who are like a barren woman, who have not borne children destined for hell as you have."]

One should also mention here the knowledgeable maidservant of Rabban Gamliel in BT *Niddah* 6b:

Come and listen: Once a maidservant of R. Gamliel was baking . . . [*continued:* loaves of *terumah* (bread sacrifice), and between each loaf she would wash her hands with water and examine herself (for menstrual blood), and at the last one, she found herself to be unclean. She came to R. Gamliel and asked him, and he decided the loaves were all unclean. She spoke to him: "Master, I have examined myself each time between each one!" So he said to her: "If that is so, then only the last one is unclean and all the others are clean." (It relates to whether the bread for the sacrifice becomes unclean through being touched by a woman who is menstruating.)]

She knew the *dinim* [laws], even if only those related to herself as a woman, so she still must have learned them; and furthermore, based on her opinion, the *kikarot shel terumah* [bread sacrifices] were seen as suitable. A mistake on her part would not only have affected herself personally but would have had further halachic implications. The fact that later there were quite learned women need only briefly be mentioned for now; however, it will be discussed in greater detail. Considering the Talmud's statements on the subject of "study," one should proceed to the words of Rambam.

Rambam, *Mishneh Torah,* Regulations for Torah Study, Chapter 1, Halacha 1: Women and servants and minors are exempt from learning Torah.

On that,

Kesef Mishneh on "Women and servants, etc.": In the first chapter of *Kiddushin* 29 we have determined that the man is *not* obligated to teach his daughter Torah, for it says in the Torah, "and teach them," their sons and *not their daughters,* . . . and in the first chapter of *Kiddushin* we have ascertained, as it is stated in the Torah: "and teach them, etc.". . . in another passage in the Torah it says: "And teach it to them, and pay attention that they carry them out," [Deuteronomy 6:4–9] we derive from this that everyone that others are responsible to teach is also obligated to learn on their own, and all who are not . . . are not . . .

See BT *Kiddushin* 29b. However, Rambam says in the same *perek* [chapter], Regulations for Torah Study, Chapter 1, Halacha 13, that

A *woman who studies* Torah *receives a reward,* but the reward is not the same as that of the man, for study was not imposed on her as a duty. . . . and although she has a reward, our Sages have ordered that the man should *not teach* his daughter Torah, *because the majority of women do not have the appropriate concentration* for study, rather they tend to use the words of the Torah *for nonsense because of their defective concentration,* therefore the Sages say, "Anyone who teaches his daughter . . ." [*continued:* "it is as if he performed frivolities." What is this about? *About the Oral Torah;* when it comes to the *Written Law* (Torah), he should ideally not teach it to her (the daughter), but if he teaches her it will *not* be seen in retrospect as if he taught her frivolities.]

On that, see Lechem Mishneh:

"A woman who studies Torah" in BT *Sotah,* Chapter "Haya Notel" (20a), it says in the Mishna, . . . that the reward supports her; in the Gemara it is said: Do you wish to say that she receives a reward through Torah study? Is she not in the category of one who is not required to do so and does it? . . . And her reward is not the same as that of the man; others say here: anyone who teaches his daughter . . . [*continued:* "commits frivolities."]

On this, Rashi is quoted in BT *Sotah* 21b, Tosafot "Ke'ilu":

Rashi, of blessed memory, said: "as if he *taught* her *promiscuity,* for she understands the contents of the Torah as *clevernesses, and she pursues her machinations secretly.* [In this case adultery is meant; knowing through Torah study how she has to behave in case her adultery is uncovered; because the reward for her Torah study will support her.]

Furthermore, the Lechem Mishneh:

They discussed the word *tiflut* [frivolities] in the Gemara. Is your opinion valid [that he actually taught her promiscuity]? Or do you prefer to say it was as if he taught her, etc. [promiscuity]. R. Abahu asked: What is the basis of Eliezer's statement? It says in the Torah: "I, wisdom, live with intelligence" [or rather cleverness, Proverbs 8:12], "therefore: If wisdom enters people, then cleverness enters with it; Rashi said that women understand the cleverness contained in the Torah and they pursue their promiscuity secretly; Rabenu [R. Yehudah Hanassi, editor of the Mishna] interpreted *tiflut* as trivial words and parables [that is, not as promiscuity]. He interpreted the Mishna as follows: Because most women cannot concentrate, etc., and in relation to women he repeated the saying put forward by R. Abahu: In what situation does this apply? In a case where wisdom enters a man, cleverness also enters, that means—only when she [wisdom] enters a man, cleverness enters. But if wisdom enters the woman, *she uses this for trivial words, and nonsense enters her as well.*" [Because the man has good intentions, he uses wisdom with cleverness; because the woman however has frivolous intentions, she employs cleverness alone, from the outset.]

We shall pause with an overview, considering what Rambam and the *poskim* [interpreters of halachic law] said, before seeing what the Tur and the *Shulchan Aruch* have to say for and against her studying and what conclusions may be drawn.

As mentioned, only sons were permitted to be taught, because it says *beyneychem* [your sons] in the *pasuk* [verse]. It is once again to be emphasized and constantly kept in view that these were only opinions, good advice of our Sages of blessed memory. Because it only says "sons," thus one should not study with one's daughter. But if she were *not allowed* to learn, how could one then say that *yesh lah sachar* [she gets a reward in the next world] *if* she studies? She would then in fact be transgressing and receiving "a reward" for this, whether or not her reward were greater than that of the man, exactly the same as his, or less.

Enough; she gets some kind of reward, and this reveals that voluntary learning on her part is not only permissible but in fact even commendable. That her learning in itself is permitted emerges from this point. It is said, as is known, that "most women are unfit for Torah study and make out of the Torah idle talk, useless nonsense." But when, as noted above, she *voluntarily* seeks to study without being required to do so, she demonstrates the wish to dedicate her attention and intellectual energy toward serious study. However, the tough reason given by Rambam is far more difficult, *"lefi aniut da'atan"* [because of the poorness of their intellect]. Here, the following might be said: First of all, if she displays "intellectual poorness" or inferior appreciation for the things to be learned, *she* cannot be condemned for the contention that the woman is naturally incapable of intellectual pursuits. Is it any wonder, given that women were kept so long from free exercise of their intellectual powers, that her lack of education resulted in her being less able than the man to follow a subject deeply when confronted with it? Is it any wonder that she remains intellectually awkward in the sense of a more profound understanding of difficult issues, if the Talmud and other texts constantly make concessions for dressing up and beauty, if her only occupation were in the home and her education only oriented toward family matters?! Too often, others directed her attention to superficial matters, leaving no room for anything more difficult. But as we have seen, nevertheless, important women have lifted themselves above the rest exactly with regard to *this*. There is just *one* single *remedy* for all these deficits that "cling" to the woman, and that is *intellectual education;* because the powers available to humans will atrophy if not used! To give a contemporary example, today it is obvious from women's intellectual pursuits and other work that they are more than *capable of concentration and possess the intellectual capacity* necessary for scientific work.

It also is clear from the previously mentioned examples that the Jewish woman *successfully* can master a talmudic style of thinking. One look at the present situation also shows that the woman increasingly is an intellectual match for the man, whether within Jewish realms or outside Jewish realms. A consideration of the intellectual features of the male sex unfortunately reveals sometimes that he, too, has a "poor intellect," estranged from the essence of Bible and Talmud, due to the abandonment of holy study in favor of worldly attractions. Much of what was *valuable* to him now seems *laughable* and it is all the worse to find this in a man, because he is appointed by G-d as a special guardian of the Torah. Both sexes today must enthusiastically acquire our Jewish knowledge. As was already said about the woman in the Talmud, she certainly has no lack of intellect; furthermore, Written Torah is allowed to her, ultimately *bedi'avad* [in retrospect], only *lechatchilah* [ideally] one warns against it as *etzah tovah* [good advice].

That which speaks against *the Oral Torah* should no longer have validity, because women who study today are not fighting for this possibility in order to commit *divrey znut* [harlotry] or to figure out how to apply what they have learned toward impure purposes. Here, too, current developments show that women *want* to learn out of *ahava tehorah* [pure love].

Naturally, there also are sad exceptions among women, but should all others suffer on their account? Are all *men* constantly mindful of their high responsibilities?! In reality, female youth are taught Talmud, for example, in the conservative Religious School on Annenstrasse.[18] And are not so many girls instructed in this discipline privately by observant teachers?! This only strengthens their love for Judaism, because through diligence and intellect they are working hard for that which had long been kept from them. The father is merely not *required* to let her learn or to teach her himself. Perhaps today's women who *wish* to learn are not among the *rov hanashim* [majority of women]—by the way, the very word *rov* implies that there must be *still others* who have very good intellect—and display this through their honest pursuit of instruction. It is possible that some lines of argument in the Talmud suit neither her nor the man. These could be then left out or dealt with later, when the intellect is better prepared for it over the course of years. Because as with every intellectual field there are also people *particularly* cut out for Talmud study and those who are *less so*. The above only touches the question of the *choice of material* and the amount, but not the principle [that she may study]. This principle remains unshaken despite some talmudic arguments that the woman must be denied *study*. Anyone who has ever taught knows that a large number of the privileged male youth are *not receptive* to *all* talmudic learning. It is also surely not possible to suggest that all men understand and are in command of every subject. It is only meant that one should give one's life in service of the Torah to the *greatest possible extent*. Each according to his abilities; one will be able to achieve more, another less.

See BT *Brachot* 5b:

Both the effort of one who accomplishes much and the effort of one who accomplishes little are equally pleasing to God, provided he directs his heart to heaven.

To return to the subject of the woman, one can learn a lot about what kind of person she is, if she sits in the house of learning and asks questions, if she stands out from the "majority" of women, and if she can be granted further teaching. I am sure that more women today are knowledgeable than before.

In the following, the halachic sources should be examined further. It reads

Tur, Yoreh De'ah, Regulations for Torah Study, cipher 245: Commandments that apply to every member of the people of Israel . . . he [the father] is not required to teach *his daughter;* we have interpreted "your sons" *and not* "your daughters"; the woman *is not required* to teach her sons.

The Bet Yosef presents the known reason for this:

"See to it that you carry out the commandments." . . . that one who is required to learn also is required to teach.

A new important point is stated in the Darkey Moshe:

The Agur[19] wrote in cipher 2 in the name of the Smag [Sefer Mitzvot Gadol (Great Book of Laws)], that the woman is required to learn those laws that relate to her. [See "Smag" in the Glossary.]

Her seriousness, as discussed above, emerges from the well-known verse cited in Darkey Moshe. Her respect for learning, her knowledge that one must bring sacrifices for this and not give so much weight to *tashmish* [sexual relations] as both Tosafot "Rotza" and Rashi state to BT *Sotah* 21b.

Rashi: "The woman prefers one measure and frivolities"—She prefers to have a smaller amount of food and provisions, along with the frivolities to be found in sexual relations, rather than nine measures (nine times as much) along with the need to separate herself from frivolities. Therefore, it is not good if she learns Torah.

Tosafot "Rotza": R. Chananel explained, a woman wants a husband who is a donkey driver who will be with her every Shabbat, to fulfill the marital duties, even though he only brings her one measure of wheat, rather than that he be a camel driver, who goes a long way, and can only fulfill his marital duties once every thirty days, even though he brings nine measures [of wheat] to support her. [*Context:* It deals with the frequency of sexual relations that the man is required to perform with his wife according to his job. A donkey driver must perform once a week on the Sabbath; the camel driver, who must travel great distances, once each month. From this R. Chananel concludes that the woman prefers one measure frivolities, that is sexual intercourse, to nine measures abstinences connected with Torah study. The rabbi furthermore believed that, particularly because the woman so desired sexual relations, it would be better to give her this one measure than to cause her to abstain over nine measures and thereby bring her into contact with the Torah.]

However, she waits for her husband, as it says in the original verse, in BT *Brachot* 17a; and in the related commentary by Rashi, she allows her husband to move to foreign cities in order to learn.

Rashi: "They wait for their husbands"—the women who support their husbands' Mishna studies and allow them to travel to another city in order to study Torah.

A wonderful example of female *zniut* and willingness to sacrifice, which delivers proof for that which Rashi (*Brachot* 17a) says, can be found in BT *Ketubot,* 62–63a:

Rabbi Akiva was the shepherd of Ben Kalba Savua [one of the richest people in Jerusalem]. His daughter saw that he [Rabbi Akiva]was modest and outstanding. [*Continued:* She said to him: "If I become betrothed to you, will you go to the Academy?" He said to her: "Yes." She became betrothed to him in secret, and she sent him away. Her father heard and banished her from his house and vowed she should not derive benefit from his property. He went (and) sat (for) twelve years in the Academy. When he returned, he brought along twelve thousand disciples. He heard an old man saying to her: "For how long will you behave like a widow during (your husband's) lifetime?" She said to him: "If he would listen to me, he would sit (there) twelve more years." He (Rabbi Akiva) said: "I am acting with her permission." He went back and sat twelve more years in the Academy. When he returned, he brought with him twenty-four thousand disciples. His wife heard (and) went out to (greet) him. The neighbors said to her: "Borrow something to wear and dress yourself!" She said to them, "A righteous man knows the soul of his cattle" (Proverbs 12:10). When she reached him, she fell on her face and kissed his feet. His attendants were pushing her away . . . (Jonas continues from this point, with her own emphases added)]: he said to them: "Leave her. *What is mine and what is yours is hers.*" [And furthermore: What comes to me through the Torah and what comes for you through the Torah, comes through her.]

The Darkey Moshe also says:

A woman who encourages her son to study Torah and is prepared to wait for her husband until he comes home from the house of study (who would not share this view?); End of citation. It is so written in the Smag [Sefer Mitzvot Gadol (Great Book of Laws)].

On that, see P'rishah [Joshua Falk Hakohen's commentary on Tur]:

"He is not obligated to teach his daughter, etc." In cipher 246 *it is written regarding the difference between the Written and the Oral* Torah (to teach Oral Torah is to teach frivolities; see there according to the correct reading, up to here the quote), that ideally he is forbidden to teach the woman [or in other words, in "retrospect" it would not be forbidden]; in any case, our teachers applied the expression *"chayav"* [*"obligated"*] because from the text it appears only that he is not required to teach it [the Torah] to her; the Sages said however: Not that he is *exempt* from teaching her [the woman], it is *actually forbidden.*

It is noted that the Rif says in Seder Kiddushin [order of marriage regulations] 12a about Perek 1, *Kiddushin*, in BT 29b:

"To teach him Torah": How do we know "teach them" means therefore the sons? In the case that the father does not teach Gemara to his son, the son must teach it to himself.

The entire line of argument is *kol shemetzuveh lilmod vachulu* [everyone who is obliged to learn, etc.] and closes with *velo benoteychem* [and not your daughters].

It is now followed by the continuation of the text in the Tur, in cipher 246:

The Rambam, of blessed memory, wrote: The woman who studies Torah receives a reward, but not the same reward as that of the man.

Rambam's entire previously mentioned citation follows immediately. It must still be noted that in the end he notes

The Sages say: One who teaches Torah to his daughter behaves as if he teaches her frivolities. What is the issue here? It is *about the Written Torah.* In fact though he should not ideally teach his daughter the *Oral Torah,* if he does teach it to her, *it is not* as if he is teaching her frivolities.

Here the opposing view is presented, fully different from what Rambam says. Rambam allows the Written Torah and the Tur allows the Oral

Torah. In this regard, Bet Yosef remarks that the various opinions are based on a *ta'ut sefer* [error].

Now the P'rishah [Yoshuah Falk Hakohen] adds his own remarkable opinion.

"Because most women do not have the ability to concentrate, and so on." But for the case in which she has taught herself and we see *that she rises above the majority,* therefore it is written that she receives a reward. This means to say, if she studies words of Torah in their place and does not misuse them for trivial words. The father, however, *is not permitted* to teach her, because perhaps she will trivialize the words of the Torah, for he does not know what is in her heart. And that is set down for us.

Furthermore:

"To what does this relate? To the *Written* Torah, but the *Oral* Torah etc.:" In Maimonides *[Mishneh Torah]*—and in the Smag [Sefer Mitzvot Gadol (The Great Book of Laws)] it says the opposite; it says in Bet Yosef that this is an error. Here as well as in the *Shulchan Aruch*. In any case, it is possible to give an interpretation for the version in the books by the Tur, which are all so written and published this way. The damages would namely be greater if she [the woman] were to abuse the *Written* Torah for trivial purposes, as if she abused the Oral Torah, and that is made clear to us. In any case the woman is *obligated* to *learn those laws that relate to her.* (This is what the Agur wrote [Jacob ben Yehudah Landau, fifteenth-century Italy], cipher 92, in the name of the Smag.). And the woman who helps her sons or husband to be occupied with Torah study receives a part of the reward *together with him* (Hagahot Maimoni [commentary on Maimonides, *Mishneh Torah*], Chapter 1, about Torah Study).

Let us look once again at what Bayt Chadash says:

Yoreh De'ah, Regulations on Torah Study, cipher 246: It is written, that one [the man] should not teach his daughters Torah, Mishna, Chapter "Haya Notel."

What Bayt Chadash states here is known already, so the view expressed in BT *Sotah* 20a and further need not again be recorded. The following is very interesting and noteworthy considering his aforementioned confrontation:

Bayt Chadash: Ideally women should not *learn according to a set manner, rather they should simply listen,* as is put forward in the commandment in the Torah portion "Hakhel"— so that they know how to follow the commandments, but as far as learning according to a set manner, ideally they should not. However, if someone *teaches her, it does not*

mean in retrospect that he had taught her frivolities; otherwise it also would be only frivolities for her to have *learned through listening, which then must equally be forbidden,* there
would be no *commandment to learn* in "Hakhel" that applies also to the women. As
always: The commandments *that the woman needs, she must learn,* thus women recite the
blessing over Torah study on all days [for example within the framework of a morning service or at Shabbat services], as it is written in Orach Chayim, cipher 47.

At first Bet Yosef says regarding Orach Chayim in cipher 47 in the *Hil-chot Birkot Hashachar* [regulations for the morning blessings]:

The Agur also wrote in the name of R. Yehudah of Molin that women do make the
blessing over the Torah even though they are not obligated [to learn Torah], and
not only that but also about the father who teaches his daughter Torah, it is as if
he teaches her frivolity, that this relates to the *Oral Torah,* but not to the *Written*
Torah. And although the formulations contained in the blessing are "to deal with
the words of the Torah," which implies the Oral Torah, in any case one is not
allowed to change the formulation of the blessing. In addition women also pronounce the *blessing over the reading about the sacrifices.* According to the rabbinical
decree, *the prayers are the counterpart of the sacrifice,* and they [the women] *are obligated
to pray;* therefore they are also obligated to *read the passage of the burnt offering and the
offerings in general* [which also contain passages from the Oral Torah]. All the more
so according to the words of the Smag [Sefer Mitzvot Gadol (Great Book of Laws)],
who wrote that women are obligated to learn the laws that apply to them. [In other
words: if a woman must say the prayers, or rather the blessings, which count as a
substitute for the former sacrifices, to which she was equally obligated, then she is
also obligated to those prayers, or rather blessings, related to Torah study, in this
case regarding the regulations for offerings, which are contained in the prayer itself.
That is, the woman not only is allowed, rather she must learn.]

On that, *Shulchan Aruch,* Orach Chayim, Regulations for the Blessings,
cipher 47, paragraph 14:

Women recite the blessing over the Torah.

Also on that, Taz:

Although they are not required to learn . . .

He continues as in the Tur with almost exactly the same view. Because the
Shulchan Aruch adds little to the Tur that is new on the theme of study,
his view now can be presented here, so as to stop and look back.

Shulchan Aruch, Yoreh De'ah, cipher 246, paragraph 5: A woman who studies Torah receives a reward, but not the same reward as the man.

He brings out the same references as Rambam and the Tur, saying that her studying would be *tiflut* [frivolities] due to her ignorance. The Mapah [of R. Moses Isserles] also introduces the important comment that will be handled in this discussion.

Mapah: In any case the woman is obligated to learn those laws that apply to her.

Taz adds something interesting to *aval Torah shebichtav* [but the Written Torah], according to which he shows an interest in the various views of the Tur, whether Oral or Written Torah may be studied. He states the following:

It seems to me that there [this refers to the commandment of hakhel in Deuteronomy 31:10–13. Every seven years the king assembles the people and reads them the text of the Torah] the king dealt only with *simple interpretations.* And this is truly permitted *even ideally,* according to our opinion, as is the daily custom. But this is not the case when learning methods of wisdom for studying *profound explanations* of Torah passages, which is ideally prohibited. And this is clearly substantiated in the Talmud: "The men [come to the hakhel gathering] to learn and the women to listen." That means that women *do not pay any attention, aside from listening to the simple explanation.* [In other words, there are clearly two "parts": on one hand the simple things for hearing, and on the other hand the profound explanations for study.]

The Tur and *Shulchan Aruch* have had their say, so one pauses. It will be observed what kinds of views these are and what conclusions one can draw from them. It should be once again emphasized that reasons are given for the negative offensive measures against women's study and that the reasons themselves already have been debated variously in the sources themselves. In their order, the excerpts shall be reviewed.

There is nothing to say about the *panim* [reasons] of the Tur, which are covered by previous citations. What is new is the comment of Darkey Moshe, which turns up frequently.

He says she *must* study *dinim* [laws] "related to the woman." Fine, but anyone who knows how *dinim* are made must say, in order to be able to correctly grasp the *niddah, chalah, hadlakat haner* [regulations regarding menstrual impurity, on the separating of dough when baking bread, and on the lighting of Shabbat candles—the three main areas assigned to women according to Jewish religious law]—just to name only the specific *reshut* [area under the rule] of the woman—one already must possess seriousness and insight in order not to fulfill these matters bluntly and insensitively; but then they would have failed their purpose. (See BT *Shabbat* 31b, "Bameh madlikin" ["With what to kindle"]: Three infringements lead to the death of a woman during delivery: If they are not careful in their menstruation, with the separating of dough, and in lighting candles.) Therefore one must proceed from Written Torah to Oral Torah; because the woman is not so limited that she does everything slavishly, without putting life into these things through her questions. But aside from the three aforementioned obligations, a woman must fulfill other things, or if her husband is absent or has died; one thinks of *Chanukah, Havdalah, Kiddush, Megillah,* the redemption of the firstborn son,[20] *Brit Milah,* and the great realm of kitchen matters[21] among others.

One should not say that women in times gone by fulfilled all without immersing themselves in the "Sea of the Talmud."[22] The matter is just not so simple.

Here again the circumstances of time testify. If women earlier did *not* understand something, it was easy enough for them to ask their well-informed husbands or, if they were not married, their father or other relatives. Not to mention, one must not forget that Jewish life overall in those days was still a beautiful life steeped in Halacha. Today, as already pointed out earlier, our Jewish life has become distant from its direct relation to Halacha, due to changed life circumstances. But what effects the woman in particular—it must be said once and for all, openly and undisguised—is that she is in fact distant from the thinking of the Talmud, because she was not prepared for such thinking due to the constant distancing from learning across the generations. With shocking clarity this holds true for the *modern* woman, because modern times and the *notions of man* as of *woman* are turned toward completely different pages of life.

If a Jewish woman with such "preparation" were encouraged to fulfill our holy obligations, she would likely ask why, with amazement: I was not raised with these things! To guard against the danger of her rejecting it all out of accidental ignorance, because one cannot treasure what one does not know, it is an *urgent necessity* to make the incomprehensible comprehensible, in stunningly clear description. Then the terms "light-headed" and "intellectually poor" soon will make way for better terms and the sad *takanot* [rabbinical statutes] of our Sages of blessed memory also will become obsolete, particularly considering that great scholars of the past seriously wondered whether these arguments always would exist.

One recalls, for example, the important observation that particularly capable women who are eager to learn for themselves stand out from the *rov hanashim,* "majority of women," and thus are rewarded for their study.

It also is fitting in this connection "that the father does not know what is *belibah*" [in her heart]. But if she says, I *want* to learn, then one can today easily assume, according to what the Talmud and Bible report about noble women, that they will remain true to these things with distinguished matter-of-factness and loyal love. In general the Talmud says one should judge the people *lechaf sechut* [decide in favor] [*Pirkey Avot,* "Teachings of the Sages"]. Even if in times past unfortunate experiences led our Sages to make negative decrees, today we have evidence that optimism regarding women's dedication is not unjustified.

Even if unpleasant impulses appear in the course of her spiritual work—somewhat more than for the man—due to her lack of experience, one must have faith, according to the old talmudic view; see BT *Pesachim* 50b:

> A person should always engage in the study of Torah and the performance of mitzvoth even though it is not for its own sake, because from learning Torah and performing a mitzvah not for its own sake he will eventually come to learn Torah or perform a mitzvah for its own sake.

The religious power of Jewish scripture certainly ignites the woman's mind if clever teachers can clarify the sometimes abstract themes of the Talmud. Time and humanity change; but the expression *Ayn bor yiray chet* [No boor fears sin, "Teachings of the Sages," 2:5] always remains; if one gives women only "scattered crumbs" of the delicacies of Jewish wisdom, then it is little wonder that, due to limited understanding, she considers it all to be pointless. One need only think of the regulations regarding *niddah* [menstrual impurity], which go into minute detail and are understandable only in the context of the entire body of talmudic regulations.

If one looks more closely at the term *hashayachim*—"what relates to the woman"—here, too, time raises her voice of warning. The responsibilities of being a woman and mother are today *greatly increased!* Apart from the nonmarried woman, who must hold an independent job and also might want to choose a career in Jewish theology, a mother has much more difficult things to manage nowadays than before.

One must remember, today the critical voices of children penetrate their mothers' ears; skeptical expressions through which the environment external to Jewish life and cultural activity apply the tone of doubt and criticism to our sacred values. The mother can arm her child with the knowledge and Jewish self-confidence, due to the wisdom and gentleness that the Talmud attributes to her, particularly those mothers who learned much about Judaism in their own childhood and are, like the son and the father, steeped in the Jewish spirit. But if the mother stands ignorant before these questions and before her unsteady child, then her son or daughter will turn from her. One must be honest and admit that one factor that creates a gap between parents and children and destroys our beautiful family life is the inability of parents to understand the doubts of youth. But a mother who herself has studied also has had her time of doubting, and so she can recognize that which her own child must go through as a reliving of her own past. She will therefore hold fast to the child by sharing her own tribulations and showing how she herself found the way from darkness to light. No matter that the child then goes its own way—that must be the case; but understanding and love, harmony, and thankfulness unite young and old and those of varying views.

From this digression into practice, let us return to theory. We do not distance ourselves from the foundation of Judaism and Halacha if she is permitted to learn. It is *never* said that woman absolutely may *not* study anything. Some permit "written teachings," others "oral teachings," still others only written teachings but also that which "is related to them," in other words, part of the oral teachings.

The word *ha'ozeret* [helpful woman] is not violated if one adds that she allows her husband to go to study, that she urges her children to study, helps explain difficult matters, and so on. So one sees that the sources, too, consider her helpful intervention indispensable. Today it is even more necessary, as has been shown.

There is the view that it would be an *issur* [prohibition] to teach her, according to the P'rishah's interpretation of the Tur. Nevertheless it is interesting to see that particularly the P'rishah later expresses the broad-minded view, which however is not completely new, that she will be rewarded if through her own enterprise she stands out from the "majority" of women who are concerned only with trivialities.

The father is not permitted to learn with her. This is not categorically declared, but rather the aforementioned reason is given: that he does not know what foolishness hides in her heart. One must be allowed to note that if he knows she possesses—instead of foolishness—a burning inner enthusiasm for Jewish teachings, then one may in fact study with her. That this humble opinion is not to be dismissed out of hand is made clear by the fact that there have been learned women. From whence came the knowledge of Rashi's daughter and granddaughter, as we will later see; whence comes a Beruria, a Yalta?! One such as Beruria cannot possess such enormous knowledge through simple listening or meager self-education.

Many women could have reached similar heights of knowledge if they did not cling overwhelmingly to the basic principle of "*Ayn ishah ela leyofi*" ["a woman only for beauty" from BT *Ketubot* 59b].

For natural beauty wins out, whether or not women spend time thinking about makeup and "fraudulent beautifiers." If, rather, her spirit is
exercised through learning, her horizon extended, her essence refined, so
will she increasingly hold to the belief that the true worth of people consists in their *inner* beauty.

One can naturally say, remaining within the halachic line of thought,
that few women exclaim, "I want to learn!" However, this objection does
not hold water because here again one's upbringing has a major influence.
What one does not know, one cannot want. If the son announces, "I want
to study," it is only when one "offers" him the opportunity to study in the
form of lessons. If one were to induct both [daughters and sons] into study
darkah and *al pi darkoh* [according to her ways and his ways], then both
would love our Torah, or in any case show their loving appreciation for it.

Regarding the controversy between the Tur and the others, as to
whether one should teach girls Written Torah or Oral Torah, the P'rishah
gives a *ta'am kizat* [lesser reason], namely that it is worse to turn the Written Torah into *divrey havay* [trivial words] than to do the same with the
Oral Torah. Now, if a stricter *issur* [prohibition] were imposed regarding
these matters, is it possible that there was difference of opinion among the
scholars?!

One sensed at that time, too, that women cannot exist without any
instruction whatsoever. A clear *command for* her studying was not available, a clear *prohibition* against teaching her also was not available, thus
there was an allowance for various opinions.

The Bayt Chadash, too, says clearly that study by women—even if not
covering such a broad field—cannot be seen as *tiflut* [frivolities], for in
that case "a simple listening" may also not be allowed. For the purpose
of fulfilling mitzvot, "simple listening," he says, is a mitzvah; however it
should only not take place as *limud derech kavah* [studying according to
a set manner]. However, it is stated that this is only *lechatchilah* [ideally],
bedi'avad [in retrospect] it is not *tiflut*.

We have seen from this exposition that study even of the Written Torah
without further explanation is no longer possible today. One finds oneself therefore, due to our changing times and conditions, in the predica-
ment that one can well describe in Hebrew as *bish'at hadchak* [in times
of need],[23] and it is fully appropriate to say what *bedi'avad* [in retrospect]
is allowed is then also *bish'at hadchak lechatchilah* [ideally in times of
need]. See Yoreh De'ah 23, Pithe Teshuva, small paragraph 6:

In addition it is written that if a man who performs ritual slaughter expects to find
something in the gullet of a bird [a stone or a worm, which would make the animal
nonkosher and thus unsuitable for consumption] it is nevertheless permitted ideally

- 29 -

Berurias talmud. Gewandtheit und Feinheit der Seele gehen

aus b. Berach. 10a hervor. ....משום דכתיב יתמו חטאים מי

כתיב חוטאים חטאים כתיב ועוד שפיל לסיפה דקרא ורשעים עוד
אינם כיון דיתמו חטאים ורשעים עוד אינם

Ebenso, wie R. Abahu als Autorität befragt wird, so auch sie.

cf. das. Berach. 10a. אמר לה ההוא צדוקי לברוריא

.... אמר ליה החוא צדוקי לרבי אבהו ...

Erwähnt sei auch hier die kundige Magd des Rabbon Gamliel in

b. Niddah 6b מעשה בשפחתה של רבן גמליאל שהיתח אופה...

Sie musste mit ד"ים Bescheid, wenn sie sich auch auf ihre

Person bezogen, gelernt musste sie sie haben, und es geht

ja noch weiter, dass auf Grund ihrer Aussage die כברות של

תרומה als geeignet anzusehen waren. Ein Versehen ihrerseits

hätte ja nicht nur ihre Person betroffen, sondern weitere

halach. Folgen gehabt. Dass es später Frauen gegeben hat,

die viel gelernt hatten sei hier nur angedeutet, es wird das

noch in den späteren Ausführungen erörtert werden.

Nachdem der Talmud zu dem Punkte "Lernen" gesprochen hat, soll

zu dem übergegangen werden, was Rambam sagt. משה בר מיימון

משנה תורה -- יד חחזקה , הלכות תלמוד תורה : פרק א" הל"א

נשים ועבדים וקטנים פ ט ו ר י ם מתלמוד תורה
נשים ועבדים וכו": כבתרא משנה Dazu

פ"ק דקדושין (כ"סו אמרינן ד א י ן אדם חייב ללמד את בתו

תורה מדכתיב ולמדתם אותם את בניכם ולא את בנותיכם ...

ואמרינן ... בפ"ק דקידושין דמדכתיב ולמדתם וכו" ...
ואותן/ את

וכתיב בדוכתא אחרינא ולמדתם אותם וסמרתם לעשותם ילפינן

שכל מאחרים מצוים ללמדם מצוה ללמד עצמו ובכל שאין ..אינו

cf. b. Kidd. 29b. Weiter sagt רמב"ם im selben פרק aber

חל" י"ג א ש ה ש ל מ ד ה תורה יש לה שבר אבל אינו

כשבר האיש ..ואע"פ שיש לה שכר צוו חכמים ש ל א ילמד אדם את

בתו תורה מפני ש ר ו ב ה נ ש י ח א י ן ד ע ת ן מ כ ו ו נ ת

להתלמד אלא הן מוציאות דברי תורה לדברי ה ב א י לפי

ע נ י ו ת ד ע ת ן אמרו חכמים כל המלמד את בתו ...במה דברים אמורים

בתורה שבעל פה אבל תורה שבכתב ל א ילמד אותה

ל כ ת ח ל ה ואם למדה אינו כמלמדה תפלות

to slaughter after only one cut, *for in a time of need it [the law] is like "in retrospect,"* end of the citation of his statement, "and it is written . . . etc.," see above, the small paragraph 3. [In other words: If a chicken or goose or other normally kosher fowl is slaughtered for food, the slaughterer must first check the gullet to see if the animal is really kosher. For this purpose he must make two cuts in the neck. With this he fulfills not only the ritual requirements but also carries a social responsibility. For a poor, hungry family the assessment of the man who performs ritual slaughter that the animal is not kosher could mean a great misfortune. "Ideally" the slaughterer should make two cuts. But in difficult times it is satisfactory—"in retrospect"—if he only makes one cut. That means that in times of hardship, relationships reverse. "In retrospect" becomes "ideally."]

If this reason were not, as I believe, key, how could one maintain public girls' schools, where even Oral Torah and Written Torah are taught *derech kavah* [according to a set manner]? One would then be required, if one were to take this strictly, to *close* all current Jewish girls' schools! But it is impossible to be content today with what girls learn "by chance" or through listening. That should be noted with regard to Written Torah. It is very much worth pointing out that the previous remark is followed by the interesting, lenient comment that we so often encounter. With this comment we enter the realm of "oral teaching"; for it means, again, that *those* matters related to the woman *must* be studied by her. As is demonstrated in this work, it is not enough for these passages meant for women to be simply learned without talmudic concepts, whose essence was not received only from the realm of the Written Torah, and secondly, without explanation they would not be understandable to her.

Thus if she already is allowed to learn *some Torah sheba'al peh* [Oral Torah], for which one must credit her with understanding, is it then so difficult to deliver *more* to her; yes, also the extended areas of the Talmud, to breathe that very spirit of the Talmud which contained the first regulations she *had* to learn!? Were it halachically not permissible to study, then one could not allow those things to be studied that relate specifically to her, for it would be a violation of principle. But she *must* be allowed to learn something, as is well enough known, thus more Talmud can be offered according to the mental faculties. (What is said above applies here as well; that today "times of need" prevail, so she *must* learn; and it has been shown that to learn "in retrospect" is also permissible.)

The reason that the Taz now gives, that only *peshutey hadevarim* [simple meanings of words] enter women's heads, is just as weak as many other reasons put forward, but at least it is a very flexible reason. He does not consider it an *issur* [prohibition], despite his opinion that she can only grasp the simple words of Torah; however, modern experience speaks against this!

But even if one accepts this reason, one can also say, if the teacher notices from questions or such that there are women whose spirit can grasp *more* than "simple meanings of words," then one is permitted certainly to give her more difficult and deeper explanations. Therefore one can again say that if the circle of intelligent women grows, one does not in *principle* need to ban learning; and the circle has grown: not only today, but in previous times, there were women, as has been and will be noted, who clearly have shown that they understand far more than *peshutey hadevarim*!

According to my modest knowledge and possibilities to draw conclusions, study for women is at the very least not prohibited by religious law. *Direct permission* in full clarity cannot be found for *everything;* for the "written teachings" in some cases study expressly is allowed; for the other branches of learning a directly stated ban is not found.

Thus one can conclude that study of both "written teachings" and "oral teachings" is permitted, that in fact the reasons no longer apply in *our time* in all its difficulty. As Rambam says, "teaching should only be given to a worthy student who is also distinguished in his deeds."

Rambam, *Mishneh Torah,* Regulations for Torah Study, 4:1: No one should be taught Torah except for the worthy pupil of distinguished behavior.

The woman of today may similarly be counted in the group of students who are worthy of receiving God's teachings. As has often been stressed, women must also have learned and have had the necessary understanding if they received the *kabalah* [certificate permitting kosher slaughter], to *pasken* [render a Jewish legal decision] on various matters in the household, as will soon be demonstrated in detail here; if they could write difficult answers—as Rashi's daughter did for him—and if they—as the learned Kröndel, wife of Rabbi Steinhart—could make important commentary on the Midrash [interpretation of sacred scriptures].

In terms of the learned Kröndel, see the *Jahrbuch der jüdischen literarischen Gesellschaft* [Yearbook of the Jewish Literary Society], 1908, page 197. It states

R. Joseph Steinhart had three wives. The second wife was the well-known "Rebbetzin Kröndel," daughter of R. Löb of Berlin, sister of R. Yeshaya Berlin (Pick),[24] of R. David Berlin, of R. Lipmann, rabbi in Eisenstadt, and of R. Hirsch, rabbi in Lissa, sister-in-law of R. Naftali Hirsch Katzenellbogen, rabbi in Mergentheim and Mannheim; granddaughter of Mordechai Moshiach of Eisenstadt, who died in 1729 in Bratislava. Kröndel's first marriage was to Yehiel Pressburg (also known as Michel Simon), and after his death in 1754 she became the wife of Steinhart. She was a *G-d fearing, clever, and learned* woman held in high esteem by her husband. He reported in the preface to [his book] *Zichron Yosef* [Memories of Yosef] that it was his wife who first urged him to publish this work.

Surprising explanations of Midrash and *Piyut* [interpretations of sacred texts and liturgic poetry] were *cited* in her name. (Rabbi Yeshaya Berlin calls her "My sister, whose fame reaches to the furthest corners of the earth." She died after six months of suffering, on the first day of Sivan, May 30, 1775.)

These few examples wish to testify for a hopeful view, which would support to a much greater extent the attempt to teach women.

Substantially less halachic source material is to be found regarding the second very important point of the rabbinical role, whether she may be engaged as a *teacher* for the community. Again, the sources themselves should provide the initial picture; afterward, a personal view shall be stated. First,

Rambam, *Mishneh Torah,* Regulations for the Study of Torah, Chapter 2, Halacha 4: One *who has no wife should not teach* children, *because of the mothers* who pick up their children; *women should not teach* children because of the *fathers* who pick up their sons. [In other words: If an unmarried man teaches little children and encounters their mothers, who have come to fetch their children from the school, it can come to awkward contact; and just the same in reverse, if women teach children and their fathers come to pick them up at the school.]

The Kesef Mishneh adds only sources from BT *Kiddushin* 82a, saying the following:

Mishna: *Someone who is single* may not teach children, just as a woman may *not be a teacher* for children. R. Elazar said, even one who has *no wife may not be a teacher for children.* End of quote.

The Gemara on this says

What is the reason a bachelor may not teach young children? . . . [*Continued:* for it was taught in a Baraita: The Sages said to R. Yehudah: Jewish people are not suspected of homosexual acts or acts of bestiality.] Rather, a bachelor should not teach because of the children's mothers, and a woman should not teach because of the children's fathers. [*Continued:* R. Elazar said, also one who has *no* wife. They asked: One who has no wife at all, or whose wife is not living with him? Come and listen:] Also one who has a wife who does not live with him may not teach small children.

A second section on the teaching of others is found in Rambam, *Mishneh Torah*, Regulations on Sexual Prohibitions, Chapter 22, Halacha 13. It must be particularly emphasized here that more exact reasons are given as to why she should not teach others. Let us first see what is written:

Whoever has no wife should not teach children, because of *the mothers* who *come* to the school to their children, which could bring him to condition of excitement; and so should women *not teach* children, because of the fathers who come to their children, whereby she could find herself *alone in a room* with them [the fathers]. The teacher does not need to be together with his wife in the school, rather she is in their home and he teaches at his place of work.

Tur and *Shulchan Aruch* should be added here immediately, in that they do not differ much from Rambam.

Tur, Yoreh De'ah, Regulations for Torah Study, cipher 245: The woman *is not* obligated to teach her sons.

The verse cited by the Bet Yosef regarding the issue of "study" also applies here to "teaching."

Whoever is obligated to learn is obligated to teach; and whoever is not obligated to learn *is not obligated to* teach.

Furthermore, the Tur says the same, as is known from Rambam:

Yoreh De'ah, Regulations for Torah Study, 245: He who has no wife *shall not teach* children, because of the fathers.

And in addition the well-known line [from the same text]:

And the woman *shall not teach* children because of their fathers.

The D'rishah says she should not teach because her husband is not always at home:

It is not man's way to stay at home.

Thus it already is mentioned here, as is to be carefully noted, that if she is to consider teaching *at all,* she therefore (1) must have learned something herself, and (2) actually, in principle, *nothing opposes* her teaching as such.

The D'rishah also gives *reasons* for her not to teach: *mishum giruy* [because of stimulation] for the man and *mishum yichud* [because of being alone together with a man] for the woman.

D'rishah: Rather the prohibition, because she is together with them, it will mean that she prepares herself for being together and could enter into adultery.

The Bet Yosef also discusses and cites this in the same way as does the Gemara. The well-known prohibition appears that a man may not teach if he has no wife. In that context, the well-known, controversial question appears, as to whether that condition of not-having-a-wife means that he has *absolutely* no wife, or if she is simply not in the city where he stays; he follows the opinion, "She is in her house and he is teaching at his workplace." Even if this passage on the prohibition of teaching for the man does not relate directly to the prohibition of teaching for the woman, nevertheless it is important as evidence to be shown later and they belong together in this connection.

It should briefly be noted that the Bayt Chadash says:

Yoreh De'ah, Regulations for Torah Study, cipher 245, paragraph 9: The woman is not obligated to teach her sons. One who has no wife should not teach.

He too hints at the controversy as to whether it means that the man has no wife, that is, that he has never married a woman, or whether she is not with him. Yes, he goes even further: even if she has died, it is also prohibited for him to teach.

Even if he has a wife, if she is not with him but stays in another city, it is also *forbidden*.

An exception is given if it were a location where it is not common that the mothers bring their sons there; see also:

In a place where it is not *common that women bring their children* to the teacher, there one may teach, even if he has no wife, and we do not need to fear that there would be sexual relations between men.

With regard to teaching by women, he does not want to approve because of *yichud*:

Paragraph 10: "The woman should not teach children": Because the woman doesn't teach in the school but rather in the home, there would be truly reasons to fear a forbidden meeting with a man, when her husband is not there.

Even if she is married and her husband lives in the same place, there is a danger of *yichud* when teaching in the home. It is interesting to note already here that there is no mention of her teaching in a *public* school.

The *Shulchan Aruch* should only be mentioned briefly here, as it does not add anything new:

Yoreh De'ah, Regulations for Teachers, cipher 245, paragraphs 20 and 21:
20: One who has no wife should not teach children, because of their mothers, etc.
21: The woman should not teach children, because of their fathers, etc.

The Shach provides the parallel of Tur, Even Ha'ezer, regulations on marriage, conclusion of reference 22. It says the following:

One who has no woman should not teach children, because of the mother who comes to her children at the school; he could find himself in *a stimulated state because of the women;* and so also the woman should *not* teach children, because of their fathers, who come because of their children and find themselves in a room *together with her.*

The commentaries of Bet Shmuel, for example, add nothing new aside from *mishum giruy* [because of stimulation] and *mishum yichud* [because of a man and woman being alone together].

Following the aforementioned sources, an opinion now will be drawn from the conclusion. What conclusion can be reached from these sources? May women teach in *public institutions*?! The answer appears to be No, and one apparently should draw the necessary consequences already regarding studying; for the case mentioned here, it means all female Jewish teachers would have to be removed from public educational service and be prohibited from teaching privately. However, one should not forget in this connection, that at the same time, if one were to take this prohibition to its ultimate consequences, also all *"Bachurim"* [single men], perhaps even those whose wives do not live in the same place, would have to be dismissed from teaching posts, whether they are working as teachers or heads of religious schools.

We see in contemporary Jewish life that, in observant circles, ladies, unmarried gentlemen, and widowers are teaching in schools. As far as it is possible to see, the consequences feared in the Talmud do not occur.

If one sets practice aside and turns back to Halacha, the matter is clear, that the explicitly stated *ta'am* [justification] has begun to sway once again with the progress of time and the resulting new circumstances. Even where *yichud* is mentioned—in teaching and in other situations with few exceptions where the *yichud* commandment must be followed—it is no longer maintained.

The reason is likely to be found in the fact that the sensual life of both sexes—aside from those with abnormal personalities—has changed. A further essential condition—as already depicted—is that woman and man work together in career and social life, so their presence is not accompanied by anything stimulating in the sense of *yichud*, even if the man and the woman are alone (together). As a small digression it is suggested to refer one's attention to the following for clarification. It is almost taken for granted today that one looks harmlessly at a woman and then turns one's glance away from her without having the feeling of having done something against Jewish views; according to BT *Avodah Zarah* 20a, specifically "looking at a woman" is not permitted. That is to say,

May one observe a woman?—It is taught: [Deuteronomy 23:10] Protect yourself from all evil, one may not observe a beautiful woman, even if she is single, *nor a married woman, even if she is ugly, and also not the colorful clothes of a woman.*

Does any Jewish man who naturally sees the Talmud and legal codes as *binding* still take such things into consideration?! One is reminded in this context also of the handshake and the counting of money into a woman's hand, and such.[25] I believe the reason for *this* is not that he is a *poretz geder* [one who "breaks the fence" (Ecclesiastes 10:8)] but rather it lies in the development of time, that necessarily brings with it *another attitude* toward womankind. And who knows—it must be said here in all modesty—what other *takanot* [rabbinical decrees] related to the woman our Sages of blessed memory would have given, had the woman been granted the same status in their day as she receives now, and if she had had the possibility to appear in public life as capable and even distinguished, and yet in keeping with the sense of *zniut*?

Returning to the textual sources, one must in fact keep in mind that the matter of woman in public teaching positions is never raised, but she appears to be considered *capable* of teaching—regardless of where.

Then she must have learned something, in order to allow the possibility to be taken into consideration at all, that children should be taught, "even if at all only at home." One is only speaking of "at home." I assume that our Sages of blessed memory never considered the possibility of her working in a school because taking on a public role was impossible for her; see in this connection only Rambam, as tracing this in the other sources would lead too far. According to *Mishneh Torah*, Regulations for the Service to King, Chapter 1, Halacha 5,

A *woman should not* be placed in the position of king, because it is said: [Deuteronomy 17:15] "You shall appoint a king over you," . . . and *not a queen; in all public positions* of Israel, only *men* shall be installed.

On this, Radbas says:

And in case you protest that it is in fact written: *"Deborah, the prophetess, judged* Israel," this is not a contradiction, *for she taught* the laws, or also, it was *on God's command.*

It is also a reason why women cannot be introduced into public service, and the position of teacher is also a form of public service.

A new perspective can however be won through the commentary of the Radbas regarding the actions of one Deborah. How was it possible that she taught men?!? If it occurred by a command of G-d, then why should she not be considered a judge, as she clearly was a prophetess?! If one does want to assume an intervention by G-d, why then should not the highest form of his intervention be accepted, for just as she, as a prophetess, taught men and stood over them, so can that also happen with a judge, for G-d appoints people according to his wishes. If she had however only told them the legal regulations that had to be fulfilled according to which one judged, that would not be anything new in relation to her status as prophetess, so that one would have had to assume an intervention by G-d.

There are, however, also views that do not assume *al pi hadibur* [God's command]; one is reminded of the related passages of Tosafot. If her teaching took place not through special intervention, how then, first, could she have learned so much, and second, how could she work as a teacher, if only teaching of great scholars, where the concern about *yichud* no longer applies; perhaps, though, according to former attitudes the justification of *giruy* [sexual stimulus] might have come into consideration. Thus she breaks through the lines of convention and enters the scene as a teacher.

As far as taking on a public role, which is not permitted to woman, there is one woman, as mentioned earlier—Queen Salome Alexandra—who also breaks the chain of women who remain distant from public life. After all is said and done, it is not too revolutionary or un-Jewish—in consideration of all the points discussed up to now—to in fact see it as permissible for her to work as teacher or rabbi.

All peoples have a common law, in addition to *written* law. Today in practice the woman has more tasks to fulfill than before; she must take on public roles, and so it has also occurred that among us Jews she gradually has begun to work as a teacher. Even in former days some women held public positions, apparently despite Halacha, as has been shown. Life does not allow itself to be fully controlled by *theory*.

It is certainly in keeping with the sense of our Sages to examine here the reasons for prohibiting women from teaching. They themselves say, "in a city where the mothers do *not* bring their children to school, then a man without a wife can teach. Let us examine in this sense the prohibition aimed at female teachers: In our cities and in our schools today there is *no* danger of *yichud*. Even when the female teacher pauses in a room alone with a father, they are not in fact "alone"; the building is filled with activity and there is a chance that students, the headmaster, and other officials would enter the classroom. That is to say, *yichud* in the conditions of today's public schools completely ceases to be an issue; and since *nothing* else stands in the way, she therefore also could be a teacher.

It could happen that those wishing to take the law extraordinarily strictly would say, even if the *ta'am* [reason] given for something is no longer valid, the prohibition or commandment that it supported remains valid. I believe, however, that I may say that here it has nothing to do with an absolutely strict prohibition, as for example with *treyfot* [unkosher food]. From the spirit of the *takanah* [rabbinical decree], it is by the way clearly seen that the *reason* was primary in banning teaching; thus the "decree" stands or falls together with the reason for it.

However, an opinion that may speak on behalf of learning would be the *takanot* [decrees] according to which "the majority of the community cannot honestly stand by them" [they are too strict, thus unrealistic]. It will soon be demonstrated how this is to be understood.

Let it first be stated that the girls' schools of today, and we do have Jewish girls' schools, would not be *permitted* to exist without female teachers. According to the size of the teaching staff, the number of female teachers must be taken into consideration at least with institutes of higher education.

Thus we see that in an era where we Jews in the world have entered this realm, too, as equals, the taking on of public teaching roles for women has become essential.

Admittedly, today we have no *Bet Din* [religious court], to come back to what was brought up on the previous page—but from the spirit of the Jewish world of ideas, which draws its support from Rambam, the following is to be inferred:

Rambam, *Mishneh Torah,* Regulations on Rebellion, Chapter 2, Halacha 5: A court that considers it urgent to pass a law, enact a decree or decide on a custom, *must advise and know in advance whether the greater part of the community is prepared to adhere to it* or if they are *not* able to adhere to it. There should be no laws passed over the community, *except for those to which the majority can adhere.*

Halacha 7: They passed a law and it appeared *to be valid in the whole of Israel,* for many years. After much time had passed, another court arose, which investigated and found that this law was in fact not followed everywhere in Israel. This court is justified to *nullify* the law, even if it [the court] *has less wisdom and influence than the preceding court.*

From this one can conclude, even if we have no *Bet Din* and certainly have much less *chochmah uminyan* [wisdom and influence], that one cannot eliminate women from the teaching role. This view is to be inferred from the *spirit* governing this decree. As proven, "the greater part of the community" *cannot survive* without the participation of the woman, also in the realm of teaching. There is no danger of a violation against a direct prohibition: the reason for which the prohibition was introduced has changed; an urgent necessity is given that the woman must work as a teacher and tutor.

To substantiate the opinion that teaching by the woman is in fact not forbidden according to Jewish opinion, the following important and interesting text is cited.

Sefer Hachinuch [Book of Education] by R. Aharon, of blessed memory, and published in Venice: Regarding Commandment 158 (in other editions, 152): There is the *prohibition,* when the Temple was in existence, not to enter in a *state of drunkenness,* for men *as well as for women. The prevention of teaching* at all places and at all times applies to men, and also *to the intelligent woman worthy of being a teacher.* Also the great Sage, *on whose teachings men depend, it is forbidden to teach* his *students* if he is drunk, because his lessons are like instructions, as we have said. . . . And so it is for anyone who teaches while drunk, whether a Cohen [priest] or an Israelite [a member of the common people], he has committed an offense, whether he is intoxicated on wine or another drink.

One can gather from this that it was assumed that at later times "intelligent women" who are *ra'uy* [worthy], that is, in fact, only those who understand something and are reliable, would be given permission to make "decisions." They are permitted *lehorot* [to teach]; that can indicate that they are qualified to *pasken* [render a Jewish legal decision], and to teach, because as it is said, all teaching is an act of "deciding," every *limud* a *hora'ah* [instruction]. Thus from a Jewish standpoint, as is here apparent, it is not far-fetched to see a woman as a teacher, even if in a smaller range and in a closer circle. What is important here is simply seeing the principle of whether *nothing* may be argued against her teaching—it just may not be *public*—but this question regarding public teaching already has been settled through the circumstances of changing reasons and demands.

After the treatment of the questions related to learning and teaching by the woman, let us go to point 5, *pasken* [render halachic decisions], as it is an assignment related to one of the aforementioned tasks of the rabbi. For this last branch, there is no direct halachic material. Conclusions must be drawn from practical cases and from the previous material.

As already mentioned, women in past ages worked in this field. It already was stated clearly above that "intelligent women" are suitable to make halachic decisions. This would be enough to provide a positive answer to the question regarding *pasken*. But in this connection all the women should be mentioned who served ably precisely in the area of *pasken*—even though it deals to a great extent (with one exception) with "questions related to the kitchen." In this context see L. Zunz *Zur Geschichte and Literatur* [On History and Literature], page 172.[26] He produces a list of women who achieve exactly those things, which should provide evidence here of what is halachically possible or not.

The text states:

1. Chillit, Rashi's sister (Hapardes folio 4b), was seen as trustworthy in decisions regarding ritual.

2. The wives of his grandsons and his granddaughter were just as much trusted to offer trustworthy decisions on certain ritual matters (see Hagahot Maimonides R.G.A. on *ma'achlot assurot* [forbidden foods] §5).

3. Dolce, wife of Rabbi Elazar of Worms, understood the rules regarding prohibited foods, taught women the regulations, nourished her husband and children; she was later murdered (handwritten account by the Rokeach).[27]

4. The wife of Joseph Ben Yochanan in Paris was practically a *rabbi* (see Simon Duran R.G.A. Th. 21c).

5. Rashi dictated his responsa to his daughter when he was ill (Hapardes folio 33c).

6. Brune Mainz wore a garment with fringes (Minhagot Maharil, *Diney Tzitzit* [regulations of the Maharil regarding the fringed garment]).

For the sake of completeness, all the names of the women are included here, even if their achievements do not deal *directly* with the question of *pasken*. Point 6, Brune of Mainz has been mentioned earlier. As far as the sources were available to me, the texts will be given here. (The details of page numbers according to Zunz is related to the very oldest editions. I have used the newer ones.) Sefer Hapardes Lerashi, of Blessed Memory, Budapest 5684 (1924), page 8, Regulations Regarding the Menstrual Impurity of Woman (previously the question was discussed as to how and in what way the immersion[28] should take place, and if the teeth must be cleaned beforehand or not):

Resh Lakish said: Women should only immerse themselves in a natural manner in the ritual bath—that is, without pressing the lips together. Yet we do not agree with the interpretation of Resh Lakish. Also in his book, R. Isaac bar Menachem the Great does not agree. *His sister, Mrs. Klelet (Beyla), introduced* in his name for the daughters of his region to clean their teeth before the immersion, said our teacher, whose soul rests in Eden, and from his answer it may be deduced that women must brush their teeth for the time of their immersion.[29]

It continues:

Sefer Hapardes Lerashi, of Blessed Memory,[30] p. 161: Here am I, a young person condemned to suffering and pain, lying on a sick bed, now I have only the time for brevity, which is not common, but my strength is at its end, and my hands are too weak to hold a quill, therefore I *read these lines aloud* to my *daughter,* and *she wrote them* to my *honored lord,* my *teacher.*

Now come the following important passages:

Responsa to the Regulations Related to Prohibited Foods, Rambam, paragraph 5: In the case where one bakes a "Pashtida" in the oven and covers it with a pan of iron or clay, and afterwards bakes it a second time on the underside of a "Paldon" without first having checked its ritual cleanliness, I asked the widow of my uncle, R. Yizhak ben Shmuel. She said her husband did not protest if she baked a "Pashtida" and covered it with a pan and the "Paldon" with another pan, as long as the oven was heated according to the baker's technique. So it was common in the house of our Rabbi Meir, my grandfather, and *in the house of Mrs. Miriam, the daughter of his daughter, who belonged to Rabbi Shlomo.* But some treat it more strictly. *Mrs. Miriam, my uncle's wife, of the Rabbi Tam, interfered,* she treated the oven until the metal was red. . . . If I had known that Rabbi Tam interfered, I would have taken back my words because of his words; but as long as no one is certain, *we will continue to depend* on our common sense and on *the witness of the daughters of the Great Sages of their generation.*

Furthermore: According to the Amsterdam edition of Responsa of Shimon ben Zemach [Rashbaz], Part III, 5495 [1735], page 21:

Question: I asked, why did my teacher praise every pupil who says: Why may one not pick olives in purity? Should he not have praised the pupil who said: Why does one pick olives in impurity? For the second one expressed himself briefly, and it is always said: One should teach students the art of expressing themselves succinctly—as it is written in the first chapter of *Pesachim* in the Babylonian Talmud.

Answer: You have asked well, and there are many possible answers. Because of this question they say in the Tosafot, that he only praised those who said: Why should one pick [olives] in a state of impurity? But I heard from Abba Mari, of blessed memory, who *in the name of the Rabbanit* [female form of "rabbi"] *the wife of Rabbi Yosef, son of Yochanan,* father of R. Mattityahu the grandfather of R. Yochanan, who lived in our generation, that the reason for the hymns of praise were those who said: Why may one not pick in a state of purity?; the fact is that he expressed himself in a clear manner, although he thereby extended his expression. Correspondingly they say: One should always teach one's students the art of expressing themselves succinctly. So said the teacher to his pupils, so that they would not use this extended language, rather the questioning students used a clean, well-considered language when speaking with the rabbi and did not ask in a brief manner, so that the heart of the rabbi was generous and he was not perplexed by the longer speech; so goes the lovely explanation. [In other words: though one pupil expressed himself more succinctly, he used the word *impurity.* The other avoided this, using the word *purity,* but to do so he had to express himself using more words.]

A passage mentioned earlier leads to a field closely related to *pasken*; it is found reprinted in the responsa of Isaac b. Emanuel Lattas, who gave two women the *kabalah* [certificate permitting kosher slaughter]. They therefore must have studied everything—meaning parts "of both the written and oral teachings"—related to slaughter. They had to be working openly with men, and the work was such that they must have taught and made decisions, in that they had to answer questions posed to them. In cases of doubt, as often occurs with ritual slaughter and that which is related, they also must have had to make halachic decisions as to whether everything had been followed in the correct order, and one *depended* on their *testimony.*

Imagine if *that* were to happen today almost four hundred years later; some might believe that Judaism would be G-d forbid "destroyed." What would the principal difference be between such a diploma and that which would be given to a female rabbi today?

In the following, first the text of this *kabalah* is given (page 139 and 140, Vienna 1860, responsa of R. Isaac ben Emanuel Lattas, of blessed memory):

(1.) I conferred *on a young woman the full authority to slaughter ritually.* . . . because there was an admirable, modest woman, a lady and a virgin, who had researched the regulations of ritual slaughter and was found to be informed in all the written laws in this matter. My ears heard that it made sense and was honorable to teach her. She repeated for me her qualifications, how her teacher presented it and passed it to her from the mouth of another teacher, who also vouched for her and her qualifications. *As regards the worthiness, of depending upon her slaughter, I therefore grant her the full authority to slaughter and permit all in Israel to eat from the animal that she has slaughtered,* but only after she has performed the slaughter two or three times in front of an expert, to see if she faints [because of the blood] and if her hands are experienced to carry out precisely the task of slaughtering according to the laws engraved in her heart and *focuses even more on* the regulations written in this book. Mantua [Italy], Rosh Chodesh, Shevat 5360 (1573), the young Yizhak, son of our honorable teacher, *Emanuel Lattas,* of blessed memory.

   (2) Formula of the Power of Authority, another Power of Authority that I granted a woman a certificate to slaughter . . . it was common *among the daughters of Israel* to *learn* the regulations of kosher slaughter, and this honorable virgin of Israel, this chaste woman did not forbid her soul from all splendor and all treasures that her eyes had seen, and became an *expert* for the teachings of the Torah about the regulations of ritual slaughter, which appear in this book, which a former teacher *taught her,* who vouches for her and her competence. So she deserves to have one depend on her kosher slaughtering. I support her and open the door for her and allow her to slaughter, in order to feed others, but only if she performs the slaughter before experts for three months twice daily, before she goes to sleep or after she rises, so they can see if she faints [because of the blood]; once a day for another three months; then an entire year once per week, and for the rest of her life once every month, so that she does not forget the things that she has learned.

From all noted heretofore, from what has just been cited, from what is stated in the Sefer Hachinuch [Book of Education] and from what has been quoted from Zunz and here repeated word for word, it emerges that *pasken* definitely is not prohibited.

The passage in Sefer Hachinuch is clearly in favor. The remaining passages show us that in times of old there were very learned women who possessed authority and on whose decisions much weight was placed.

Thus one recognized her logical, moral, and intellectual awareness. It is a mistaken objection to suggest these facts could be shaken by saying that these are only the abilities that relate to the "sphere of the kitchen." It also should be considered here, as has often been stressed, that much seriousness and keen intellect must be summoned in order to understand and keep our *dinim.* If a woman is, for example, not careful, "thoughtless," does not take it so literally, poses no *she'elah* [question], and is unable to decide whether one thing or another is *kasher* [kosher], she not only makes herself "culpable," but also the one who eats the "unsuitable" food through no fault of his own. But to know what is really *kasher* or *treyf* [unsuitable] she must learn much and then be capable of making "a decision," such as to declare kitchenware and food unsuitable, and many more related issues.

But how much she would have to know, and how much "decisive power" would be ascribed to her, if she worked as a *shomeret* [watcher] in restaurants, hospitals, and such institutions! How is it possible that the wife of Rabbi Yochanan was counted as one who handed down traditions, and that one depended on her statements, unless it was because she first studied long, and second because the thought was alive in the people, that women—by virtue of what has been transmitted to them through teaching or by example—are suitable to decide difficult questions in cases where it is not possible to ask men.

"Wise women" who are *ra'uy* [worthy] *lehorot* [to teach] thus are given the right to make decisions. So there apparently were in fact women who, in addition to possessing intelligence—for that alone did not suffice—had acquired the professional knowledge and applied it, as emerges from the citation above. The only thing is, there were relatively few. Their entire work as household "supervisor" is a *pasken*. This is possible for in this area she knows something; no one else can represent her and therefore she had the chance to demonstrate in practice that she can summon the requisite understanding and seriousness for such matters.

If she now has a career as a rabbi and must make decisions in other areas in which she has studied, then nothing revolutionary has happened. With the seriousness that her job entails, she puts into practice something that women long were allowed to do in the household, only to a greater extent; but it lies within the *same level* and therefore does not offend Jewish sensibilities. It is written that "one relies upon women" so it is not foreign to Judaism if this "support" is broadened from the narrow, *permitted* range into a larger one of *pasken,* to which in principle there is no objection.

I believe that the question of whether a woman may make halachic decisions as a *Rabbinerin* may *very* clearly be seen as permitted, and *it is not necessary* to continue to linger over this matter.

Aside from studying, teaching, and *pasken,* today's rabbi is also a preacher in the synagogue and on special occasions. Now the question arises: can the woman as rabbi also fulfill these tasks? To answer this question one must define the sermon, as there is no halachic material on the *sermon as such* available in the sources. I believe one may understand the sermon as *teaching* the community. Whereupon we must see how far her work as a teacher may go. It has been shown that it is not halachically improper that the woman today takes on the teaching profession. This teaching profession extends not only to children from the age of six to fourteen, but in higher educational institutions the woman must also teach young people between the ages of seventeen and eighteen. Then what is the difference if she teaches eighteen-year-olds, females as well as males, or that she therefore teaches people between the ages of twenty and eighty through her *sermons* in the synagogue?

The hindrances that can arise already have been handled in the beginning of this work. One is reminded here of the pulpit, separation of the sexes, and the calling up to the Torah. It is not necessary to consider the oft-mentioned citation on *yichud* here, for she speaks to the *multitudes*. That something such as *zniut* should prevent her from preaching is also not acceptable, for certainly in her dress she would not be taken in by the "fashionable frivolity" to which unfortunately the world of our women today have surrendered, as she must wear the clothing befitting to her job. Her hair likewise is covered and the appearance of the woman to men during the sermon need not give rise to any halachic objections as it can only be a fleeting glimpse, and it is to be expected that a serious man pays attention in a strictly *religious* mood during services.

Just as both female doctors and teachers in time have become a necessity from a psychological standpoint, so has the *female rabbi*. There are even some things that women can say to youth, which cannot be said by the man in the pulpit. Her experiences, her psychological observations are profoundly different from those of a man, therefore she has a different style. One need only consider the areas of fashion and contact of youth with each other as ones to which she can dedicate her particular attention. That was however already dealt with in another passage. If Jewish culture is to be maintained, the woman must contribute particularly in this way and *both* sexes must deliver their great service.

G-d created the world with *two* sexes, and the world cannot continue to be supported by only *one* sex. In her private circle the woman was always a servant of G-d but today's times demand that she also serve *in public life*.

This brings one to points 7 and 8, those of so-called "pastoral care." That women can and do work for others with tact, sympathy, and a sense of sacrifice need not be demonstrated from the historical past and in the present; what the Talmud says and what other passages add on this have been mentioned often in this work. Welfare, care, the ability to speak and hold community evenings already have been enriched by her contribution and her independent actions. That her ability lies particularly in caring for youth almost goes without saying. After all, the Talmud ascribes to her insight into human nature and gentleness, and armed with these abilities she is capable of easing the pains and fears and hardships of their lives.

At any rate, no halachic material can be found regarding the question of *female preachers*, and the analogous passages to be cited here indicate no halachic difficulties. While one might touch upon the question of active and passive voting rights in this connection, I cannot address it in this work; but it is to be emphasized that much evidence supporting the other points works here as well. Furthermore, one knows that opinions vary on this and not a few favor double voting rights [both to vote and to be elected].

Someone may wish to object that it may well be that there is no direct halachic *prohibition* found, and that times have changed, but up to now it has not yet been the case that a female rabbi was working in the community. But that is *not* proof that she may not do this from a legal standpoint; for it is written in the Mishna, Eduyot 2:2: "*Lo ra'inu ayno ra'ayah*" [not having seen is no proof]. Or if someone should say: "*Minhag Yisrael Torah Hu*" [A custom common in Israel has the power of Torah] [Yoreh De'ah, 242, paragraph 14—Mapah], here too this is not correctly applied; for one *cannot* apply this sentence to a *minhag* [custom] that was never practiced; for the question of a female rabbi was never current. Aside from that, numerous responsa deal with and answer fundamentally new questions, which would be an impossibility if one kept to this false interpretation of *minhag*. Thus it is to be seen that for the points up to now, the woman even in a halachic *sense* is suitable, and may take on these functions as a rabbi. It can only be a question of *emotional reactions*, for those who cannot bear to have a woman work *rabbinically* and on the *pulpit*; but the force of prejudice related to feelings should not dominate over understanding and logical argumentation.

As its final point, this work will handle the halachic issues related to the function of the woman as a rabbi with the *get* [divorce decree] and *kiddushin* [marriage]. Here the challenges are more difficult than heretofore, but not irresolvable. What does the rabbi actually do *al pi din* [according to law] in these aforementioned cases? Properly speaking, *nothing* except for a minor involvement with the *get*. That he is present at marriages in his rabbinic capacity and delivers a talk is a modern custom that has *nothing* to do with *Halacha*. Similarly with the *get*, his presence is not *absolutely* necessary. For the *kiyum haget* [establishment of a divorce decree] a collegium of three men must be present, which used to be the *Bet Din*. As a substitute for this *Bet Din* today three rabbis serve; which is not thoroughly the law, that it must be three rabbis; rather the *Bet Din* can also consist of three *well-informed private* men. This *Bet Din* according to the simple *din* [law] is *not necessarily* imperative, as we will learn in the forthcoming discussion. It may therefore be important to touch upon whether the woman can function somehow on a *Bet Din*.

First the sources will again be examined and initially with regard to *kiddushin*.

There is little material to find regarding *kiddushin*. The Rambam introduces the following:

Mishneh Torah, Regulations for Marriage, Chapter 3, Halacha 1: How is the woman wed? Through money . . . and it is given to her *in front* of *witnesses.*

and further,

Rambam, *Mishneh Torah,* Regulations for Marriage, Chapter 4, Halacha 6: If one has wed before unsuitable witnesses, the woman is *not* considered *married.*
BT *Kiddushin* 65b: R. Yizhak, son of Shmuel . . . said: If someone marries [a woman] before a single witness, *his marriage is invalid.*

Further, Tur, Even Ha'ezer, cipher 42:

. . . a wedding that *has not taken place* before *witnesses,* and even before one witness, *is invalid.*

Furthermore:

Shulchan Aruch, Even Ha'ezer, Regulations of the Marriage Ceremony, cipher 42, paragraph 2: The betrothal that did not take place before witnesses or before one witness is *invalid* as a *betrothal,* even if both parties agree; this applies as well to a betrothal that takes place first before one witness and afterward by another; it is also invalid as betrothal.

Mapah: Some are more stringent, if the marriage happened before one witness and two consent.

Be'er Hetev:[31] But for a wedding *in front* of *women* [as witnesses] everyone agrees, that one doesn't worry that the marriage might be valid according to Rashbaz, 2nd Volume No. 300.

Here the sources discuss only that witnesses to a *kiddushin* must be present, next to the groom and the bride. Naturally the sentence from BT *Kiddushin* 6a applies here as much as with the *get*:

Whoever is *not well-informed* in the regulations about divorce and marriage *does not deal with it.*

With the words *harey at* [with this, you are betrothed to me], where two witnesses are there, the bride is betrothed to the groom in that he gives her something. Today it is usually the ring. Anything else done to embellish the ceremony is *halachically not* necessary. Of course there can also be a difficulty at *kiddushin,* so the participants must be informed about the regulations. A *Bet Din* only gets involved if calamities arise. Nothing further is needed for the simple act of the marriage ceremony, according to the *din* [law].

It is already noted that absolutely nothing speaks against a female rabbi performing a marriage ceremony *nowadays.* Always present are: bride and groom and two witnesses. There is *no* halachic objection to her observing the ceremony; just as little that she, just as would the male rabbi, delivers a small talk and reads out the marriage document.

Matters related to the completion of the *get* are somewhat more difficult. First of all, the sources should be considered:

Rambam, *Mishneh Torah,* Regulations for Divorce, Chapter 1:

Halacha 13: How does one know that the divorce decree must be given before witnesses? Because the Torah says: with two or three witnesses [Deuteronomy 17:6] the matter is *established.*

Halacha 15: It is a decree of the Sages that a divorce decree has to be signed by *witnesses* lest it is handed to the wife [by the husband] in front of the two [witnesses] and they die, the *get* is as worthless as a piece of clay. . . .

Halacha 3: This teaches . . . that she is not divorced until the *get* is placed in her hand or in the hand of her envoy, which is the same as her hand, or was given to her court, where all is the same as her hand.

The Tur says:

Even Ha'ezer, Regulations for Divorce, cipher 133: *"There must be two kosher* [suitable] *witnesses* present at the moment of the handing over of the divorce decree; it will be given to her in front of them. . . . [but if the decree was signed by two witnesses] and if he [the husband] comes over and *gives it to her between the two of them, it is "kosher"* [suitable].

The Bayt Chadash agrees with the opinion of the Tur:

It is common for a divorce decree to be delivered in the presence of a minyan [a quorum] *of ten men.*

So far it is established that the *get,* at any rate, is preferably seen in the presence of a minyan and two "kosher" witnesses, as is common today in observant circles. It is also common today that a *Bet Din* is present. The woman cannot function as a witness; the *Bet Din* still must investigate the matter.

But let us follow the sources a bit further:

Shulchan Aruch, Even Ha'ezer, Regulations for Divorce, cipher 130, paragraph 1: There must be *two kosher witnesses* who sign under the last line of the divorce decree.

Furthermore:

Shulchan Aruch, Even Ha'ezer, Regulations for Divorce, cipher 133, paragraph 1: There must be two *kosher* witnesses present at the moment of the handing over of the divorce decree (so that he [the husband] gives the divorce decree to her [his wife] in the presence of these two); and also, *it must ideally be signed by witnesses,* but in case there were only the two witnesses—*to the signing*—and he [the husband] gives it to her between the two of them, it is *in retrospect kosher.* And similarly, if there are witnesses at the handing over, but *no* witnesses at the signing, it is *kosher.* Some say, if it is known, that he gave it to her without the presence of witnesses, although there were witnesses at the signing, it is *unacceptable.* At any rate, if they see the signatures on the divorce decree, they can assume that of course it is delivered in front of the witnesses.

Mapah: See above at the start of cipher 130: One should have the same group of witnesses for both the signing and the handing over, and not *two groups.*

The text discusses *edey messirah* [witnesses to the delivery] and *edey chatimah* [witnesses to the signing]; a rabbinical role is not mentioned. However we are going to illuminate the question more thoroughly.

Shulchan Aruch, Even Ha'ezer, Regulations for Divorce, order of the divorce decree, cipher 154: At the time of the Sages of the Gemara, it was common to name a *wise specialist;* so it is found in the words of the Kadmonim [first generation of codifiers], that the divorce decree normally would be handed over *only in front of the great scholars of the generation;* the husband therefore tried to engage *only an expert* for the delivery; *whoever was not an expert for divorces and marriages, should not deal with these matters.*

Cipher 123, paragraph 1: *All are kosher* to write the text of the divorce decree. . . . *even the wife* herself. If her husband assigns her to write it, she can write it and give it into the possession of her husband, so that he can return and present it to her.

The following will explain the instructions of the *get* more explicitly and the decree regarding the *Bet Din. Shulchan Aruch,* Even Ha'ezer, small edition, instructions for divorce decrees, paragraph 2:

. . . the rabbi invites the scribe and two witnesses.

On that, see Pithe Teshuva [on paragraph 4, Commentary 8]: From this we determine that *for the handing over of the divorce decree a court consisting of three rabbis is not necessary;* this is consistent with the *Shulchan Aruch* and the *Achronim* [last generation of codifiers from the fifteenth and sixteenth centuries until today] from all regulations related to divorce. *From no place is it known that there must be a rabbinical court,* except with a divorce decree delivered by a messenger; here the Rema explains in cipher 142, paragraph 4, that one should be more stringent, and deliver the divorce decree, even if the messenger is not a relative and is not unsuitable—in front of the three [the rabbinical court], etc. In their answers, both the Radbas in part 1, cipher 84, and the Re'em[32] in part 2, cipher 35, explicitly explain that even if one is more stringent, if the event occurs in the night, in any case it will be agreed *that there is no requirement for a rabbinical court*—as it is explained explicitly there in his sense, see there; so is it explained in the sense of Rema. Although in the answer of the Noda Bi-Yehuda, cipher 114, that I presented, it is said that one must in this case *make it more stringent,* and in his view a court of three rabbis is necessary in the delivery of the divorce decree, and also in the case of a divorce decree, that it goes from the hand of the husband into the hand of the wife. Nevertheless he differentiates between an engaged and a married woman [a divorce decree is also required to dissolve an engagement]. There in cipher 105, he lashes out at a rabbi who delivered a divorce decree *on his own,* as was not common in any community of Israel, as even the *greatest Ga'on* [honorary title for a sage] convened a rabbinical court for the delivery of the divorce decree; according to his view, this [divorce] should *in retrospect* be considered invalid—see there. At the conclusion of cipher 118 it is also written, if one takes three [a rabbinical court], this is in keeping with the law, only one should not make it more stringent by reducing the intimacy between them more than is suitable according to the law—see there. And with my limited ability I take on the words of the above-mentioned Noda Bi-Yehuda and *deduce from them several proofs, according to which there is no requirement for a rabbinical court.* The core of the proof of Noda Bi-Yehuda, of blessed memory, to the words of Rashi, of blessed memory, is at the beginning of the BT *Sanhedrin.* Accordingly, the three [a rabbinical court] is necessary at rejections [within the marriage that give cause for divorce; see also Genesis 39:8]. All decrees of the rabbi are to be compared with the Torah. *The Noda Bi-Yehuda interpreted the intentions of Rashi:* If the divorce decree is Torah, this proves that a rabbinical court is necessary [In other words: if the rabbinical decrees have Torah ranking, it is necessary, for confirmation of the "rejections," to have a rabbinical court at a divorce.] About this I write that one should repress and argue in the sense of Rashi, according to which this resembles the *"enforced divorce decree,"* as in the cases in which the husband is forced to liberate the woman. Despite the limitation of my argumentation the world will agree with me that in the case of an enforced divorce decree, according to which he [the husband] is forced to free her [his wife], a rabbinical court is necessary, *which can be drawn from BT Gittin (Chap. 8). In fact, with the divorce decree* [the normal sort] *which is given according to the wishes of the husband one can say, and Rashi agrees, that there is no need for a rabbinical court.* Concerning this matter the Responsa of Chatam Sofer [mid-nineteenth century] were published this year. There I also found the view of Rashi regarding Even Ha'ezer, part 2, cipher 64, exactly as I myself had explained it, according to which what is written is to be compared with the Torah, that is to say, like an enforced divorce decree, *for which a rabbinical court, consisting of experts, is needed—and that is from the Torah,* etc. (Thank G-d, I had the privilege to be able to concentrate on the views of the great Rashi). In closing let it be said, that perhaps in previous generations a rabbinical court had to be convened for every divorce decree, *because no one lodged a complaint against it.* And it follows from the words of BT *Shabbat* part 4, and in the Tosafot, Re'em, which I compared with Noda Bi-Yehuda, see there . . . and in any case Chatam Sofer brought to light in his answer, part 1, chapter 5, cipher 51, as he wrote, *that the delivery of a divorce decree itself did not require a rabbinical court.* In fact, concerning what occurs after the recording and turning over of the divorce decree, he wrote, it is common in Diaspora communities of the people of Israel to call upon a rabbinical court for the handing over of the divorce decree. Because regarding the theme of *Gittin* [divorces] it relates to serious regulations, many investigations must be undertaken, etc. Again I reported in the name of the responsum of Chatam Sofer, part 1, cipher 51, which he brought to light, *that the delivery of the divorce decree itself does not require three* [no rabbinical court]; that does however happen after the recording of the divorce decree and before its delivery, if the rabbi called an inquiry, and asks questions of the scribe, and the witnesses, which are named in Sefer Halachot Gedolot ["Sahag" (Great Book of Laws)], paragraph 66, and further, *if the witness's statements are to be heard, this requires the three* which comes from the Torah, and *if there is none,* the divorce decree cannot be delivered, etc.—see there. About this I wrote, correspondingly, if the wife stays at the place of the separation, it is not necessary to give the divorce decree before a rabbinical court. As it is written above, cipher 142, small paragraph 7: *the importance of the three is not performed with such severity;* in any case one should from the outset surely make it more stringent because it comes from the mouth of the *Ga'on* Noda Bi-Yehuda, of blessed memory, and aside from that, because in the majority of the Diaspora communities of

Israel it is common. As it is written in the answer of the Chayim, whose question is mentioned above, in the chapter on divorce decrees at the end of section 3, at the side of 80, I share his view according to which no rabbinical court is required by law; he, too, wrote that in any case *among the majority of rabbinic courts of Israel it was common to gather at least three wise students* [rabbis] *so they could better inquire into* [the truth] and "not treat it lightly as flatbread" [an Aramaic expression], as it says in BT *Sanhedrin,* that there must be at least three people for a rabbinical court—see there; (and see in the answer of the Chayim in Even Ha'ezer, part 2, cipher 5; that is the answer that is referred to Orach Chayim, cipher 51, as mentioned above), according to which he dealt for a long time with this issue. He concluded from this, *that there was simply no doubt that* a rabbinical court *of three was not required for the delivery of a divorce decree by a husband to a wife. It has nevertheless become common among us* [Jews] *to call upon a rabbinical court because of the questions* that the witnesses and the scribe *ask before the delivery,* if everything has been carried out as required according to the religion of Moses and Israel, so that they can sign the divorce decree. And he himself of blessed memory agreed that it likewise is not necessary that the woman . . . makes the contents of it public.

According to the above, [for the *get*] one must have *minyan* [quorum of ten men], a *sofer* [scribe], two *kosher* witnesses, and the couple, or the *shaliach* [messenger] for one or both. There are divided views on the question of the *Bet Din,* as has been shown. The cited commentator says that for the *get* a three-member *Bet Din* would be unnecessary unless a messenger delivers the *get.* Not even the *Shulchan Aruch* speaks of a *Bet Din.* The Radbas also endorses this position. But the Noda Bi-Yehuda on the other hand believes that even for a *get* without a *shaliach,* a three-member *Bet Din* must be present; he even—as one sees in the text—takes offense at one rabbi for giving a *get* on his own, so that he considered it *bedi'avad* [in retrospect] invalid.

The Noda Bi-Yehuda bases his views on Rashi. But the opinion of the Pithe Teshuva fails to support this, as he believes that Rashi is speaking of a so-called *"get ha'me'usseh"* [enforced divorce decree]; there must be a *Bet Din* according to BT *Gittin;* but otherwise, according to the Pithe Teshuva, *no Bet Din* is needed. Thus two different opinions confront one another. Others take the view that while the *din* [law] may not require a *Bet Din,* still, as it is such an important matter, one should nevertheless be "more stringent" and stick to the *minhag* [custom] and appoint a *Bet Din.* It is important to consider the view of the Chatam Sofer, who believes ten people are absolutely necessary and also is of the opinion that for the *get* itself no *Bet Din* is needed; *only* when

she'eylot [questions] and *chakirot* [investigations] are directed at witnesses must there be a *Bet Din* present. But in the end one comes to the
conclusion—which ultimately the Pithe Teshuva also supports—that
though actually according to the law a *Bet Din* would not be needed,
still one should be *machmir* [more stringent] and consult a *Bet Din*
"from the very beginning."

In any case it is common in most rabbinical courts in Israel to gather three wise students [rabbis] or more, *so that they can investigate correctly.*

Personal observations are set forth here: How did the completion of the
get proceed according to the much earlier citation? In fact it must have
been done by a *chacham beki al hagitin* [knowledgeable expert on
divorce] or *lifney gedoley hador* [in front of the greatest of the genera-
tion]. Where are these "*gedolim*" [great] today? So, since we live in other
times, one must be satisfied with a single well-informed expert.

Where is it forbidden that the woman can be *mesader haget* [one who
sets up the order of a divorce decree], I mean such as in that she calls
together the *minyan, sofer,* and *eydim* [witnesses] and—as has become
common today—three well-informed assistants for a *Bet Din* or such as,
if that is not possible, she calls in three men who are not knowledgeable
on this matter and teaches them beforehand about what is to occur? She
then would supervise the *get* to see that it is correctly written and they
would direct the usual questions to witnesses and other persons concerned, for the main point is that the answers would be given to the *Bet
Din,* which consists of men. One naturally also could do it in such a way
that one man from the *Bet Din* asks the questions, but only after she has
made everything clear to him—if he is not an expert—and then she herself *strictly* guards the procedure so that no mistake can be made. So I
believe that the woman herself can carry out even this disputed function
according to Halacha. One should not underestimate, with regard to this
procedure in religious life, particularly with what precedes the delivery of
the *get,* that women have a special ability to overcome some of the difficulties that arise through the ill will of one member of a couple, or even
to prevent the divorce.

Before this topic is concluded, one ought to ask why it should be
impossible halachically for a woman to fulfill the function of *judge.* It does
not appear to me that general unreliability would be ascribed to her, for
as we already have seen in other connections, one grants her trust on that
respect. First, again, the sources will be introduced; for it goes hand in
hand with this investigation to determine whether she is capable to bear
witness and be considered believable.

On this see the passages in Tosafot on BT *Gittin* 2b:

Why *do we depend on women* when it comes to kosher slaughter, although they do not know the regulations of slaughter? Because it is within her capacity to learn to slaughter, or she can assign a substitute who can slaughter for her, as if by her own hand.

If she had learned how to perform ritual slaughter and can practice it, too, then *trust* must have been granted to her in this and all connected with it. I know well that this accreditation is different from that granted to witnesses and in the judicial office; but it is on the same level with *credibility overall*. If someone strictly speaking were considered untrustworthy, one could *never* trust in him. One is either to be credible in everything or in nothing. From the following it will also become evident that there are *substantially* different reasons that *hinder* women halachically in this regard. Rambam should be the first to speak on this.

Rambam, *Mishneh Torah,* Regulations for Witness Testimony, Chapter 9, Halacha 2: *Women are unsuitable as witnesses* according to the Torah, for it is written, "by two witnesses," which [according to Hebrew grammar] is the male form and not the female form of the word.

On this, Kesef Mishneh:

I don't know why our rabbi [Rambam] expressed satisfaction in signing this grammatical proof; I cannot express satisfaction, because the entire Torah is written in the grammatically male form.

He proves it from BT *Shevuot* 30a:

[Deuteronomy 19:17] "Two men should stand as witnesses". . . *the woman is not* kosher to bear witness.

That is the *basic position* according to which women are disqualified from *eydut* [bearing witness]. On this, what the Tur said should be mentioned first.

Tur, Choshen Mishpat, Regulations for Judicial Office, cipher 7, paragraph 5: Women are not suited to judging, and Deborah was not a judge, but she instructed the judges of Israel.

In addition,

Bet Yosef: "The woman is not suitable to judge, *and Deborah was not* a judge, etc." At the end of the first chapter of BT *Bava Kama* 15a it is written in the Tosafot that woman is not suited to judging; in Chapter "Bo Siman" (BT *Niddah* 49b), we have learned, *that all those suited to judge are also suited to be witnesses.* As we said in Chapter "Hachovel" (BT *Bava Kama* 88a) and in Chapter "Shevuot Ha'eydut" (BT *Shevuot* 30a), the *woman is not suited to witness;* although it is written in the Bible that Deborah judged Israel, this is not proof that women were kosher to judge; perhaps the Israelites *accepted her* [Deborah] *over themselves* because of the purpose given to *her by the presence of God.* In Chapter "Hacholez" (BT *Yevamot* 35b) it says that the woman is not worthy to be a judge, as we taught: anyone who is kosher to judge is also kosher to judge. The Talmud Yerushalmi makes it clear in tractate *Yomah that the woman should not witness, nor should she judge;* and Deborah was not a judge, rather she instructed so that the judges could judge; aside from that, a destiny given by God is something different. This all comes from the passage at the end of Chapter 3 in BT *Shevuot* (30a).

The Bayt Chadash contributes nothing new, only a comparison between *ishah* [woman] and *katan* [minor, child]. What has been stated up to now clearly shows the difficulty of the problem and articulates the woman's lamentable fate in this matter, which prevails up to today, that is that she is still *passul l'eydut* [unsuitable for testimony] and therefore also *passul ladun* [unsuitable for judicial office]. But one can note the following in this matter: One glance at life in *general* shows that the woman in today's society can take on the position of judge, lawyer, and witness. From the latter it thus emerges that the social order is *mekabel* [accepting of her] and adjusts to her activity in respective forms, as it says in *Shulchan Aruch*, Choshen Mishpat, Regulations for Judicial Office, cipher 22, paragraph 1:

Who accepts a relative or someone unsuitable, regardless of whether this person should be the judge or witness *over him* . . .

It is to be drawn from the spirit of this decree that if one chooses a person for himself who strictly speaking is "unsuitable" to judge or be a witness, then it is halachically acceptable.

To go on in this spirit, assume the following: When the people go to a female rabbi for the purposes of a *get* or something similar and wish to have her in the judicial office or as a witness, then it is permissible. If the community is *mekabel* [accepting of her] as a leader just as it would a man, this is analogous to what has been stated here. She is therefore a *mekubelet*, as Deborah was, in that society adjusts to her. For today she already has been granted trust in many functions; it is nothing new for her to be "accepted" by the community. If now also in Jewish affairs this trust were given, in the sense to which we have referred, this would simply be the realization of something that is basically not new but actually already is in effect to a great extent.

In the following, proof is presented for cases in which, strictly speaking, leniency is possible regarding the granting of trust.

Rambam, *Mishneh Torah,* Regulations for Witnesses, Chapter 5:

Halacha 2: In two passages the Torah gives a single witness credit: in the case of the Sotah [adulteress], so that she does not drink the bitter water . . . and also *from the words of the Rabbis, the testimony* [from one witness] *about a woman, that her husband has died.*

Halacha 3: At any place where a single witness can testify, a woman can testify as well.

If the first referred to cases where trust was granted to one "witness," then another passage follows related to Sotah in which the woman is certified as trustworthy. See Talmud Yerushalmi, *Sotah,* Chapter 6, Halacha 4:

. . . If a woman witness says a woman has made herself impure [committed adultery], and another woman witness says she has not made herself impure then she must drink the bitter water. If one witness says she made herself impure and two witnesses say she did not make herself impure then she must drink the bitter water. If two say she made herself impure and one said she has not made herself impure, she does not have to drink the bitter water.

Gemara: . . . In all places where the statement of a woman is declared as suitable *as that of a man,* the man can prove the woman guilty of lying and [the reverse is also true] the woman can prove the man guilty of lying.

As already suggested, strictly speaking it relates to simpler cases, or rather, the cases are difficult in *theme,* but to be more lenient with women regarding the results that these matters bring with them, the terms for granting trust are more lenient; that is, *one* witness is accepted, together with people who otherwise would not be seen as "trustworthy."

Here it will be shown simply that *in fact* it is not foreign to the Jewish spirit to accept witness from a woman, for if she were *passul* [unsuited] in the sense of *unworthiness* one could never permit exceptions in which she delivered witness. One simply cannot forget that the testimony in Sotah similarly *assumes* [the woman's] conscientiousness and an *understanding* for the *significance* of the actions, apart from the fact that the accused can choose *p'ssulim* [unsuitable witnesses]; see in this regard the annotated glossary of the Bayt Chadash on the Rosh in BT *Bava Kama* 15a:

Let them be accepted as masters of the law, as testifiers in their communities.

See the Rosh on BT *Shevuot*, Chap. 4; he also uses the term *mekubelet*:

Where does the view originate, that only men and not women can give testimony? It is taught in the Torah: So should two men stand as witnesses: the scriptures speak of witnesses [male form], and as women are unsuitable to testify, they also are unsuitable to judge, as we have learned; everyone who is kosher to judge, etc. . . . And also in the Talmud Yerushalmi, where we gave the argument that "two" is recorded here, and further it says, "and two men stayed in the camp." Just as there it speaks of men *and not of women,* and not of children, here also it speaks only about men and *not of women* and not of children. So we have learned that the *woman cannot bear witness, so now we know that she can not judge.* And though in the story of Deborah it is written that she judged over Israel . . . we explain that she *taught the judges of Israel.* Another opinion: *because of her prophecy she was accepted over them.*

It is mentioned again in that passage that Deborah judged because she was "accepted." Perhaps today there would be even more "Deborah-women" who would fulfill that role well. In principle it is immaterial *who* turned this Deborah into a judge; the *fact* is simply that a woman practiced as a judge, and not to the detriment of the community. And here, too, habit plays a role. One used to say that a woman should not go before the court, "because all glorious is the royal daughter within " [Psalms 45:14]; see also BT *Shevuot* 30a. But today this no longer holds water, as already shown. If there had been such a great need for the women as judge and witness as there was a need for her as teacher and educator, then perhaps life might have brought with it, that—just as in the teaching profession, where in a way a prohibition exists, she also would have had great achievements in judicial office.

It is interesting to note what Leopold Löw writes in his *Gesammelte Schriften* [Collected Writings], volume 3, Szegedin 1893, page 340:

The Karaites however, do *not* disqualify women as witnesses. Attacking the Rabbanites, Yehudah Hadassi says: Because in Israel there are women who are *more* just, *more* prophetic and *more* godfearing than men, and why should their testimony not be accepted?

Zunz said however in 1859 that the regulations in the Karaite law book "bear the character of a constructed opposition. . . ." Löw continues:

One asks oneself, however, if right was always on the side of their opponents. In the question facing us, both *reason* and *culture* speak for them [the Karaites]. If, then, diligent Bible study, above the level of "law and history, custom and life," kept the Karaites from *repressing* women, then this researcher finds an obvious and not insignificant witness to the results of the new interpretation of writings according to which the later repression of women in the holy religious documents is baseless.

Thus says Löw.

It is in fact a misjudgment of the Jewish spirit to suggest that the woman is never to be considered capable of giving witness and of trustworthiness, as if she were a "subordinate." The interesting material that has been and will be stated illuminates this point.

It does not work to uphold the *rigid principle* that *completely* shuts her out. I am aware that in the stated examples often the *eved* [servant] and instead of *two* witnesses *one* witness are seen as capable of testifying, but this will not be elaborated further here. At any rate, all other things aside, surely it opens *new* perspectives for the woman, who is the only one to be handled in this connection. The trustworthiness and the confidence to which she is entitled as is shown in the stated examples are on the *same level* as the confidence and trustworthiness that one must demonstrate to her if one would recognize her as a witness in a totally unrestricted sense, just as one does the man.

From the following passage of Tosafot comes the approach that the principle—saying that he who is "suitable" *"ladun"* [to judge], also is suitable to *"lehe'id"* [to testify], and vice versa—refers actually *only* to the *man*. One can deduce from this passage that for the woman, one point can be independent of the other. BT *Bava Kama* 15a, Tosafot "Asher tassim lifneyhem" [Exodus 21:1]:

"These are the ordinances that you shall set before them." The Torah compared the woman with the man. It is astonishing. Does not *"lifneyhem"* [before them] refer solely to those who are suitable to *judge*? As we learned in the final chapter of Gittin 88b, "before them, and not before the laypeople." And the woman is unsuitable to judge, as we already learned in chapter "Bo Siman" (Niddah 49b) that, "Whoever is suitable to judge is also suitable to bear witness." But the woman is unsuitable to bear witness, as we have said in "Hachovel" (88a) and in the chapter "Shevuot Ha'eydut" (Shavuot 30a). One may say about the chapter "Bo Siman" (Niddah 49b) that it is dealing with men. *All men who are suitable to judge are also suitable to bear witness.* And from what is written (Judges 4), "And she judged Israel," about Deborah, *we can not bring proof that a woman is suitable to judge,* for perhaps *they accepted her because of the Divine Presence* [Who had appointed Deborah as a judge, which was an exceptional, unprecedented situation.] And what if you argue that we have seen in Gittin (88b) that *"lifneyhem"* [before them] is used to exclude the laypeople, and here we see that the same verse is used to include the woman? It is possible to say that there it [the verse] excludes because *"lifneyhem"* refers to judges, who are written about in that section of the Torah (Exodus 21:6). And could you say that we could have learned that we are required to have suitable judges without *"lifneyhem"*, since the verse uses the word "elohim" to describe the judges? We would answer that *"lifneyhem"* is necessary [to the argument] for all issues where the court uses force, even though it is not by law required to have qualified Jewish judges in those cases. And so it is proven in the first chapter of Sanhedrin (page 7b), where we learn from the verse "and you shall place before them" that these are the instruments of the judge.

Further evidence for the theory introduced up to now, that the woman in many matters would be seen as *quite trustworthy*, follows here. BT *Kiddushin* 73b:

R. Chisda said: Three persons are *believed* only when testifying *immediately*—but not when they testify later . . . [*continued:* and they are (the parents of) a foundling; a midwife; and a woman who testifies to free her female companions (from possible impure status). In the case of the foundling, we already have explained. The midwife, because it was taught: *The midwife is believed* if she says about twins, this one was first and is thus the firstborn, the other one came out second.]

BT *Kiddushin* 73b:

The Rabbis taught in a Baraita: A *midwife is believed* if she says, "This child is a Cohen, this one a Levi, this one is a *natin* and this one a *mamser* [illegitimate child]. . . . "

Her trustworthiness as a midwife was granted by the Sages, in that her seriousness and feeling of responsibility would be recognized, if one thinks of the religious consequences that arise on the basis of her *statement*, (for example the redemption of the firstborn).

New evidence for the woman's trustworthiness as a witness is found in the following citations. In matters of argument (slander) even if it deals with *money*, the woman is granted trust, expressly when there is no *man* to take her place relative to the situation.

(1) Book of the Responsa of Our Teacher R. Josef Kolon[33] of Blessed Memory, published in Lemberg 5555 (1795), cipher 179: In addition, I found in another passage written in the name of our Rabbi Tam of blessed memory: *The woman or the relatives are to be believed in this* and are indicated [as witnesses] in every case of argument in which there is none of the usual witnesses, and as a result are to be relied upon for judgments in cases of slander *where there are no witnesses*—end of citation. So there you have it: in fact in any case of argument a woman or a relative is to be believed. In addition, the following statement is found in the answer to the question asked about Mordechai

in the name of Chovel: We were asked about situations of argument, quarrel and slander, *whether women and relatives can bear witness. It is clear that she* [the woman] *can bear witness,* even in a situation *that involves money;* as we also explain there, that the woman in childbed is qualified to testify that her son is the first born, even when it involves *the payment of money, five Selaim,* to the priests [for the redemption of the first-born son].—End of the citation.

The same principle applies in a place where *only* women are present and an argument has arisen. Were the woman according to the view of the Sages in her manner untrustworthy or unreliable, then this kind of exception would never have been made.

(2) "Terumat Hadeshen," Responsa of R. Isserlein, part 1, published in Warsaw in 1882—*Laws on testimony, page 73a,* Question 353: Leah and Rachel fought about the places for women in the synagogue. Leah brought *two women,* who stated that the places belonged to her; and Rachel brought *one man,* who stated the places were hers. Which report is preferred, the one from the mouths of two women or that from a man? Answer: It appears that in this case the law is . . . and although normally there is *absolutely no testimony from women, in this situation where there normally are no male witnesses, it is better to trust in them* [the women], and thus I found, as I copied down the collections of great rabbinical laws, *that women are to be trusted to testify.*

Even in difficult situations, that is, where the results are far-reaching from the halachic standpoint, the woman's statement is granted full faith, as the following examples prove.

(1) Rambam, *Mishneh Torah,* Regulations for Witnesses, Chapter 5, Halacha 2: In two passages the Torah gives a single witness credit: in Sotah, so that she [the suspected adulteress] does not drink the bitter water . . . [that is, if only one witness blames her for adultery, she is considered guilty; but if there is no witness she must drink the bitter water, and its effect (she dies or lives on) shows if she is guilty] and so it is also with the words *of testimony of a witness who testifies about a woman that her husband has died.*
      (2) BT *Gittin* 5a: All are qualified to bring a *get* except for a deaf-mute, an insane person, and a minor. . . . But there is the case of a woman who delivers her own *get,* which is also not common. Yet we learned: The *woman* [wife] *herself may bring her* [own] *get,* but she must say, "*It was written in my presence and signed in my presence.*"
      (3) BT *Gittin* 23b—Mishna: Even those women who are not granted trust to say, "Her husband died," *are trusted to bring her get.* . . . *The wife herself may bring her get only that she must say:* "[The *get*] *was written in my presence and it was signed in my presence.*"
      (4) BT *Yevamot* 117a—Mishna: *All are acceptable* to submit testimony for [a woman] about the death of her husband, except for her mother-in-law, the daughter of her

mother-in-law, her rival, her sister-in-law—who can become her rival through the law of marriage to the brother-in-law and the daughter of her husband [these have a hostile orientation to her]. *What is the difference between divorce and death?* The documents are the proof.

(5) BT *Yevamot* 122a: It was then introduced, to allow the marriage on the grounds of the statement of a witness from the mouth of the witness, from the mouth of a slave, *from the mouth of a woman* or the mouth of a female slave.

(6) BT *Yevamot* 118a: If a woman traveled with her husband overseas, comes back and says *her husband has died, then she may marry and receive her bride price.*

(7) BT *Pesachim* 4a—last line: *All are believed concerning the disposal of chametz* [leavened bread] *even women, even slaves and even minors.*

Father and *mother* testify in the sad case that their son is a misfit. Here, *both* stand as equals, side by side in the Torah as educators and as witnesses.

(1) Deuteronomy 21:18–20: If one has a stubborn and rebellious son who will not listen to his father's voice and *his mother's voice* and even if *they chastise* him, he does not listen to *them,* then his father and *his mother* shall take hold of him and *bring* him to the elders of the city and to the gate of the place and say to the elders of the city: "This, *our son,* is stubborn and disobedient and does not listen to *our voice* and he is a glutton and drunkard."

In No. 2 we see that when it comes to *issurim* [prohibitions] the woman is regarded as trustworthy, so that one depends on her testimony, with the exception of the opinion of the Maharshal.

(2) Shach, *Shulchan Aruch,* Yoreh De'ah, Regulations Regarding Worms, cipher 84, small paragraph 11, comment 35: "A woman who finds herself etc." According to the opinion of the Maharshal about eating and drinking, in his book, women, *who are required to be exacting* during the investigation [as to whether food is kosher], were not considered trustworthy, because there is a lot of difficult work, and we say that *they*—women—*are lazy.* In the section Orach Chayim, the author focuses on the tasks that do not require great concentration; but in relation to the painstaking sorting of legumes and small fish and other things, they are not to be relied upon for [the checking of] prohibitions of the Torah. The Rema writes in the Tach (Torat Chatat, p. 82): *"that this is not the custom, rather women* may examine *legumes and fruit and one depends on her,"* even though when it comes to the sorting of small fish, he says in the Mapah at the end of cipher 127, the trustworthiness of the woman is evaluated differently, particularly as the prohibition is not yet fixed *and there also are many aspects on which the regulation is lenient.* Therefore although we are of the opinion that it is prohibited, *one should in any case rely on her* [the woman]. As it is also written in the Tach, which says in closing: "Go, see how the people handle this!"

However, the above-mentioned view of the Maharshal is made obsolete by that of the Rema:

(3) *Shulchan Aruch,* Yoreh De'ah, Regulations for Heathen Wine, cipher 127, paragraph 3—Mapah: The woman is trustworthy if it relates to prohibitions, that is, if she mends something, making it kosher (there Ran,[34] Chapter "Ha'omer" and at the beginning of BT *Chulin*). *But this applies only to clear prohibitions from which it is clear that something must be fixed, to make the meat kosher, for example.* If there are doubts about the prohibition, for example if unclean fish must be sorted from clean, or a prohibition that involves aspects that involve a lenient application of the regulations (see Ran), the woman is not trustworthy. [In other words: If the prohibition is strictly formulated, the woman would also follow it strictly; if the prohibition offers possibilities of interpretation and contains points of flexibility, it is to be feared that the woman would not be able to summon the necessary strictness.]

Example 3 also shows us that the woman is "granted trust" in matters related to an *issur* [prohibition]. (An exception in which she is not granted trustworthiness is in a case of *sofek* [doubt], for one believes she would "be more lenient.")

Rema, paragraph 1: All who are unsuitable for testimony are suitable in relationship to ritual prohibitions.
    BT *Gittin* 2b: . . . a single witness is believed with regard to ritual prohibitions.

Enough with examples!

As has already been explained often, from the presented passages it becomes *manifestly* evident that the statements of the woman, and even in some cases her *official testimony,* receive full validity. Our Sages of blessed memory have attributed to her a rather large area in which she is trusted and even the halachic results that come about through her statement did not put off our Sages of blessed memory from seeing her statement as trustworthy. How much seriousness one must have attributed to her, how much awareness of responsibility must have been granted her, if she were permitted to present genuine testimony to the *Sotah* [adulteress]! One considers those difficulties that could have arisen if she had been careless or dishonest or superficial when she had to bring her *get* or had to declare the death of her husband or the like. Thus, because these relate to difficult cases, our Sages of blessed memory already have been *lenient;* but it must be observed that if it is necessary, she delivers *genuine testimony,* with all the difficulties of responsibility inherent in such matters. It is thus not stepping away from the Jewish worldview—if one grants trustworthiness to the woman as a witness in an *emergency*, then one extends this to cases in which there is *not an emergency;* because in fact her character is not in question regarding *trustworthiness.* One thinks of the other examples, those still to come from *issurim* [prohibitions] as midwife, in searching for *chametz* [leavened bread that must be removed before Passover], in cases of contention, educational matters, not to mention the area of "supervision" [of *kashrut*], which already has been discussed. In all the realms mentioned up to now, unreasonableness and carelessness of the woman would inflict dreadful damage in the halachic sense, if she were *unable* to fulfill the full weight of her testimony.

Our Sages of blessed memory, however, appear to have considered her capable and thus granted her trustworthiness. It must have been due to the times, the circumstances, and the "rote learning" of a *psak* [rabbinical decision] that one regarded her as *passul le'eydut* [unsuitable as a witness] in the great field of testimony. If one binds oneself *strictly* to the *word*, she *cannot* be admitted as witness and judge. But whoever *considers the spirit of our Jewish sources* and draws conclusions from it—and that is surely permitted, for the position of the woman today is different from before—may say the following: If one considers the sources, it is well within one's right to say that from the stated material it is only a small step to the extended testimony and to the judicial office which would be based on this, and it does *not* lead away from Judaism if one permits the latter to the woman. It is only extending a line already sketched out by our scripture, for it must always be stressed that the limitations in this area are explained by the position of the woman overall. It must in fact prompt consideration, that one finds distinctly in the Torah (see Exodus 21:7), *veki yimkor ish et bito le'amah*, that one *may sell a daughter as a maidservant,* something that cannot happen with the *son.* It will not be decided here what this is based on. From later regulations, also concerning marriage and such, the view is displayed that the wife (also the daughter) is presented as a kind of "property" of the father or the husband. It can be questioned whether that is for the benefit or to the detriment of the woman (it probably was seen in those days as necessary). Enough: the fact remains that from our *standpoint today* it must be seen that the woman in earlier times was paternalized (for example, it is well known that it was essentially different [in terms of consequences], whether the father or the mother married off the daughter).

Mishna, Sotah 8:3: The man sells his daughter; the woman does not sell her daughter. The man marries off his daughter, but the woman does not marry off her daughter.

But as one gathers from the presented material, from time to time the woman *rose against* the many "regulations," emerged from the secluded and "protected" position, and enriched Jewish life with her energy; and then one must deal with the woman as a factor and perhaps make concessions. The words in BT *Brachot* 45a, "Go, see what the custom of the people is," supports this view, first of all as evidence that one had to make concessions to her because *life* demanded this; for example, in the household *only* she could fulfill the sorting of legumes, despite the halachic considerations as stated in the *Shulchan Aruch* (perhaps one might say today that the woman no longer spares any "effort," as one used to think she did). Nevertheless the Rema says in Torat Chatat, Hilchot Tola'im, paragraph 9, the above-cited line from BT *Brachot* 45a.

Second, the line above applies to the much-discussed issue of the woman's "testimony and judicial service." Here, too, one can repeat: "See what the custom of the people is." Among us Jews, the woman today works as a teacher, a school principal, and head of other educational institutions where one must depend upon her testimony and where she acts on her own behalf. In addition, one must establish—because we Jews live in the greater world—that here, too, the Jewish woman will be admitted to *all* professions. One thinks for example of Jewish female lawyers and Jewish female judges (including in youth courts). These last-named professions are from the standpoint of Jewish welfare *an urgent necessity* today.

So what is the custom of "the people?" They need the woman and call her, because she *must* come and help. Despite the explicit prohibitions against her taking on any public profession, the *needs* of the day require that she *in fact* assume a public role. One almost can say that it has become a *minhag* [custom] that women work in public. Just as with other professions that she has had to take on out of *necessity,* so do today's conditions in the meantime require her to be a rabbi. One cannot say that the job of rabbi in the sense of "clerical work" is *chukot hagoyim* [laws of the nations],[35] for the other religions also have not permitted this kind of work to women up to now. If the other professions that women fill are *halachically* permissible, then so is the job of rabbi, which, as has been demonstrated, comprises almost all the other professions within it.

It can certainly happen that she could make mistakes in her job as rabbi or that one or another unworthy person would dedicate themselves to this post, not understanding Judaism; it is to be explained from this that one must accept that there always are *beginnings* to overcome. In addition, it hardly needs to be emphasized that anyone who seeks the truth can also go astray. Did not Elisha ben Abuya change into *Acher* [the other]?! (See

BT *Chagigah* 14b.) These are consequences to which *human beings* are subjected, but *not only* women.

One may assume that if a woman takes on such a position she will manage it with seriousness and love. Nowhere would it be denied that the woman has sensitivity, honesty of aspiration, willingness to sacrifice, love for humanity, and a sense of tact—the basic requirements for the job of rabbi. The objection that it is against *zniut* has been illuminated sufficiently; first of all this term itself is much changed, and some elements have been abolished, which goes against the *din* of the *Shulchan Aruch,* as mentioned, and it would have been better to maintain those elements in order to preserve the *kedushah* [holiness] in Yisrael.

It is *not only the women* but also *the men* who have deeply offended *zniut* and *hitrachek min ha'arayot* [refrain from sexual indecency] (see *Shulchan Aruch,* Even Ha'ezer 21). It is *impossible* to maintain the principle of holiness if only one part of the Jewish people fulfill the related requirements. Second, the term *zniut* has changed for the better with regard to the societal position of the woman, in that she has become accustomed to *harmless* association between the sexes. Times have called into action the female doctor, teacher educator, lawyer, judge; their work is a blessing in the Jewish sense, it does not lead to *prizut* [licentious behavior] nor does it offend *zniut*. If these professions of the Jewish woman are *halachically* possible, then so is the rabbinic profession, as already mentioned above (for she already carries out in detail almost all the tasks in the jobs previously delineated, on a smaller scale).

If one objects, but the woman still cannot be counted in a minyan, one can quote the ironic joke of a great Jewish leader of our time: "Woe unto the *kehillah* [Jewish community] that only has its minyan when the rabbi shows up."

When it comes to her *religious majority,* this is not in such a bad state, as has been attempted to show here. One must only recall the BT *Megillah,* in which *yesh omrim* [there are some who say] that she should not be *motzi* [to enable others to fulfill their obligations] for others; one can gather from that that there is another opposing opinion that in fact did allow her to be *motzi* for others. There is no question about her religious majority, according to the Taz, when it comes to *Kiddush*. Not to mention all the other examples presented in this work.

That women are also active in other fields of religious life has been mentioned often already. The both beautiful and instructive book by Meyer Kayserling should finally be noted: *Die jüdischen Frauen in der Geschichte, Literatur and Kunst* [Jewish Women in History, Literature, and Art] (Leipzig, 1879).

Whoever reads this book will be amazed to see what women have accomplished. But he must also ask: How is this possible? That despite the remote position of the woman she could accomplish such great things? The answer can only be that despite all the prohibitions, time has drawn our Jewish ancestors along, so that women in fact did study, teach, and do good works. There are however also dark points in this book, reports about women who did not honor Judaism; but they are far outnumbered by the noble ones. Whoever strives toward truth and light sometimes goes into the darkness instead of into the sun. That is the secret of the struggle of life!

Let us now turn to these women who are of outstanding accomplishment in the realm of Judaism. Page 136 of the book guides one to Rachel, Bellejeune, the sister of Rashi; to Miriam, and Anna, his daughters and granddaughters; pages 134–141 carry the title "rabbinically educated women.". . . [Also] Mrs. Händel Cohen, widow of Paltiel Cohen of Breslau. Page 136 mentions Muallima, who was considered by the Karaites as a *theological authority*. Page 137 says that in Rome there was a Paula dei Mansi, daughter of Abraham b. Joab Hasofer and wife of Yechiel b. Solomon, who was well versed in the Hebrew language and rabbinical scholarship. Page 137 also refers to the daughter of R. Samuel b. Ali in Bagdad, who had thousands of pupils gathered around her, *was learned in Bible and Talmud, and delivered public lectures to young people.* According to the report of the traveler Petachya of Regensburg, this female scholar called Bat Halevi—similarly to *Olympia Fulvia,* who taught *openly in* Basel and whose writings were published there—sat at her lectures in a box covered with dark glass so that the young people would not see her and stare at her. The same regulation was followed one hundred years later by *Mirjam Schapira,* daughter of the learned Solomon Schapira and sister of Peretz of Constance, who later became the matriarch of the famous *Luria* family of rabbinic literature.

She, too, was a *weighty expert in the Talmud* and *rabbinic literature;* for years she headed a *college* and, *sitting* behind a *curtain* during the lessons, counted *numerous followers as her students.*

Enough examples from this book, which we could long continue. In this connection the interesting story should be noted, regarding the intelligence of the well-known Beruria and her *talmudic knowledge* (see Tossefta[36] Kelim—Bava Metzia, Chapter 1, Mishna 3) through her argument against a *Tanna* [learned of the Mishna-generation]:

Klustra [a button that belongs with a latch]—R. Tarfon says that it is impure; the Sages say that it is pure; Beruria says: *Let* it fall through the opening and hang there during the Sabbath. When these things were told to R. Yehoshua, he said: *Beruria spoke correctly.*

It is interesting to see from these examples that, despite prohibitions, women studied and taught, although this prohibition is repeated in many passages, while on the other hand it *is not* so often repeated that one must "be covered from the view of the man." Still, the latter is more strictly observed than the former, for the daughters of Israel gladly submitted to *zniut*. For the behavior of those days, when a woman so rarely came out into public, these precautionary rules were used. Today, as already often stressed, *this* kind of *zniut* with these precautionary measures can be abandoned, for the woman in today's society and in public life *regularly* must work together with *men*. Naturally, it must be stressed to *both* sexes that, particularly today, *both* must observe the holy commandment of *zniut* in a broader sense, to preserve the customs and purity of Israel.

Even if, in keeping with today's views, one rejects the regulations of *zniut*, which go into the smallest details, *one still may not deny the spirit of these serious decrees.* That is why both sexes must set barriers so as not to become distant from the foundation of Judaism.

Briefly, points 8 and 9 of the tasks that the rabbi must fulfill—and thus also the female rabbi—should be addressed. That she is suitable to settle conflicts need not be proved. Even with a *din hatorah* [court for the Laws of Torah], if one sees it as a judicial hearing, she could officiate if the opposing parties *choose* her, and at the very least work as an "observer."

Finally, the lifestyle of the rabbi is addressed. It goes without saying, but it still must be firmly emphasized, that only those men and women should devote themselves to the job of rabbi, teacher, and custodian of Jewish ideas who are *suffused* with Jewish spirit, Jewish self-confidence, Jewish morality, purity, and Jewish holiness, who could say, together with the Prophet Jeremiah (20:9):

But his word was in my heart like a burning fire shut up in my bones. . . .

I *must* fight for G-d. In BT *Yomah* 72b it says: "A scribe whose heart does not match his exterior is no scribe."

That must be the leitmotif for those people who wish to practice such a job as that described here. *Life* and *teaching* must *be one,* if they wish to set a true *example* for the ones they guide. There is no great halachic conflict regarding the fact that Jewish people, when they consecrate themselves to G-d, consecrate themselves *fully.* Whoever dedicates their life to others, in particular one who wishes to dedicate oneself through work, must not only comfort with *words* but also through *deeds*. It says in BT *Avodah Zarah* 17b:

If someone only is occupied with Torah, without carrying deeds of loving kindness, it is as if he had no God.

The taking in of *gerim* [converts] could not be dealt with here, as it would be too much.

If this is true for *every Yehudi* [Jewish man] and *every Jewish woman*, how much more so for one who wishes to commit his life's work to the service of G-d and thus to his people. May it not be forgotten, in all loyalty and love for our scripture and its holy regulations, *that the spirit of freedom speaks through the texts*. It must be this spirit that speaks in favor of the woman and that has an *illuminating effect* on this question. Meyer Kayserling says in his book: "*The more free and unfettered their influence, the more richly* the female virtues, too, will *blossom* in connection with the inner *religious life*, to whose nourishing and care the *women* of *today* are *excellently suited*" (Kayserling, p. 336). Aside from *prejudice* and *unfamiliarity*, there is almost *nothing* halachically opposed to the woman taking on the rabbinical role. So may *she*, too, through *such* work, promote Jewish life and religiosity *lishmah* [for the sake of Torah] in future generations:

Sources

1. *Gesammelte Schriften* [Collected Writings of] *Leopold Löw* (Szegedin, 1893).

2. *Real-Encyclopädie f. Bibel und Talmud* [Encyclopedia of Bible and Talmud], by Dr. I. Hamburger (Leipzig, 1886).

3. *Frauenwahlrecht* [Women's Voting Rights], by Alfred Freimann Posen (manuscript).

4. *Die rel. Stellung des weiblichen Geschlechts im talm. Judentum* [The Religious Position of the Female Sex in Talmudic Jewry], by Dr. P. Holdheim (Schwerin, 1846).

5. *Die Frau im jüd Volke* [The Woman in the Jewish People], by Dr. Adolf Kurrein.

6. *Die jüdischen Frauen in Geschichte, Literatur and Kunst* [Jewish Women in History, Literature, and Art], by M. Kayserling (Leipzig, 1879).

I declare, in lieu of an oath, to have produced the work on my own and not to have used anything other than the cited literature.

Occasionally, if something appeared unclear to me, I allowed myself to consult knowledgeable acquaintances.

Regina Jonas
June 24, 1930

tam venishlam berich shemey
[concluded and completed, blessed be his Name]

NOTES

1. Eduard Baneth (August 9, 1855–August 7, 1930), rabbi and professor of talmudic science at the Lehranstalt [College] and later Hochschule für die Wissenschaft des Judentums [Academy for the Science of Judaism]. Among other duties, he was also responsible for granting the rabbinical diploma.

2. This and other emphases are, unless otherwise noted, Jonas's own.

3. "Taking off the shoe," that is, a prevented levirate marriage. It relates to the custom of the widowed, childless sister-in-law removing the shoe of her brother-in-law before a judge, when her brother-in-law does not wish to marry her after the death of her husband, his brother. (See Deuteronomy 25: 5–10.)

4. That is, judgments on the basis of Jewish religious law (Halacha).

5. This shows clearly that Regina Jonas operated within the bounds of traditional, if not fully Orthodox, Judaism and was not one who promoted Reform Judaism, according to which men and women should sit together during religious services. The image of the female rabbi that she draws here maintains the separation of the sexes in the synagogue: the female rabbi accesses the pulpit through a special entrance. According to her description, women are not called up to the Torah reading, a central event in the Jewish service and an honor usually given to men. Jonas did not stress this privilege, because in her opinion this was a superficial "honor."

6. An expression in Hebrew that also is beloved today, meaning that true beauty is on the inside. Alongside the citation in the original is written in pencil: "Inner female beauty." All Jewish daughters are considered to be "royal daughters," just as "All Israelites are royal children," for example, in BT *Shabbat* 67a.

7. Salome Alexandra—the only Jewish queen, Hasmonean dynasty, ruled from 76–67 BCE; she was considered a successful politician, above all because she

-86-   95

gilt das für j e d e n יהודי und für j e d e

J ü d i n, so erst recht für den, der seine Lebens-

tätigkeit in dem Dienst G,ttes und somit seiner

Menschen stellen will .

Möge bei aller Treue und Liebe zu unserem Schriftum

und seinen heiligen Vorschriften doch auch nicht ver-

gessen werden, d a s s d e r G e i s t d e r

F r e i h e i t a u s i h m s p r i c h t.

Dieser Geist möge es sein, der f ü r die Frau spricht

und auf diese Frage e r h e l e n d wirkt. Es sagt

M.Kayerling in seinem Buche:"j e f r e i e r u n d je

u n b e e n g t e r i h r e W i r k s a m k e i t, des-

to r e i c h e r e r b l ü h e n auch die weibli-

chen Tugenden in Verbindung mit dem innigen r e l i-

g i ö s e n L e b e n, das zu nähren und zu pflegen

die Frauen der G e g e n w a r t v o r z ü g l i c h

B e r u f e n sind." (dass.S.336),ausser Vorurteil

und U n g e w o h n t s e i n steht hal.fast n i c t s

dem bekleidenden des rabb.Amtes seitens der Frau ent-

gegen. So möge auch s i e in einer s o l c h e n

Tätigkeit jüd.Leben und jüd.Religiosität לשמה

in kommenden Geschlechtern fördern.

   Benutzte Literatur:

1.) Gesammelte Schriften v.Leopold Löw (Szegedin 1869)

2.) Real-Encyclopädie f.Bibel und Talmud v.Dr.I.Ham-

burger (Leipzig 1886).

3.) Frauenwahlrecht v.Alfred Freimann Posen (Handschrift
4.Die rel.Stellung des weiblichen Geschlechts im talm.
Judentum v.Dr.S.Holdheim, (Schwerin 1846) .
5.)Die Frau im jüd.Volke v.Dr.Adolf Kurrein)
6.) M.Kayserling die jüd.Frauen in Geschichte, Literatur und Kunst (Leipzig 1879).

   Ich versichere eidesstattlich, die Arbeit allein
angefertigt zu haben, und keiner anderer als die ange-
gebene Literatur benutzt zu haben.
   Manchmal, wenn mir etwas sehr unklar schien ,
erlaubte ich mir kundige Bekannte zu fragen.

Regina Jonas

Last page of Jonas's treatise

Signed "Regina Jonas" at the bottom of the page.

brought peace to the land after an epoch of unrest. Among other things she set great store by the content of Jewish religious laws and supported the party of the Pharisees.

8. Citations refer to German text.

9. Citation refers to German text (Leipzig, 1906).

10. The opinions about Queen Salome Alexandra vary. Meyer Kayserling wrote about Salome Alexandra in *Die Jüdischen Frauen in der Geschichte, Literatur und Kunst* [Jewish Women in History, Literature, and Art] (Leipzig, 1879), for example, p. 16 (translation from the German original): "The first woman from this generation that was as famous as it was unfortunate, who had an essential influence on the fate of the Jewish state, who even herself wore a crown, was Salome Alexandra. With the fact that the few still available sources regarding the characterization of this woman do not concur, in that the scribes of Herod's dynasty (Flavius Josephus) depict her as a tyrannical, weak-willed tool of a party, it becomes difficult to portray her accurately."

11. Proverbs 31:10: "*Eyshet Chayil:* In Praise of the Capable Wife":

A capable wife who can find?
For her price is far above rubies.
The heart of her husband safely trusts in her,
And he does not lack grain.
She does him good and not evil
All the days of her life.
She seeks wool and flax,
And works willingly with her hands.
She is like the merchant ships;
She brings her food from afar.
She also rises while it is still night,
And gives food to her household, and a portion to her maidens.
She considers a field and buys it; With the fruit of her hands
    she plants a vineyard.
She girds her loins with strength,
And makes her arms strong.
She perceives that her merchandise is good;
Her lamp does not go out at night.
She puts her hands on the distaff,
And her hands hold the spindle.
She stretches out her hand to the poor;
Yes, she reaches forth her hands to the needy.
She is not afraid of the snow for her household;

For all her household are clothed with scarlet.
She makes for herself coverlets;
Her clothing is fine linen and purple.
Her husband is known in the gates,
When he sits among the elders of the land.
She makes linen garments and sells them;
And delivers girdles to the merchant.
Strength and dignity are her clothing;
And she laughs at the time to come.
She opens her mouth with wisdom;
And the law of kindness is on her tongue.
She looks well to the ways of the household,
And does not eat the bread of idleness.
Her children rise up, and call her blessed;
Her husband also, and he praises her:
"Many daughters have done valiantly,
But you excel them all."
Grace is deceitful, and beauty is vain;
But a woman who fears the Eternal shall be praised.
Give her of the fruit of her hands;
And let her works praise her in the gates.

12. The terms "for shame" and "for praise" are defined by Rashi; Genesis 6:9 relates that Noah was righteous "in his generation"; Rashi comments: "In his generation—some of our teachers see this as praise: all the more so if he had lived in a time of righteousness, he would have been a person of greater righteousness; and some see it as shameful that he was righteous in relation to the age in which he lived, but if he had lived in the time of Abraham he would not have been counted at all."

13. The context is a list: "Ten kab of wisdom came down into the world, Israel received nine and the rest of the world received one. Ten kab of beauty came down into the world, Jerusalem received nine and the rest of the world received one. Ten kab of wealth came down into the world, Rome received nine and the rest of the world received one. Ten kab of poverty came down into the world, Babylon received nine and the rest of the world received one. Ten kab of arrogance came down into the world, Eilam [an ancient nation in what is now Iran] received nine and the rest of the world received one, etc. Ten kab of power came down into the world, the Persians received nine, etc. Ten kab of lice came down into the world, Persia received nine, etc.; Ten kab of wizardry came down into the world, Egypt received nine, etc.; Ten kab of promiscuity came down into the world, Arabia received nine, etc.;

Ten kab of talkativeness came down into the world, women received nine, etc.; Ten kab of drunkenness came down into the world, Ethiopia received nine, etc.; Ten kab of sleep came down into the world, slaves received nine and the rest of the world received one."

14. Beruria, one of the few recognized female scholars in the Talmud, was born in the first half of the second century and lived in Tiberias. She possessed such rich knowledge that she entered into halachic discussions with many scholars. She also explained verses of the Bible, closing with the words "Look at the end of the verse"; this expression would become the norm among later Talmud scholars during discussions.

15. During the Torah reading, it is traditional to call up first a Cohen, then a Levi, and then Israelites, that is, Jewish men who are neither Cohen nor Levi. If there is no Levi present at the service, the Cohen reads the blessing again for the second reading, on behalf of the Levi. If there is no Cohen, the Levi reads the Cohen's blessing first and then the Levi's.

16. The expression "to be *motzi*" is derived from "bringing someone out of debt." For example, a *Motzi* is a Torah reader or prayer leader who takes over someone's Torah reading or recitation of Kiddush or Havdalah and thereby brings the man, who is obligated to fulfill the commandment, "out of debt." Jonas's argumentation pertains to whether someone who is not obligated to fulfill time-bound commandments—in this case, the woman— can serve the function of bringing someone "out of debt."

17. "Leaning": see Leviticus 4:29 or 16:21. The priest lays his hand on the sacrificial animal so that his sins or those of the people donating the sacrifice will be transferred to the animal. BT *Chagiga* 16b relates to whether one may place one's hands on the head of the sacrificial animal during the sacrifice on a holy day—see Leviticus 1:4; some agree, some disagree, and ultimately it also relates to whether women "may lean."

18. One of the schools in Berlin where Jonas also taught; in January 1924— before the start of her rabbinic studies—she delivered a lecture on the theme "Youth and Synagogue Service" to "Esra, 1b," the association of former students of the Religious School in Annenstrasse 1b. Following her ordination in 1935, the former rector of the school, Isidor Bleichrode, sent her his congratulations from Palestine, where he had emigrated.

19. Agur: Jacob ben Yehudah Landau, fifteenth-century Italy.

20. The redemption of the firstborn son on the thirtieth day after his birth through the payment of five shekels to the priest (Numbers 18:16).

21. Guarding over the ritual purity of food and the condition of the kitchen.

22. A saying about the endless breadth and depth of the Talmud.

23. A halachic term providing the conditions under which Jewish religious laws may be temporarily voided.

24. Yeshaya Löw Berlin (also called by his father-in-law's name, Pick), Talmud researcher, born in 1725 in Eisenstadt, died in 1799 in Breslau; student of R. Hirsch (Biala) Charif, elected Rabbi of Silesia in 1793.

25. Here, Jonas inserted a page with the following remarks:

> BT *Eruvin* 18b: The rabbis taught in a Baraita: One who counts out money for a woman *from his hand into her hand,* or from her hand in his hand, in order to gaze at her, even if he is in other ways comparable to Moses, our teacher, who received the Torah at Mt. Sinai, he will not be freed from the judgment of *gehinnom* [hell]. About him the writings say: "Hand to hand, he is not spared from evil; he is not spared from the court of Hell [Proverbs 11:21]."
>
> It appears as if this passage, which properly speaking does *not* prohibit the payment of money into the hand of a woman—except in case of dishonest intentions—was developed as a preventive measure, to refrain completely. Dancing of the sexes together is considered in the same context. Nevertheless, both happen in almost all Jewish circles, and not always to the benefit of the Jewish character; but it also serves as evidence that the times or the opinions of people overtake the law. The only answer is not to close one's eyes to reality; to guide and help through understanding of change, through teaching of both sexes, so that the conscience is more awake and dominant; however, the making of harmless small concessions prevents the result that all or a part of our teachings would be abandoned out of too great strictness; to describe these things more closely here would divert us from our theme, thus only these suggestions must suffice.

26. Following is the full citation from Leopold Zunz's *Zur Geschichte und Literatur* [On History and Literature], reprint Berlin 1845 edition (Hildesheim: Georg Olms Verlag, 1976), I:172–173 (translation from the German original):

> With all the severity with which female modesty was gauged and guarded, one was also somewhat lenient, if, for example the strictures of Sabbath observance were not equal with consideration to what women deserve. Only they were permitted to play with nuts on the Sabbath—Tosafot, Eruvin f. 104a; Piske Tosafot, Eruvin §. 211, Sabbat §. 470—to weave their hair and to go out with jewelry—Kol Bo No. 31 f 22a, 23b. Even regarding the preparation for the Sabbath meal, certain activities of the woman were overlooked—Zeda laderech 4, 1, 13. In love of Judaism women were not outdone by men; they

had an equal part of martyrdom and more than one woman has been mentioned, who was prized for her virtue and knowledge. Chellit, Rashi's sister—Hapardes f 4b.—likewise the wives of his grandchild and Miriam, his granddaughter—Hagah. Maim, RGA, on Ma'achalot Assurot No. 5.—were cited as trustworthy voices on decisions about certain ritual matters; he dictated a testimonial to his daughter when he was ill—Hapardes f 33c. The wife of Elazar of Worms, Dolce, who was murdered by armed men, understood the rules about prohibited foods, taught women the regulations, and herself stitched more than 40 Torah Scrolls; she sustained her husband and their children, and was so charitable and so gentle, that R. Elazar, who mourned her death—p. 173—in a poem, that begins with Proverbs 31:10, said he had never been angered by her (handwritten tales of Rokeach). The wife of Joseph b. Yochanan in Paris was almost a rabbi herself—Simeon Duran RGA. Th. 3. F. 21c; Brune of Mainz did what normally was incumbent only upon men, by wearing the fringed garment—Minhagot Maharil.

27. See also Kayserling, 138 (in German original): "A remarkable woman is Dolce, wife of the multifaceted, learned Rabbi Elazar of Worms. She knew all the rules about prohibited foods, taught women in the order of prayer as well as in synagogal songs, delivered public talks on Shabbat. She was very pious, and in her piety she never neglected to prepare candles for Shabbat and the holy days in the House of God; she stood during the entire Day of Atonement and also did not allow herself even for a moment to sit. She fed her husband and their children, was extraordinarily charitable and had such a gentle nature that her husband honored her in a song of mourning, saying he had never been distressed by her in his life. This rare woman suffered a martyr's death, together with her two daughters, Bellette and Anna; they were killed by two Crusaders on December 6, 1213 or 1214, in Erfurt."

28. The observant Jewish woman goes to the mikvah, a ritual bath, seven days after the end of her monthly period and immerses herself three times completely in the water. From that point on, she is ritually "pure" and may resume sexual relations with her husband.

29. Regarding Beyla, Jonas inserted the following lines as a footnote in her text: "Meyer Kayserling, *Die jüdischen Frauen* [Jewish Women], Leipzig, 1879, refers on p. 136 to Bellette, the sister of R. Isaac ben Menachem; and Rahel, called Bellejeune, daughter of Rashi, so that it appears that here one is not speaking of Rashi's sister, but rather of ben Menachem's sister."
Full citation in Kayserling:

France, too, had numerous richly gifted women. In Orleans we encounter: Bellette, sister of the old, well-known talmudic authority R. Isaac ben Menachem, who lived around the year 1050, and Hanna, sister of R. Jacob of Orleans, who was beaten to death on the Coronation Day of King Richard I of England in London. Bellette instructed in the name of her brother the women of her home city in their religious duties; Hanna taught her female co-religionists about the blessing that women are to make by the obligatory lighting of the Shabbat candles. A whole group of learned women came from the family of the famous Bible and Talmud commentator Salomon ben Isaak [Salomon bar Isaac], or Rashi, from Troyes in the Champagne region. Rahel, called Bellejeune, Rashi's daughter, was like her sister very well educated. With her husband Eliezer she did not live happily and divorced him. Miriam, Rashi's granddaughter and the daughter of R. Yehudah ben Nathan, was so well versed in the rabbinical laws that her questions, in connection with cuisine, were submitted to her for decisions and were quoted by later rabbinical authorities as trustworthy voices. Anna, another of Rashi's granddaughters, daughter of R. Meir of Ramerü, taught, like Bellette, the women in religious matters. Etc.

30. Sefer Hapardes Lerashi, of Blessed Memory, commentary on the Babylonian Talmud (Budapest: Chaim Judah ben Kalonymous Ehrenreich, 1924).

31. *Be'er Hetev* [A Good Explanation]: a book with interpretations of the *Shulchan Aruch;* its three authors lived in the seventeenth and eighteenth centuries.

32. Re'em: R. Eliah Misrachi, Turkey, 1455–1526.

33. Josef Kolon died in 1480 in Pavia.

34. Ran: R. Nissim ben Ruben Gerondi.

35. "Laws of the nations" refers to idolatry and other practices and cults forbidden to Jews (for example, Leviticus 20:23).

36. Tosseftah: A work parallel to the Mishna, but which was not taken into the canon and is seen as a supplement to the Talmud.

GLOSSARY

Translations of foreign words and phrases appear in square brackets following the term. Quotation marks indicate terms that also appear as entries in this Glossary.

Ashkenazi Hebrew pronunciation of Hebrew typical of central and eastern European Jews before the Shoah; in contrast to "Sephardic Hebrew," spoken by Jews of Spanish origin and from other southwest European countries, referred to as modern Hebrew in Israel.

Baraita a mishnaic law that was not codified in the Mishna, but quoted elsewhere in rabbinic literature.

Bayt Chadash [New House] commentary by Joel Sirkes on the "Tur," always printed in combination with Joseph Karo's "Bet Yosef." Sirkes was born in 1581 and died in 1640; he lived in Lublin.

bar mitzvah [son of the Covenant] Aramaic and Hebrew; one obligated to fulfill the commandments; celebration for Jewish boys, who at the age of thirteen assume adult religious responsibilities.

bat mitzvah [daughter of the Covenant] one obligated to fulfill the commandments; celebration introduced by Reform Jews in the nineteenth century for Jewish girls, who at the age of twelve assume adult religious responsibilities.

Be'er Hetev [Declare It Good] commentary of Yehudah Ashkenazi on the *Shulchan Aruch*, seventeenth-century Poland.

Beruria one of the few recognized female scholars in the Talmud. She was born in the first half of the second century and lived in Tiberias. Beruria was married to Rabbi Meir.

Bet Din Jewish court consisting of at least three rabbis.

Bet Shmuel commentary of Samuel ben Uri Shraga Faibush (seventeenth century) on the *"Shulchan Aruch."*

Bet Yosef [House of Yosef] commentary by Joseph Karo on the "Tur," always printed with and seen as a basis for understanding the *"Shulchan Aruch."* Parts I and II were published in 1550 and 1551 in Venice; parts III and IV were published from 1553 to 1559 in Sabbioneta. Joseph Karo, who was born in 1488 in Toledo and died in 1575 in Safed, laid out the sources in Bet Yosef, gave references from talmudic and other halachic writings for all his decisions, and included the decisions of other authorities of the post-talmudic era.

brachah blessing, benediction; plural: *brachot.*

Brit Milah circumcision of the newborn boy, eight days after birth.

BT Babylonian Talmud. See "Talmud."

Chanukah [dedication] eight-day Festival of Lights beginning on the twenty-fifth day of the Hebrew month of Kislev, commemorating the rededication of the Temple after the victory of Judah Maccabee in the second century BCE.

Chatam Sofer [Sealed by the Scribe] six-volume work of halachic decisions, composed by Moses Sofer (or Schreiber), who was born in 1763 in Frankfurt am Main and died in 1839 in Pressburg, where he was rabbi from 1803 through 1838. He founded a well-known Talmud Torah school there, which produced countless rabbis and Talmud scholars. His work, published from 1841 to 1861, remains a basic text in Orthodox rabbinical circles.

Cohen Priest, member of the family of Aaron. Descendants of the Cohanim (plural of "Cohen") are still honored by being called up to the Torah reading during the service.

Darkey Moshe [The Paths of Moses] see "Rema."

D'rishah [Research] together with "P'rishah" [sorting out], the commentary on the Tur by Yehoshuah ben Alexander Falk Hakohen (who died in 1614 in Lemberg).

Gabba'im member of the synagogue board; male is *Gabbai* and female is *Gabba'it.*

Ga'on title of honor for a rabbinically learned person.

Gemara see "Talmud."

get divorce, certificate of divorce.

Halacha [path] a law or the body of Jewish religious law and the rabbinical discussion about the law.

halachic based on Jewish religious law.

Halachot religious legal obligations; plural of "Halacha."

Hatarat Hora'a rabbinical diploma, rabbinical teaching certificate.

Havdalah [distinction] blessing at the conclusion of the Shabbat or holidays, marking the separation of that day from nonholy days.

kashrut ritual laws related to food.

Kesef Mishneh commentary by Joseph Karo (1488–1575) on the *Mishneh Torah,* the main work of Rambam (Maimonides), in which Karo prepared a list of sources for Rambam's codified laws; see also "Bet Yosef" and *"Shulchan Aruch."*

Kiddush blessing over wine.

kiddushin marriage.

kosher suitable, permitted.

Lattas, Isaac b. Emanuel an itinerant rabbi, author of numerous responsa. Born around 1570 in southern France, he moved to Italy where he became a private tutor in the family of Isaac Abravanel.

Lechem Mishneh [Double Bread] commentary of talmudist Abraham de Botan (born around 1545 in Turkey, died around 1603; lived in Saloniki) on Rambam's *Mishneh Torah.*

Levi third son of Jacob and Leah; ancestor of Moses and Aaron; the priest and the Levite. Descendants of the Levites are still honored by being called up to the Torah reading during the service.

Levush main work of Mordechai ben Abraham Jaffe, born in 1530 in Prague, died in 1612 in Posen. Levush is partly based on the *Shulchan Aruch.*

lulav palm branch used in a ritual for the holiday of Sukkot.

Maggid Mishneh commentary of Vidal de Tolosa (fourteenth-century Spain) on Rambam's *Mishneh Torah.*

Maharil shortened form of the name Jacob ben Moses Halevi (with the nickname "Mölln" or "Molin," thought to refer to his grandfather's name), who was born in 1355 in Mainz and died in 1427 in Worms. The Maharil belonged to the Rhineland school, the focus of which was the collection and recording of synagogal customs as well as the customary order of daily and holiday prayer services. He preserved the western German tradition.

Maharshal shortened form of the name of Solomon Luria, who was born in 1510 in Brest Litovsk and died in 1573 in Lublin. His main accomplishment was the work Yam shel Shlomo [Solomon's Sea], an elucidation of seven talmudic tractates.

Mapah [tablecloth] critical glossary on the *"Shulchan Aruch"* assembled by Moses ben Israel Isserles (also called "Rema,") who was born ca. 1510 and died in 1572. Isserles lived in Cracow. Originally, Isserles wrote a commentary that always accompanies the "Tur": "Darkey Moshe" [The Paths of Moses]. When he encountered the work of his contemporary Joseph Karo, Isserles transformed his work into glossaries, which are included in Karo's *"Shulchan Aruch."* He called this the Mapah (the table-cloth for the well-ordered table); they have become essential for Jews of German and Polish background. (The first edition was published in Cracow in 1578.)

megillah [scroll] "Megillat Esther" is the parchment on which the story of Queen Esther is written.

mezzuzah [doorpost] a prayer written on parchment that is rolled and placed in a special container the cover of which bears the word *Shadday,* one of the names for God. The mezzuzah is placed on the entrance to a home and most rooms within the home, on the right-hand doorpost, according to the literal instructions in Deuteronomy 6:4–9; 11:13–21, which are written on the parchment.

Midrash research, interpretation of text, or a talk related to and following upon the Torah reading in the synagogue.

Mishna also *Torah sheba'al peh* or Oral Torah, six volumes of Jewish law, which were codified by Yehuda Hanassi in the second century in Palestine. Orthodox Jews believe that the Oral Torah was equally revealed at Mount Sinai as the Written Torah *(Torah shebichtav).* See also "Talmud."

Mishneh Torah [Repetition of the Law] fourteen-part religious work by Rambam (Moses Ben Maimon, or Maimonides), who was born in 1135 in Cordoba and died in 1204 in Fostat, near Cairo, which unites the religious legal decisions, reflections on ethical and philosophical matters, and the entire spiritual work of the Talmud and other rabbinic literature into a systematic, organic entity; also called Yad Chazakah [Strong Hand]. It was completed in 1180.

mitzvah commandment; plural: "mitzvot." The Torah contains 613 mitzvot governing the daily life of observant Jews.

Noda Bi-Yehuda collection of legal opinions of Yeheskiel Landau, who was born in 1713 in Opatov and died in 1793 in Prague. The first edition was published in 1776.

Pesach [Passover] seven-day holiday beginning on the fifteenth of Nissan, which recalls the exodus of the Israelites from slavery in Egypt.

Pithe Teshuva [Gateways of Return] collection of halachic opinions on the *"Shulchan Aruch"* by Abraham Eisenstadt (born in 1813, died in Koenigsberg in 1868; he lived in Kovno, Lithuania).

P'rishah [sorting out] see "D'rishah."

prizut unchaste, licentious behavior.

Purim [lots] festival on the fourteenth of Adar, celebrating Queen Esther's rescue of the Persian Jewish Diaspora from Haman's planned attack; so called because Haman used a lottery to determine the date on which his goal would be accomplished. On Purim, the Megillat Esther is read aloud.

rabbanan [our teachers] the rabbis who discuss Mishna and Talmud.

rabbi "my master" or "my teacher": a position of learning that replaced the priest following the destruction of the Second Temple, the driving of the Jews out of Palestine, and the end of the practice of animal sacrifice. The rabbis interpreted the correct application of Jewish religious law in the talmudic academies of Israel and Babylonia. (See also "Talmud.") In the Middle Ages, rabbis had a judgelike power. After the French Revolution and the loss of civic legal autonomy, Europe's Jewish communities redefined the rabbinical role to resemble the spiritual role of Christian clergy. From that point on, rabbis functioned primarily as spiritual leaders—preachers and ministers. The observance of Halacha by the Jews became a matter of private choice.

Radbas shortened form of the name David ben Simra, who was born in 1480 in Spain and died in 1574. He wrote a commentary to Rambam's *Mishneh Torah.*

Rambam shortened form of the name Moses ben Maimon, also Maimonides. He was born in 1135 in Cordoba and died in 1204 in Fostat, near Cairo. Author of the *"Mishneh Torah"* and *Guide for the Perplexed,* Rambam was the most important Jewish philosopher and codifier in the Middle Ages.

Ran shortened form of the name Nissim ben Reuben Gerondi, also Rabbenu Nissim. Ran was born in 1320 and died in 1380. An astronomer and physician, he lived in Barcelona and was one of the most important teachers of Jewish law in his era.

Rashal shortened form of the name Solomon Luria; he was born in 1510 in Brest Litovsk and died in 1573 in Lublin. See "Maharshal."

Rashbam shortened form of the name Samuel ben Meir; he was born circa 1080 in Rameru, son of Rashi's daughter Yocheved and brother of Jacob b. Meir (R. Tam). He died in 1174.

Rashbaz R. Shimon ben Zemach Duran, fifteenth century, Algiers.

Rashi shortened form of the name Solomon ben Isaac; he was born in 1040 in Troyes and died there in 1105. Rashi studied in Worms and founded a Talmud academy in Troyes. He wrote commentary on almost the entire Bible and Talmud. His commentaries are included in all editions of the Talmud.

rav sir, great master, teacher; a rabbinical title (see also "rabbi").

Rema shortened form of the name Moses ben Israel Isserles. He was born ca. 1520 in Cracow, where he died in 1572. His commentary on the "Tur"—"Darkey Moshe" [The Paths of Moses]—is always printed together with it as well as with his "Mapah," the critical annotation of Joseph Karo's *"Shulchan Aruch."*

responsa see *"She'eylot Ut'shuvot."*

Rif shortened form of the name Isaac ben Jacob Alfasi, who came from Fez—in Arabic, "Al-Fasi." One of the most important Talmud scholars of the Middle Ages, he was born in 1013 in a village near Fez and died in 1103 in Lucena (Spain). He is considered the unquestionable, authoritative successor to the Babylonian scholars and the first to completely systematize the Talmud. The views of Rif in connection with the compendium of "Rambam" and "Rosh" became the basis for Joseph Karo's *"Shulchan Aruch."*

Rosh shortened form of the name Asher ben Yehiel, the talmudic authority. Known as the father of the Tur, he was born in about 1250 in Germany and died in 1328 in Toledo, Spain.

Rosh Chodesh beginning of the month; new moon.

Rosh Hashanah [beginning of the year] Jewish New Year holiday, which falls on the first and second of the Hebrew month of Tishrei.

Second Temple see "Temple."

Sefer Hachinuch [Book of Education] an explanation of the 613 commandments in Torah, compiled 1302 to 1308 by Aharon Halevi of Barcelona for his son and his companions; first published in Venice in 1523.

Sephardic Hebrew Hebrew spoken by Jews of Spain, France, and other Mediterranean lands; accepted as modern Hebrew in Israel.

Shabbat Sabbath, the holy seventh day of the week.

Shach shortened form of the name Shabtay ben Meir Hakohen, who was born in 1621 in Vilna and died in 1662 in Holleschau (Moravia). His work Siftey Cohen [The Lips of the Priests] is a commentary on the "Shulchan Aruch."

Shavuot [weeks] the festival of weeks, of the harvest and pilgrimage, commemorating the giving of the Torah at Sinai. It is held on the sixth to the seventh of Sivan.

she'eylot ut'shuvot [questions and answers] also called "responsa" or legal opinions; questions put to and answered by rabbinical authorities. They are an essential part of the commentary and codification literature to which they correspond. In that the responsa are decisions regarding legal questions that are not answered in the Talmud, they interpret Bible, Mishna, and Talmud. The responsa relate not only to practical, legal, ritual, and ethical questions but also deal with scientific theoretical matters, such as problems of religious philosophy, astronomy, mathematics, chronology, geography, and the calendar. The responsa literature covers a period of seventeen hundred years (from the third century CE up to today); one thousand extant collections contain several hundred thousand responsa.

Shema recognition that there is only one God, as stated in Deuteronomy 6:4–9 and 11:13–21; and Numbers 15, 37–41. The Shema is considered the most important prayer in Jewish liturgy, and is recited at daily morning and evening services.

shofar ram's horn, sounded daily in the month of Elul, on Jewish New Year, and at the conclusion of Yom Kippur.

Shulchan Aruch [well-ordered table] systematic compendium of Jewish ritual laws; assembled by Joseph Karo (born in 1488 in Toledo; died in 1575 in Safed), first published in Venice 1564 to 1565. It consists of four main parts, according to the structure of the "Tur" codex of Jacob ben Asher: Orach Chayim [Path of Life]; Yoreh De'ah [He Imparts Knowledge]; Even Ha'ezer [Stone of Help]; and Choshen Mishpat [Regulations for Judicial Office]. The *Shulchan Aruch* remains the most important ritual and legal codex for observant Jews. It was appended with Moses Isserles's "Mapah" [tablecloth] on Ashkenazi customs (first edition published in Cracow in 1578). The foundation of the *Shulchan Aruch* is Bet Yosef, a commentary on the "Tur" by Joseph Karo, always published together with it.

Simchat Torah joyful holiday honoring the Torah, at which the annual cycle of Torah reading is concluded and begun anew; during the celebration, all the Torah scrolls in a synagogue are carried through the sanctuary.

Smag shortened form for Sefer Mitzvot Gadol [Great Book of Laws]; a ritual codex completed around 1250 by Moses ben Jacob of Coucy.

smicha rabbinical ordination.

sukkah temporary hut, decorated with branches and fruit, in which the holiday of "Sukkot" is celebrated.

Sukkot [huts] Feast of Tabernacles.

Talmud [teaching] next to the Bible, the main text work of Judaism. Begun around the second century BCE and completed in the sixth century CE, it consists of the "Mishna" (religious laws) and the Gemara (discussion on religious laws). The "Mishna" was compiled in Hebrew; the Gemara in Hebrew and Aramaic. One must differentiate between the Jerusalem Talmud *(Yerushalmi)* and the more extensive Babylonian Talmud *(Bavli)*, which alone is recognized as authoritative.

Tanach Hebrew Bible; the word is an acronym of the first letters of the three biblical works: the Torah (Five Books of Moses); Nevi'im (Prophets); and Ketuvim (Writings).

Taz shortened form of the name David ben Samuel Halevi, based on his main work, "Turey Zahav." He was born in 1586 in Vladimir-Volinsk and died in 1667 in Lemberg. The "Turey Zahav" is a commentary on the *"Shulchan Aruch"* and is always printed together with it.

tefillin phylacteries, leather strap and prayers worn on the left arm, against the heart, and on the forehead by men over the age of thirteen during weekday morning prayers. The tefillin includes a small black box containing four Torah portions written on parchment: Exodus 13:1–10, 11–16; and Deuteronomy 6:4–9, 11:13–21.

Temple central place of cult and worship, built in Jerusalem by King Solomon in the tenth century B.C.E. It was destroyed in 586 B.C.E. by the Babylonian invaders under King Nebukadnezar II. The temple was rebuilt, known as the Second Temple in the time of Ezra and Nehemia in the fifth century and, as a result of the Jewish revolt, was destroyed by the Romans in the year 70.

Terumat Hadeshen collection of responsa compiled by Israel Isserlein, who was born circa 1390 in Marburg (Steiermark) and died circa 1460 in Vienna-Neustadt.

Torah also *Torah shebichtav* or Written Torah, the Five Books of Moses (Genesis, Exodus, Leviticus, Numbers, Deuteronomy). *Torah sheba'al peh* or Oral Torah is the "Mishna."

Tosafot "additions" to the Talmud commentary and criticism of Rashi, printed in all editions of the Talmud on the outer margins, whereas Rashi's comments take up the inner margins. Most authors were French Jews, but German and Italian Jews also contributed. The most important Tosafist is considered to be Jakob ben Meir Tam (Rabbenu Tam), a grandson of Rashi, who was born around 1100 in Rameru (Seine) and died in Troyes in 1171.

Tur shortened form of the name Jacob ben Asher, based on his main work, the Arba'a Turim [Four Rows]. Son of "Rosh," he was born around 1269 in Germany, probably in Cologne, and died around 1340 in Toledo, Spain. The title of his work relates to the four rows of gems on the shield of the high priest. It was written for the Jewish public and considers in this connection only the laws in effect after the destruction of the Temple. The four segments are Orach Chayim [Path of Life]; Yoreh De'ah [He Imparts Knowledge]; Even Ha'ezer [Stone of Help]; and Choshen Mishpat [Regulations for Judicial Office]. They are in the form of a coherent argument that leads in the end to a decision. The author's definitive authority is his father, the "Rosh." The work is the foundation for Joseph Karo's *Shulchan Aruch*.

Turey Zahav main work of David ben Samuel Halevi; see "Taz."

tzitzit fringes at the corners of the tallit, or prayer shawl.

Yalta the self-confident daughter (fourth century CE) of the arch-exile Rabba b. Abbahu; her husband, R. Nachman, became head judge through his marriage to Yalta.

yichud private proximity of a man and woman who are not married.

Yom Kippur [Day of Atonement] the most important Jewish holy day, which falls on the tenth day of the Hebrew month of Tishrei.

zniut practicing restraint, in the sense of modesty, chastity, humility.

Structure of the Talmud
(According to Maimonides)

I. ZERAIM

Berachot

Pe'ah

Dema'i

Kil'ayim

Shevi'it

Terumot

Ma'aserot

Ma'aser Sheni

Challah

Orlah

Bikurim

II. MOED

Shabbat

Eruvin

Pesachim

Shekalim

Yoma

Sukkah

Betzah

Rosh Hashanah

Ta'anit

Megillah

Mo'ed Katan

Chagigah

III. NASHIM
    Yevamot
    Ketuvot
    Nedarim
    Nazir
    Sotah
    Gittin
    Kiddushin

IV. NEZIKIN
    Bava Kama
    Bava Metsia
    Bava Batra
    Sanhedrin
    Makkot
    Shevuot
    Eduyot
    Avodah Zarah
    Avot
    Horayot

V. KODASHIM
    Zevahim
    Menachot
    Chullin
    Bekhorot
    Arakhin
    Temurah
    Kerithot
    Me'ilah
    Tamid
    Midot
    Kinim

VI. TAHAROT

    Kelim

    Ohalot

    Nega'im

    Parah

    Taharot

    Mikva'ot

    Niddah

    Machshirin

    Zavim

    Tevul Yom

    Yadayim

    Ukzin

ADDITIONAL HALACHIC COMPENDIA AND COMMENTARIES

Mishneh Torah (Rambam, Maimonides)

Commentators:
  Kesef Mishneh (Joseph Karo)
  Lechem Mishneh (Abraham de Botan)
  Maggid Mishneh (Vidal de Tolosa)
  Radbas (David ben Simra)

Tur (Jacob ben Asher)

Sections: Orach Chayim, Yoreh De'ah, Even Ha'ezer, Choshen Mishpat
Commentators:
  Bayt Chadash (Joel Sirkes)
  Bet Yosef (Joseph Karo)
  Darkey Moshe (Moses ben Israel Isserles)
  D'risha (Yoshuah Falk Hakohen)
  P'risha (Yoshuah Falk Hakohen)

Shulchan Aruch (Joseph Karo)

Sections: Orach Chayim, Yoreh De'ah, Even Ha'ezer, Choshen Mishpat
Glossaries: Mapah (Rema, Moses ben Israel Isserles)
Commentators:
  Bet Shmuel (Samuel ben Uri Shraga Faibush)
  Be'er Hetev (Yehudah Ashkenazi)
  Pithe Teshuva (Abraham Eisenstadt)
  Shach (Shabtay ben Meir Hakohen)
  Taz (David ben Samuel Halevi)

THE AUTHOR

ELISA KLAPHECK is an ordained rabbi in Berlin, Germany. She was born in Düsseldorf, Germany, in 1962 and studied political science and Jewish studies in the Netherlands and Germany. For many years Klapheck worked as a journalist for major German newspapers, radio, and TV and was formerly the editor-in-chief of Berlin's Jewish monthly *jüdisches berlin* [Jewish Berlin]. In May 1999 she helped establish Bet Debora, Berlin's first conference of European female rabbis, cantors, scholars, and spiritually interested Jews (see www.bet-debora.de). Elisa Klapheck is a devout feminist and deeply committed to the revival of Jewish life in Germany. She is active in various Jewish initiatives throughout Germany, among them the Egalitarian Synagogue of Berlin in Oranienburger Strasse.

NAME INDEX

A

Abahu, Rabbi, 130
Abigail, 106, 107
Akiva, Rabbi, 16, 112–113, 136
Albeck, Rabbi Chanoch, 31, 34
Albeck, S., 34
Alexander, H., 27–28, 31, 36
Alexander, I., 57
Alexander, Rabbi Siegfried, 57, 60
Alexander, Rabbi Ted (Theodor), 9,
    27–28, 31
Amram, Rabbi, 112–113
Anna (granddaughter of Rashi), 182,
    192
Anna O., 22
Annette, 90, 92

B

Baeck, N., 35
Baeck, Rabbi Leo, 6, 9, 29, 30, 34,
    35, 37, 38, 61, 62, 63, 70, 73, 77
Baker, L., 88
Baneth, Rabbi Eduard, 6, 20, 29, 31,
    32, 34, 37, 98, 100, 185
Bartov, O., 91
Beck, G., 63, 73, 74
Bellejeune (Rachel), 182, 191
Bellette, 191–192
Berlin, Y. L., 190
Beruria, 112, 129, 130, 143, 182–183,
    189
Beyla (Mrs. Klelet), 157
Bleichrode, Rabbi Isidor, 6, 27, 39,
    189
Bohnstedt, B. (née Norden), 69, 70

Bohnstedt, W., 69
Boyarin, D., 88
Brasch, M., 43, 49
Brentzel, M., 22, 88
Brotzen, J., 49
Brotzen, K., 49, 50
Brotzen, L., 49
Brune of Mainz, 114, 156
Burstein, B., 39

C

Callman, R., 52
Camnetzer, M., 28
Carlebach, J., 43, 90
Carlebach, Rabbi Zwi, 66
Chillith (sister of Rashi), 156
Cohen, H., 182
Collin, M., 52
Coper, E., 20–21, 24
Cronheim, R., 75

D

Dämmig, L., 88, 92
Daughters of Zelophehad, 105
David, 16, 50, 106
De Gouge, O., 21
Deborah, 35, 106, 107, 153, 170,
    171, 173, 174
Dick, J., 91
Dienemann, Rabbi Max, 6, 9, 36, 37,
    39, 43, 56, 61
Dolce (wife of Rabbi Elazar of
    Worms), 156
Dubnow, S., 107

SUBJECT INDEX

A

Academy for the Science of Judaism:
location of, 36–37; under Nazi
regime, 61–62; Regina Jonas and,
5–6, 26, 38, 98, 100; women students and, 29

Aleph Rabbinic Program, 14

Anna O., Bertha Pappenheim, Biographie (Brentzel), 22, 88

Anti-Semitic regulations, in Nazi Germany, 22, 35–36, 61, 71

Artscroll Series: Talmud (Schottenstein
Edition), 99

Ashkenazi Hebrew, in halachic treatise
of Regina Jonas, 98, 99

Aufbau (periodical), 91

Auschwitz-Birkenau, 75, 79

B

Bat mitzvah, and Rabbi Max Weyl, 24

Berlin Jewish Community: and contract with Regina Jonas, 56–57,
60–62, 65; and documents of
Regina Jonas, 80; membership of,
88; and ordination of Regina
Jonas, 36; and services with Regina
Jonas, 50

Berlin Wall, fall of, 5, 88

Berna (newspaper), 51, 86

Bertha Pappenheim: A New Look at the
Concept of the Family (Konz), 88

Bertha Pappenheim: Gebete/Prayers
(Klapheck and Dämmig), 88

Bet Debora conference, 8, 11, 13, 87,
93

Bet Debora journal, 93

Bible, description of women in,
104–108

B'nai B'rith, 50

B'nai Emunah, 6, 27, 52

Brit Milah (circumcision), 121–122

C

Census for Jews, in World War I, 22

Central Archive of German Jewry, 5,
80

Central Welfare Board of the Jewish
Community, 22

Centrum Judaicum. *See* Stiftung Neue
Synagoge—Centrum Judaicum

Chanukah, 35, 36, 62

Chastity. *See Zniut* (chastity, modesty)

"Church tax," 88

Circumcision (*Brit Milah*), 121–122

Collected Writings (Löw), 174, 184

A Concise History of the Rabbinate
(Schwarzfuchs), 92

Contract, of Regina Jonas with Berlin
Jewish Community, 56–57, 60–62,
65

D

Days of Sorrow and Pain: Leo Baeck
and the Berlin Jews (Baker), 88

Declaration of the Rights of the
Woman and Female Citizen, 21

Department for Psychological
Hygiene, at Theresienstadt, 78

Deportations, 72–73, 75, 76–79